NOSTALGIA AND RECOLLECTION
IN VICTORIAN CULTURE

Also by Ann C. Colley

EDWARD LEAR AND THE CRITICS

THE SEARCH FOR SYNTHESIS IN LITERATURE AND ART
The Paradox of Space

TENNYSON AND MADNESS

Nostalgia and Recollection in Victorian Culture

Ann C. Colley

First published in Great Britain 1998 by
MACMILLAN PRESS LTD
Houndmills, Basingstoke, Hampshire RG21 6XS and London
Companies and representatives throughout the world

A catalogue record for this book is available from the British Library.

ISBN 0–333–72813–0

First published in the United States of America 1998 by
ST. MARTIN'S PRESS, INC.,
Scholarly and Reference Division,
175 Fifth Avenue, New York, N.Y. 10010

ISBN 0–312–21664–5

Library of Congress Cataloging-in-Publication Data
Colley, Ann C.
Nostalgia and recollection in Victorian culture / Ann C. Colley.
p.   cm.
Includes bibliographical references and index.
ISBN 0–312–21664–5 (cloth)
1. English literature—19th century—History and criticism.
2. Nostalgia—Great Britain—History—19th century.   3. Great
Britain—History—Victoria, 1837–1901.   4. Great Britain–
–Civilization—19th century.   5. Autobiographical memory in
literature.   6. Nostalgia in literature.   7. Memory in literature.
I. Title.
PR468.N64C65   1998
820.9'353—dc21   98–7211
                                                              CIP

This book is printed on paper suitable for recycling and made from fully managed and sustained forest sources.

10   9   8   7   6   5   4   3   2   1
07   06   05   04   03   02   01   00   99   98

Printed and bound in Great Britain by
Antony Rowe Ltd, Chippenham, Wiltshire

For
Constance Meta Cheetham

Contents

List of Plates

Acknowledgments

Chapter 1 first appeared in *The Centennial Review*, XXV (winter, 1991); parts of Chapter 7 appeared in *Victorian Literature and Culture*, XXV, no. 2 (1997), and selections from Chapters 5 and 6 are to appear in *Victorian Poetry* and in *Reading the Interior: Nineteenth Century Domestic Space*, eds I. Bryden and J. Floyd (Manchester University Press).

I should like to thank the library staff of the Beinecke Rare Book and Manuscript Library, Yale University; the Bodleian Library, Oxford; the Cambridge University Library; the Pierpont Morgan Library, New York; and the Yale Center for British Art. I am especially grateful for the assistance given me by Diana Slatin, Eric M. Lee of Yale University, Katharine Lochnan, Curator of Prints and Drawings at the Art Gallery of Ontario, and Marjorie Lord of the Butler Library at the State University College of New York at Buffalo. I should also like to thank the Research Foundation of New York and the UUP for their support.

As the book progressed I was fortunate to have the opportunity to share parts of it with colleagues at the Northeast Victorian Studies Association meetings and at Gerhard Joseph's Victorian Studies Seminar held at the Graduate Center of the City University of New York. Their insightful responses and their interest in the work were invaluable. In this respect, I wish to acknowledge my colleagues David Lampe and Anthony Lewis, who took the time to read and comment upon parts of the manuscript. I also cannot forget the support of my colleagues at the Institute of English Studies (University of Warsaw, Poland) during my Fulbright year there. I am particularly indebted to Ewa Łuczek, whose work on memory has been and continues to be a companion to my own. My final and enduring thanks go to Irving, whose criticism is the most necessary, difficult, and demanding, and to Rachel, who in her kindness never turned away. And there is Gwen, the child of my own nostalgia.

Introduction

> Nostalgia may be mistaken for melancholia, by the restlessness and want of sleep which accompanies the disease, and the strong tendency to selfdestruction [*sic*] which attends it when the desire of revisiting the country which is longed after, cannot be accomplished; life becomes then a burden, and the *taedium vitae* leads to real insanity, terminating in suicide. From what has been said, the necessity for distinguishing nostalgia from insanity, when the distinction may prove serviceable, must be sufficiently obvious.
>
> A. T. Thomson, 'Lectures on Medical Jurisprudence at the University of London', *The Lancet*, I (18 March 1837) 883

At a time when the twentieth century approaches closure and the past presses against the borders of the present (when one can, for instance, purchase a cardboard facsimile of a nineteenth-century proscenium to frame the cyberspace of one's computer screen), and at a time when the troubling question of the relation between the past and the present lays siege to a culture's conscience, it is, perhaps, appropriate to consider the role of nostalgia as an organizing force in the imagination and memory. Increasingly one senses a preoccupation with remembrance. One notices a recurrence of the word 'nostalgia' in popular and critical discourses and comes across studies like David Lowenthal's *The Past is a Foreign Country* (1985) and Raphael Samuel's *Theatres of Memory* (1994) that document the proliferation of nostalgia in contemporary culture.

With this context in mind, I have selected a group of Victorian British writers and artists whose work emerges from recollection and whose texts consciously take their shape from a sense of loss and a yearning for home. In this study I am not concerned with the Victorians' attempts to resuscitate Camelot and their championing of a distant past – phenomena already meticulously documented. I concentrate, instead, upon their longing for a past that is confined to the span of their own lifetime – not an era they have never personally known.[1] Charles Darwin's *The Voyage of the Beagle*, Robert Louis Stevenson's prose and poetry, Elizabeth Gaskell's narratives, John

Ruskin's *Praeterita*, Walter Horatio Pater's 'The Child in the House', Ford Madox Brown's *The Last of England*, Richard Redgrave's *The Emigrants' Last Sight of Home*, and a series of J. M. W. Turner's engravings are instances of 'texts' indebted to remembrance and to this more immediate nostalgia. They offer the reader/viewer an opportunity to learn about their creators' particular experience of the nostalgic moment. They also provide an occasion to re-examine the idea of nostalgia itself – to consider its idiosyncrasies and frequently unacknowledged complexities – and to reflect upon the act of recollection that accompanies it.

As a term, 'nostalgia' first came into print in 1688 when Johannes Hofer wrote a 'Medical Dissertation on Nostalgia or Homesickness' (*Dissertatio Medica de ΝΟΣΤΑΛΓΙΑ, oder himwehe*) for the University of Basel. In his dissertation Hofer explains that *Nostalgias* is 'Greek in origin' and is 'composed of two sounds, the one which is *Nosos*, return to the native land; the other, *Algos*' that signifies 'the suffering or grief' arising 'from the desire for the return to one's native land'.[2] This definition was to become the basis for thinking about nostalgia for two centuries to come, especially among members of the medical profession who well up into the nineteenth century treated nostalgia as both a physical and an emotional disease – it was what Thomas Arnold (1782) called a form of 'pathetic insanity'. The number of tracts on the subject is considerable. Eighteenth and nineteenth-century physicians such as Jean-Jacques Scheuchzer (1705, 1719), Theodor Zwinger (1777), Robert Hamilton (1787), Albert von Haller (1788), Dr. Jourdan Le Cointe (1790), Philippe Pinel (1819), A. T. Thomson (1837), and August Haspel (1873) wrote on the illness. From their accounts one learns that the disease was primarily associated with soldiers who became acutely despondent and physically weakened when they were sent away from home to serve in foreign lands. According to their case studies, those afflicted 'frequently wandered about sad', 'scorned foreign manners', had a 'distaste of strange conversation', were 'inclined to be melancholy', thought obsessively about home, and suffered from a variety of physical symptoms such as: 'disturbed sleep', 'decreased strength', 'diminished senses', 'palpitation of the heart', 'constipation', 'unusual body movements', and a 'loss of appetite'.[3]

The cures for nostalgia, of course, reflected the physicians' understanding of the disease and standard medical practices of the time. The primary remedy was either to distract the patient from his obsession or to offer him the 'hope of returning to the Fatherland'. In most cases, doctors suggested that their patients, if strong enough, be sent home.[4] For instance, in the case of the homesick man from Berne (discussed in Hofer's dissertation), the doctor concluded that 'no remedy' was going to work 'other than a return to the homeland'.[5] As might be expected, many physicians also frequently purged or bled their patients (by opening the brachial veins). And there were less standard cures. For instance, one late eighteenth-century physician (Jourdan Le Cointe) thought he could rid one patient of his nostalgia by inciting pain or terror through the application of red-hot irons to his abdomen. Another (Jean-Jacques Scheuchzer), convinced that the sickness was related to atmospheric pressure, suggested that if his patients could not be sent back home, they should be quartered on a hill where they would be able to breathe 'lighter'. The prevailing opinion was that if a person were not treated in one way or another, he would risk death. Such was the fear that in some military quarters, doctors suggested that everything must be done to reduce the influence of the *idée fixe*. In some camps, soldiers were punished for singing or whistling tunes that would remind those around them of home.

By the middle of the nineteenth century the concept of nostalgia as an independent clinical entity began to disappear. A few articles on the subject, however, still appeared in medical journals like *The Lancet* (see introductory quotation), and army doctors continued to list nostalgia in their accounting of case histories. For instance, in the official medical history of the American Civil War, 5213 cases of nostalgia were reported among the white troops of the north during the War's first year. When the cases increased during the second year, physicians reacted by advocating more generous furloughs.[6]

Obviously the nineteenth-century writers and painters discussed in this book would not have been considered clinically nostalgic by their contemporaries. In spite of this fact, though, they, in some way, mirror the case studies described by physicians, for they experience loss and at moments feel alienated from their homeland and their origins by virtue of distance, age, or alteration. All of them intermittently suffer from a desire for reunion, for some point of correspondence between their present and their past, their immediate surroundings and home. Caught in circumstances that dispossess and trap them in the tension between the real and the remembered, these figures (or the characters in their works) write or paint toward home in an attempt to reach a place where there is a possibility of continuity and where there is a sanctuary from the changes that come with the passing of time. Often their texts offer them a form of hope, of promise, that they can, for a moment, place themselves in the track of their former selves and re-enter what is now irrevocably absent and seemingly unavailable. They can reclaim what was once themselves.

Although each of these figures lives through the nostalgic experience as if alone, each is tacitly connected to the other in an unformed and unnamed community of people who reach for the metaphor of their history to bring what is absent into the present in order more fully to integrate their lives. They tend to take comfort in the past, for they are part of a culture that finds in it a means of resolving (rather than creating) tension or difference. The past gives them a way of discovering synthesis. (An engagement with it does not necessarily expose the antitheses and ironies imbedded in our postmodern sensibility – theirs is not a perspective that tends to mock and distrust what belongs to a former time.) Neither do they participate in that part of our contemporary culture that, as Arjun Appadurai suggests, promotes a nostalgia without memory – a world in which people look back to events and places they have never lost and simply take what they need from the past out of a 'synchronic warehouse of cultural scenarios' that function as a 'temporal central casting' according to the desires of a political moment.[7] On the contrary, these figures exist in a context without this disjunctive overlapping. They are part, instead, of a sensibility in which there is a distinction and a distance between the past and the present. They belong to a world that has a memory; consequently, they move about in places that carry the burden and the authority of what was once in them. There is an object to these people's sadness.[8]

Through their nostalgia, these figures sometimes sentimentalize and fictionalize a past that, perhaps, never fully existed. At times they seem to subscribe to what has now become a standard way of thinking about nostalgia – that it corrupts reality by idealizing the past and by eradicating what had been difficult. On other occasions, though, their yearning for home does not conform to this expectation, for it readily acknowledges the troublesome as well as the blissful events of another period in their lives. Their nostalgia does not always mute the negative. Similarly, their homesickness does not necessarily contaminate their judgment so that they naively embrace something that never was, negate what is valuable in the present, and resist the possibilities of the future. On the contrary,

their longing often gives them the means to move beyond themselves and their past – it creates new maps. Their nostalgia is a
significantly more complicated experience than the easy utterance
of the word usually allows. Theirs is not a response that primarily
trivializes, simplifies, and misrepresents a former time; instead, their
writing toward home is an event that brings into itself all the
intricacies of the nostalgic experience.

In order to discuss how these figures engage the nostalgic
moment and involve themselves in the act of recollection, I have
divided the book into three parts: I: Voyages and Exile, II: Childhood Spaces, and III: The Idea of Recollection.

Part I: Voyages and Exile is about the nostalgia experienced by
those who sailed away from the shores of Britain – those who left on
voyages of discovery, of necessity, and of choice – and were, therefore, absent from the 'Fatherland' or home for extensive periods of
time, some for the rest of their lives. And it is also about the longing
felt by those who suffer displacement at home. Each chapter in this
section addresses the character and the consequences of their subsequent yearning and exile.

Voyages and Exile opens with a discussion of Charles Darwin's
nostalgia when he was gone five years from England on board the
H.M.S. Beagle. In 'Nostalgia and the Voyage of the *Beagle*' I describe
the nature of Darwin's yearning for home and consider the consequences of it for his understanding of the principles that were to
inform his work on the origin of the species. I suggest that, contrary
to what one might expect, by augmenting his sensitivity to the lost
and present memories in the landscape of his travels, Darwin's
homesickness contributed to his desire and his ability to restructure
accepted scientific thought. In addition, I propose that his mapping
of the topography of memory during the voyage helps clarify nostalgia's idiosyncratic relationship to remembrance. Through Darwin's example one more readily comprehends the paradox that
nostalgia's memory requires the obliteration of the past. Like Darwin, one needs a period of forgetfulness if one is to structure and,
thus, remember experience and restore the aura to it. Nostalgia
depends as much upon forgetting as upon remembering.

Through Darwin's experience, one also comes to appreciate more
vividly the fact that nostalgia is not necessarily a purge that rids
memory of the dangerous or the violent. It does not, as some would
claim, consistently reject the negative or cast the unwanted into
oblivion. Instead, nostalgia occasionally clears away the quieter,

edenic moments and surfaces the excitement associated with the more difficult, fearful, and threatening episodes from the past.

In the second chapter of Part I, '*The Last of England* and the Representation of Longing', I focus upon portraits of homesickness. I use the occasion of the voyages of emigration and the genre of emigration painting popular in mid-nineteenth-century Britain to examine the sentimental nature of nostalgia and to address the question: how is it possible adequately to represent longing – what kinds of images satisfactorily signify a yearning for something that is irrevocably absent? On looking closely at these paintings, particularly at Ford Madox Brown's *The Last of England*, one soon comprehends the possibilities and difficulties inherent in the task. In particular, one sees how hard it is to bypass sentimentality and find a genuine means of expressing loss. It is too easy to create a counter text to the intended subject and produce a painting that represents itself rather than what is internal to its stated purpose. The canvases of these genre painters depicting the departure of emigrants for North America, Australia, and New Zealand illustrate the temptation to let the fascination with detail overwhelm the fact of absence and, thus, compromise the character of nostalgia's memory that, as I discussed in the previous chapter, requires a forgetting as well as a remembering. I close the chapter by turning to Ovid's *Tristia*. As one of the most poignant commentaries on exile, its verses offer some insight into the malleable, metamorphic, and subjective images attending longing and absence; they help explain why the representation of these experiences can be fraught with difficulty.

In the third chapter, 'R. L. Stevenson's Nationalism and the Dualities of Exile', I explore the complex nostalgia of Robert Louis Stevenson who, as a young man and as an 'amateur emigrant', willingly sailed away from the shores of England to live a life in exile. This circumstance, though, did not prevent his feeling at once hopeful and homesick, and did not stop him from alternating between wanting to move on and wanting to return home. His vacillation was part of his acute sensitivity to the antithetical character of experience – his inclination to remark upon his own contrary impulses and to dwell between contentment and longing, approval and disapproval, collectivity and individuality, the present and the past. Because of this orientation, Stevenson readily acknowledged the Janus-like glances of the nostalgic moment in which he simultaneously engaged what is and what was or recalled what had been both painful and blissful, terrifying and golden. At times, though, Stevenson seems to have wanted to break away from this perspective by succumbing to the abstracting and contracting powers of longing that for the moment allowed him to transcend his contrary impulses. This submission, however, never lasted long, for Stevenson soon qualified the consequent synthesis by returning his attention to those ambiguities that all too easily reasserted themselves. Stevenson's exile, his nostalgia for Scotland, and his intermittent nationalism offer poignant examples of an engagement with a yearning that never completely escapes a consciousness of duality.

In the final chapter of this section, 'The "shaking, uncertain ground" of Elizabeth Gaskell's narratives', I address the experience of exile that belongs to people who never leave their native land but are uprooted by changes in their environment. To consider this form of exile and its attendant nostalgia, I discuss the ways in which Gaskell removes her characters from the protective circumference of the collective memory, places them in a nonsynchronic landscape, sends them in search of a refuge, and then requires them to imagine alternative ways of mapping their environment – a task made more complex by the coming of the railroads and the laying down of new tracks upon the land.

In the discussion I distinguish between two kinds of nostalgia: The first creates sites of memory that freeze and attempt to conserve or frame a detached moment; the second evokes places of memory and attaches one's yearning to a wider orbit and multiple dimensions that continually qualify the experience of longing. Gaskell's preference is for the latter. Hers is a nostalgia that exists not at the expense of historical understanding.

In Part II: Childhood Spaces I turn my attention away from those who were either displaced or separated from their 'Fatherland' and focus, instead, upon those who felt exiled from their childhood and longed to return to the landscape of their youth, re-enter its rooms, and reclaim the self that had once inhabited them.

To open this section I return to Robert Louis Stevenson. Reading through Stevenson's prose and poetry one soon realizes that his nostalgia for Scotland was not nearly as pressing as his desire for his early years there. In 'The Landscape of *A Child's Garden of Verses*' I point out that even though Stevenson spoke of his childhood as a 'very mixed experience, full of fever, nightmare, insomnia, painful days and interminable nights', he also remembered the happier moments that combined with the difficult to make his boyhood a more intense time than the present. As an adult he wanted to relive that intensity; consequently, he often turned his attention to the absorbing spaces of his youth and attempted to re-enter their flexible and synthetic landscape. Nostalgic for this prospect, he not only re-engaged the play, the vicarious violence, and the places of his early years but also began composing *A Child's Garden of Verses* (1885). These poems offered him a sanctuary that was more durable and satisfying than that afforded by his nationalism, for they were his means of writing toward home and reclaiming, momentarily, what was no longer fully available to him. These verses helped him walk back into the spaces of his early years and recover the 'elasticity' of childhood that had allowed him to inhabit a malleable space. The poems in *A Child's Garden of Verses* are about Stevenson's nostalgia for this flexibility. In its verses the dualities of home and distant skies, land and sea, trees and ships, are not alienating; they do not exile the child, for in his terrain, beds and books, darkness and light, meadows and seas, pillows and battlefields mingle to form a single subjective topography. Surrounded by this landscape the child belongs to a larger perspective that collapses the distant and the contiguous. With ease, he journeys back and forth between modes of consciousness and varieties of terrain without the experience of difference that can complicate the adult experience.

The second chapter in Part II moves from a longing for the expansive landscape of *A Child's Garden of Verses* to a nostalgia for the private interiors of home. In 'Rooms Without Mirrors: The Childhood Interiors of Ruskin, Pater, and Stevenson' I discuss John Ruskin's, Walter Horatio Pater's, and Robert Louis Stevenson's nostalgia for the rooms of home. I describe how each of these figures attempts, by means of his autobiographical writing, to repossess and re-enter these most intimate spaces of childhood.

In their texts Ruskin, Pater, and Stevenson dwell upon their longing for their idiosyncratic relationship to the interiors of their childhood. They are all conscious of how their physical being defines their sense of their surroundings. From their perspective, bodies, not objects, structure the spaces of home. Each, not surprisingly, experiences this phenomenon in a different way. The result is that in their autobiographical texts Ruskin, Pater, and Stevenson offer three distinct models of how the consciousness of one's physical being illuminates the interiors of home. Ruskin speaks of the invisible body; Pater, of the æsthetic body, and Stevenson of the ubiquitous body.

In addition I note that as children, Ruskin, Pater, and Stevenson, had lived in rooms without mirrors. In their early years they had no need to seek its confirming and synthetic gaze. For these young subjects the looking-glass world was irrelevant. As nostalgic and alienated adults, however, they come to require the mirror's reflection. Through their autobiographical writing they place a mirror in these rooms and through its reflection attempt to rediscover the self that once lived there. Like nostalgia itself, the mirror not only reveals but also protects. It shields those who look at it from a direct sighting of the past and prevents what lives in their memory from fading or disappearing. It urges the eye away from the stare of the direct experience that can stultify and even destroy its subject.

The final section of the book, Part III: The Idea of Recollection, examines the nature of recollection in the nostalgic experience.

When writers reach toward events and places from their past, of course, they inevitably reveal their attachment to recollection. Among those who are more than usually conscious of this indispensable companion is Robert Louis Stevenson. In the first chapter in this section, 'R. L. Stevenson and the Idea of Recollection', I consider Stevenson's commentary on the character of remembrance. His remarks on the subject allow one not only to reflect upon the moment of recollection but also to become more aware of its visual elements – to notice the optical metaphors (his references to magic lanterns, kaleidoscopes, mirrors, and thaumatropes) that help structure remembrance and, in turn, shape his prose. Stevenson's observations remind one that recollection is not merely a looking back; it also a commitment to a particular way of seeing.

With this principle in mind, I open the chapter by discussing Stevenson's visual orientation (his lifelong interest in images). I then continue by discussing his thoughts about the character of remembrance. More than many others, Stevenson had a sense of a past that is focused and available. His experience with recollection is quite different from that endured by those who are sensitive to a vanishing and shadowy past that refuses fully to be recognized. His vividly recollected and durable images are not the frail, retreating, slipping, and consumed memories that, for instance, in the next century, belong to Walter Benjamin and Michael Ondaatje who can no longer find a legitimizing referent in the world that surrounds them. The condition of empire, I propose, modifies and varies the act of remembrance and alters the nature of one's nostalgia.

In the last chapter, 'From the Vignette to the Rectangular: Bergson, Turner, and Remembrance', I continue to discuss the nature of recollection. This time, using Henri Bergson's theory of memory, I suggest that even though writing toward home seems to create texts that concentrate on a single journey from the present to the past, memory really has more avenues into consciousness than that which leads the attention from the now into an incontiguous then. In *Matière et Mémoire* Bergson insists that memory does not necessarily 'consist in a regression from the present to the past, but, on the contrary, in a progression from the past to the present'. Thus, rather than simply waiting passively to be retrieved by a searching or longing eye, memory also moves forward to meet and intersect with a present that either rejects, acknowledges, or uses it.

In order to explore this alternative paradigm and consider how it comments upon the act of writing toward home, I call to mind, perhaps surprisingly, a small selection from the numerous etching-engravings and mezzotints of J. M. W. Turner. In their own interesting way, these prints mirror aspects of Bergson's understanding of the relationship between the past and the present, and serve as visual parallels to the process of recollection. Turner's prints are appropriate analogues because their long series of intermediate proofs (printed before the plate's publication) allow one to see the successive degrees by which, according to Bergson's theory, the 'virtual state' of memory grows into the 'actual perception' of recollection. Significantly these comparisons between the Bergsonian theories of memory and the evolution of Turner's prints would not have necessarily been alienating to Turner's champion, John Ruskin, for whenever Ruskin studied the engravings, he found memory and recollection at work – he saw 'an arrangement of remembrances'. Ruskin believed that Turner, more than most artists, consciously and unconsciously beckoned remembrance to initiate, develop, and modify his pictures' images. Turner *recollected* rather than *imagined* his compositions.

After commenting upon the relationship between what is marginal and what is dominant in recollection and upon the elasticity of memory, I conclude the chapter by suggesting that if one moves from these parallels between Turner's work and the act of remembrance and returns to the autobiographical writings or narratives of Darwin, Stevenson, Gaskell, Ruskin, and Pater, one can no longer think of their texts as one-way streets, leading the reader and author from the present to the past. Darwin does not simply look back toward home; Stevenson does not merely cast his longing glances behind him; Gaskell does not elide the irregularities of memory; Ruskin does not just work his way backwards via his retrospective vision; and Pater does not retrace the fantasy of his childhood only through a narrative that travels from adulthood to childhood. Texts like *The Voyage of the Beagle, A Child's Garden of Verses, Cranford, Praeterita,* and 'The Child in the House' emerge from a plethora of directions, sources, and shifting images that intersect and revolve in overlapping circles to form a complicated network of roads. Like nostalgia, recollection revolves the eye in many directions at once – it is not a simple way of seeing and reconstructing the past.

I close with a catalogue of afterthoughts about the experience of nostalgia and recollection that have emerged in the course of writing the book.

Notes

1.   See, for example, M. Girouard, *Return to Camelot: Chivalry and the English Gentleman* (New Haven: Yale University Press, 1981).
2.   J. Hofer, 'Texts and Documents: Medical Dissertation on Nostalgia by Johannes Hofer, 1688', trans. C. K. Anspach, *Bulletin of the Institute of the History of Medicine,* II (1934) 381.
3.   For articles on the history of nostalgia, see, for instance, G. Rosen's 'Nostalgia: A "Forgotten" Psychological Disorder', *Clio Medica,* X (1975) 28–51 and J. Starobinski 'The Idea of Nostalgia' (Trans. W. S. Kemp), *Diogenes* (summer, 1966) no. 54, 81–103. See also D. Lowenthal, *The Past is a Foreign Country* (Cambridge: Cambridge University Press, 1985) pp. 10–11.
4.   In Richard Hunter and Ida Macalpine's *Three Hundred Years of Psychiatry: 1538–1860* (London: Oxford University Press, 1970) pp. 499–500 there is a case study written by an army surgeon, Robert Hamilton, who in 1781 recognized the symptoms of 'nostalgia' and arranged to have his patient sent home to Wales. According to Hunter and Macalpine, this case was the first reported in England.
5.   J. Hofer, 'Texts and Documents: Medical Dissertation on Nostalgia by Johannes Hofer, 1688', 382.
6.   G. Rosen, 'Nostalgia: A "Forgotten" Psychological Disorder', 47.
7.   Arjun Appadurai, 'Disjuncture and Difference in the Global Cultural Economy', *The Phantom Public Sphere.* ed. Bruce Robbins (Minneapolis: University of Minnesota Press, 1993) pp. 272–3.
8.   In *On Longing: Narratives of the Miniature, the Gigantic, the Souvenir, the Collection* (Baltimore: The Johns Hopkins University Press, 1984) Susan Stewart speaks of nostalgia as 'a sadness without an object'. The longing experienced by the figures discussed in this book, however, seems, very much, to have a specified object.

Part I
Voyages and Exile

The several more remote predisposing internal causes are latent entirely in the body, having the strength to excite the mind again to seek ideas of the Fatherland. Especially, moreover, some disease preceding this, whatever it may have been, in measure aggravates either the seriousness or the length of time and furnishes the occasion for the nostalgia. (The previous) disease having been badly handled, or (the patient) in some manner having been deprived of attentions, they easily become sad, continually think about the Fatherland, and because of the perpetual desire of returning there, they finally fall into the illness. The preceding external causes owe their derivation to these antecedents in the changed manner of living. First the variety of the weather contributes however little to the disposition of the blood and the destroying of the spirits; especially do the foreign manners, diverse kinds of food, make for them injuries to be borne, and various other troublesome accidents, and one might add six hundred other things.

From Johannes Hofer, *Medical Dissertation on
Nostalgia or Homesickness*, 1688

1

Nostalgia and the Voyage of the *Beagle*

> Forgetfulness, by rolling my memories along in its tide, has done
> more that merely wear them down or consign them to oblivion. The
> profound structure it has created out of the fragments allows me to
> achieve a more stable equilibrium, and to see a clearer pattern.
>
> C. Lévi-Strauss, *Tristes Tropiques*
> (New York: Atheneum, 1974) pp. 43–4

DARWIN'S NOSTALGIA

On 27 December 1832, when the *H.M.S. Beagle* set sail from Devonport, Darwin embarked upon a voyage that took him away from England for nearly five years. As those familiar with the voyage's particulars know, the ocean passage was not always smooth. Darwin suffered from seasickness. No matter how frequently he willed himself to endure the rougher weather, to center his thoughts on the future and honor his 'ambition to take a fair place among scientific men', and no matter how his poetic sensibility esteemed the sea's grandeur, he could not gain his sea legs.[1] Despairing, he occasionally kept to his hammock and complained to his mentor John Henslow that he was 'sea-sick & miserable'.[2] Worst of all, his discomfort exacerbated his longing for home; it intensified a nostalgia that, although not continuous, was more tenacious than his physical distress.[3] He yearned for his family, his friends, Shrewsbury, Cambridge, and 'long-past happy days' not only when the waves advanced but also when they receded and the sea lay calm and luminous beneath tropical skies.[4] Moreover, he longed for them on land when he rode through the plains and into the primeval forest. There his 'former home' seemed far away.

Darwin's letters, of course, often chronicle his painful wish to be back among his friends and register his fears concerning the 'enormous period of time' he is to be away. He confides to Henslow, 'I am

15

sometimes afraid I shall never be able to hold out for the whole voyage.' In other letters he speaks of his yearning to 'see anything' that 'strongly' reminds him of England. Almost apologetically, he compares himself to a 'schoolboy' who wishes to be 'there, enjoying my Holydays'.[5] The past rises, in Darwin's words, 'like departed spirits' to haunt him.[6] At times images from his past show through a translucent present to create a double image. The past and present rest within one another like superimposed photographic negatives that print into a single double image. Darwin writes, 'I find I steadily have a distant prospect of a very quiet parsonage & I can see it even through a grove of Palms.'[7] The present contains a mirage of the past. At other times, though, the doubling is disorienting. In a letter to his sister Caroline (27 December 1835) he muses, 'how strange it is, to think, that perhaps at this very second Nancy is making a vain effort to rouse you all from your slumbers on a cold frosty morning.'[8] This doubling paradoxically emphasizes the distance between the two places; thus, Darwin must regard home, in his words, 'through the long interval of the Pacific & Indian oceans'.[9] The reality that there is 'nearly half the world between me & home' startles him.[10]

Attempting to diminish this interval Darwin writes other letters that, like telescopes, illusively collapse the distance between him and home. Endeavoring to unite the disparate landscapes, he writes wistfully to Caroline, 'but how great a difference between this & the beautiful scenes of England. I often think of the Garden at home as a Paradise; on a fine summers [sic] evening, when the birds are singing how I should enjoy to appear like a Ghost amongst you, whilstworking with the flowers.'[11]

THE VOYAGE OF THE *BEAGLE*

Not surprisingly, the homesickness that, at times, is enthusiasm's companion in Darwin's letters to England also finds its way – though less explicitly – into Darwin's accounts of the *Beagle*'s voyage.[12] His yearning, for instance, often influences his narrative's perspective. The nostalgic eye that turns to regard what is left behind cannot help but indulge comparison and let the past emerge as the legitimizing referent. Thus, Darwin looks at an insect and remarks on the similarity between it and a 'water beetle common in the ditches of England', captures a landscape by observing that 'The

country on the whole resembled the better parts of the Cambridg-
shire fens', and understands the steepness of a slope by remarking
that the hill 'would have checked the speed of an English mail-
coach'.[13] These comparisons are not merely for the sake of his
English readership; they are also there for the audience of his longing. They do not seek 'splendid contrasts'[14] between the magnificent
scenery of his travels and the familiar, quieter prospect of England;
instead, they journey home to find that 'pensive stillness' which, in
Darwin's words, 'makes the autumn in England indeed the evening
of the year'.[15]

Darwin's nostalgia also sheathes the narrative's æsthetic sensibility. Although Darwin is awed by the sight of the Cordilleras and the
intricacies of a tropical forest, he never fully surrenders to them his
understanding of what is beautiful. Like beings whose proportions
are not familiar, the mountain ranges and the forest's dense foliage
stand just outside the boundary of acceptance. They are visions of
excess or exception that his nostalgia holds at bay. In his appreciation of them, he cannot help but invoke what his homesickness
considers the more acceptable proportion and beauty of the English
landscape. The pleasure of a prospect, therefore, resides in its ability
to recall 'the wilder parts of England', and a tree's splendor dwells
among its branches that project 'with the vigour of an English oak'.[16]
His longing for home even dwarfs what stands before him so that
the Welsh Mountains loom larger, more real than the soaring
Andes.[17]

In particular, Darwin, who regards himself as exiled, is sensitive to
the idea of home. His longing for the fatherland and for the familial
provokes a criticism of those who, according to his nostalgic understanding, live without any knowledge of it. He scoffs at those
'barbarians' who lack forks and knives and are in want of home's
'comforts': 'I am sure no cottage or hovel in England could be found
in a state so utterly destitute of every comfort.'[18] He disapproves of
the Fuegians; their 'want of accommodation' and 'lack of domestic
affections' distress him. The 'homecoming' of the three Fuegians
(Jeremy Button, Fuegia Basket, and York Minster) after spending
three years with missionaries in England seems especially to reflect
Darwin's discomfort. (Part of the *Beagle*'s charge was to take these
three back to their homeland.) From his perspective, these returning
Fuegians have, in fact, no home to come back to, for their relatives
are dishonest, and, worse, their dwellings are crude, bare, and
temporary. Darwin believes they 'cannot know the feeling of having

a home'; they cannot be privy to what he later, in his metaphysical notebooks, called 'a love of place'.[19] Furthermore, their reunion is not what he would have desired his to be. Whether rightly or wrongly, he senses the returning Fuegians' disorientation. Neither linguistically nor physically do the trio seem to connect with their people. They seem to belong nowhere, for their voyage to England and back has dressed them in new clothes, introduced new tastes to their palates, and pressed new words into their speech. Upon a later visit he is relieved to find them more settled.[20] They have, maybe, recovered some memory of their origins. Perhaps implicit within Darwin's attention to home and embedded within his expressions of longing is an acknowledgment of origin. The soil of home contains the deepest strata of being. Longing embraces belonging and tacitly admits a place – a fatherland – from which the individual issues. It presumes a progenitor and thus attempts to tender passage to that origin.

REMEMBERING AND FORGETTING

Most significantly Darwin's longing gives voice to nostalgia's peculiar relationship to memory. Suffering from what Darwin, in the Hartley tradition, termed 'absence of association', Darwin cannot help but acknowledge the importance of memory, especially its defense against loneliness and exile. Whenever he feels deprived of home and the familiar images seem to slip closer to oblivion by wrapping themselves in the weeds of forgetfulness, he holds fast to nostalgia's sanctuary of memory.[21] His survival depends upon it. In a letter to W. D. Fox (15 February 1836), for instance, Darwin writes, 'We are on opposite sides of the World & everything is topsy turvy: but I thank Heaven, my memory is in its right place & I can bring close to me, the faces of many of my friends.'[22]

Darwin's dependence upon memory to assuage his homesickness is, perhaps, easily recognizable. No travel account, biography, or autobiography overlooks its importance. One, of course, immediately thinks of Wordsworth's reliance on memory or recollection. Darwin's reliance upon memory, however, is not as straightforward or, perhaps, as available as it seems to be for Wordsworth because in his case the remembrance that belongs to nostalgia is replete with paradox. It is so because the memory that helps the individual endure absence and assuage his longing by blocking forgetfulness also depends upon what it hinders. That is to say, nostalgia's memory both resists and requires the obliteration of the past. This paradox infuses the sensibility of Darwin's narrative.

It is in this sense that Darwin's voyage repeats Odysseus's. Both travelers, of course, find themselves, in Homer's words, 'held back on the broad ocean'.[23] More significantly, though, each is on a journey that confronts forgetfulness.[24] Just as Odysseus must contend with beings like Circe and the Sirens who snatch memory from their victims and make them 'utterly forget their own country' or remembrance of their family, so must Darwin cope with oblivion's presence. Although Darwin, unlike Odysseus, never lets images of his country or family slip completely away from his consciousness, he must often contend with the fact of forgetfulness – the reality of the unremembered or buried past. Experiences compel him to be sensitive to change and loss. Like Odysseus's, his very wanderings from one port to another invoke a structure that continuously alters as it forms. When the *Beagle* moves up and down the South American coast, Darwin's life becomes as protean and, perhaps, as unpredictable as the sea that carries him. He laments that the voyage's plans undergo a 'complete revolution'.[25] Rarely may he return to the places he leaves behind. In a letter to Caroline (29 April 1836) he complains, 'There is nothing, which I so much long for, as to see any spot & any object, which I have seen before & can say I will see again.'[26] He wants to go back, primarily, it seems, to reinforce his memory and unseat forgetfulness. Darwin fears that the accumulating richness and variety of what he sees in his travels will stifle remembrance. Like the multitude of white butterflies that early in the voyage surround the *Beagle* and with their dense splendor block the view, the plethora of images threatens to hinder his remembrance of what has gone by and will pass before him. Darwin begins to resemble José Arcadio, in *One Hundred Years of Solitude*, who forgets 'because life at sea had saturated his memory with too many things to remember'.[27] His fears echo Coleridge's sensitivity to 'the intense *vividness of the Remembrance*' that can itself obliterate the details of a recollected landscape.[28]

The voyage's shifting reference also renders Darwin more privy than usual to the mutability of his surroundings and to the fact of forgetfulness.[29] Change and extermination are always close at hand; they are ready to move away from the margin and enter the text's consciousness. In his narrative, for instance, Darwin periodically writes about the instability of the various governments and the

wars of extermination against the Indians. As Captain Fitzroy cynic-
ally notes: revolution 'is actually the fashion in South America' (19
April 1833).[30] Darwin remarks on the desperate revolutions in St Fé
and Las Conchas – a state which underwent fifteen changes 'in the
course of nine months' – and describes the political upheavals that
turned Buenos Aires 'upside down'.[31] Forms and people change,
disappear, and drive themselves and others into oblivion.

These political revolutions, of course, have their parallels in the
upheavals Darwin observes in the natural world. Throughout the
voyage, like 'a navigator of old', Darwin registers the most trivial
signs of change in the surrounding landscapes, and, consequently,
understands that what now stands before him has altered and will
continue to change or disappear and be forgotten. For instance,
when a fox dashes in front of him, Darwin suspects that because
of man's intrusion, in years to come, the fox 'will be classed with the
dodo, as an animal which has perished from the face of the earth';[32]
and when he examines the various tropical flora he wonders, given
the evidence of physical changes, what will become of them and
who will remember them. Nothing, though, disturbs Darwin so
profoundly as nature's 'enormous convulsions' that create 'streams
of stones' and gaping fissures that rupture the earth's foundations.
These convulsions not only disturb the natural world but also frac-
ture Darwin's own sense of stability and the earth's remembrance of
itself. Horrified, he looks at the disastrous consequences of the
Chilean earthquake and writes: 'A bad earthquake at once destroys
our oldest associations: the earth, the very emblem of solidity, has
moved beneath our feet like a thin crust over a fluid; – one second of
time has created in the mind a strange idea of insecurity, which
hours of reflection would not have produced.'[33] Darwin realizes that
in one moment the earthquake consigns to oblivion the significance
of the present. The nostalgic Darwin cannot help but turn to home,
indulge his longing, and write: 'If beneath England the now inert
subterranean forces should exert those powers, which most assuredly in former geological ages they exerted, how completely would
the entire condition of the country be changed!'[34] Oblivion is not
merely the matter of the past or the future. It informs the present.

Darwin's sensitivity to the fact of forgetfulness and the threat of
extinction has, of course, other consequences for his understanding
of what he sees during his travels. As if acknowledging the power
and readiness of forgetfulness to conceal remembrance, he envies
those, like the gauchos, who have the ability to temper or restrain its

potency. He notes, for instance, that at 'one glance' the gauchos can obstruct forgetfulness's intrusion by filling in a 'whole history' of a horse's tracks. Respectfully he writes, 'Supposing they examine the track of a thousand horses, they will soon guess the number of mounted ones by seeing how many have cantered; by the depth of the other impressions, whether any horses were loaded with cargoes'.[35] He admires the gauchos' independence and their abilities to live as nomads – perhaps by moving in the tracks of change they keep pace with it and rarely experience the difference between either the past and the present or their temporary berths and 'home'. In a sense, because they obliterate forgetfulness, nostalgia is not within their ken.

Similarly Darwin praises those who by recognizing an animal's claw marks on a tree can determine whether or not a jaguar has been near and those who know by the parrots' sudden flurry among the trees where someone has arrived in the forest.[36] These individuals recover what otherwise would remain forgotten and invisible. Indeed, their custom of 'tracking' is not unlike Darwin's. He too wishes to trace and understand the vestiges of what is little known or extinct. He despairs that in Patagonia there is not the least vestige of anything because all traces of a former time are covered up by the deep entangled forest.

Subscribing to nostalgia's idiom Darwin is particularly attentive to the remains of what once had lived. For instance, he is fascinated to discover the skull of a murdered captain, to see a sailor's body perfectly preserved in the icy soil of the South Shetland Islands,[37] and to find an ancient seed buried deep in a sandpit.[38] His attentiveness to what endures within a landscape that decays and forgets predisposes him to speculate on such matters as 'How long does any vestige of a fallen tree remain?',[39] a question that obviously echoes his sensitivity to loss. At the moment he asks that question, he turns his mind back to England – a gesture that not only repeats his reaction to the Chilean earthquake but, more significantly, reflects nostalgia's desire to exempt home from mutability's authority. In fact, wishing to hold home still, Darwin, before the voyage ends, begs his sisters not to cut down the trees behind the family home. Not surprisingly, upon his return Darwin expresses his relief to find that unlike the rest of England, 'the good old Town of Shrewsbury & its inhabitants' are unchanged – they 'will go on', he wryly boasts, 'as they now are to Doomsday' (6 October 1836).[40] Comforted to discover that time has not completely unraveled and discarded the cloth of his childhood, Darwin notes that during his absence although a few individuals aged significantly, neither intimate friends nor close family members had died.

Pursued by the augury of forgetfulness, Darwin, like most travelers, wants to hold on to as many of his experiences as he can. And prompted by an impulse to memorialize and give safe custody to what he has seen, Darwin jots down impressions and notes during his five-year voyage. Like the letters he sends home, these notes help him hold on to the scattered pieces of his wanderings. He feels relieved when they arrive safely in England. In 1832, for instance, he tells Caroline (24 October – 24 November), 'I am glad the journal arrived safe . . . . I would as soon loose a piece of my memory as it. – I feel it is of such consequence to my preserving a just recollection of the different places we visit.'[41] In a similar mode Darwin, as was the practice of naturalists, also becomes an avid collector and assembles crates of bird skins, megatherium bones, plants, butterflies, insects, animal hides, rocks, fish, and fossils that he periodically ships to Henslow. Like others before and after him, Darwin worries lest they suffer from damage and mismanagement. In March 1834, for instance, he writes to Henslow, 'I have been alarmed by the expression cleaning all the bones [Darwin had numbered in sequence each of the megatherium's bones] as I am afraid the printed numbers will be lost . . . such and *many other* points **entirely** depend on the numbers being carefully preserved.'[42] To eradicate the numbers would be like losing sight of the horses' tracks. Without them he could not, of course, reassemble what had been present before and see through to the distant past. The numbers shield his memory form the blind gaze of forgetfulness. Like the cards that Pilar Ternera reads in *One Hundred Years of Solitude*, they recover what has been.

To protect his tracks, so that he like Odysseus would return with his 'treasures', Darwin sets himself the task of labeling each specimen. As if laying steppingstones across the River Lethe, he places names on each item and secures what otherwise might fade or disappear. These give him passage to the past to reclaim an intimacy with what is absent. They collapse so much of what he wanted to remember into themselves that they, paradoxically, afford him the luxury of dipping his toes into the water and relinquishing a little. The privilege allows him, as it was to permit Claude Lévi-Strauss, to see the larger outlines of his travels and compose his narrative and his thoughts about what he has seen. Darwin needs, as did

Lévi-Strauss, a period of forgetfulness in order to structure and, thus, remember his experiences. Lévi-Strauss describes the phenomenon: 'Forgetfulness, by rolling my memories along in its tide, has done more than merely wear them down or consign them to oblivion. The profound structure it has created out of the fragments allows me to achieve a more stable equilibrium, and to see a clearer pattern.'[43] Forgetfulness, then, need not destroy memory. It can also admit what it tends to obstruct. Forgetfulness must accompany memory in the traveler's narrative. (It should be added here that Alexander Von Humboldt's narratives of his travels are, it seems, a notable exception. Unlike Darwin, Humboldt was not so willing to let forgetfulness play a role. He almost choked his text with measurements and facts. The consequence is that his *Narratives of Travels to the Equinoctial Region* has, in a sense, no fictive shape.)

It is, perhaps, a recognition of these two unlikely companions (remembering and forgetting) that creates the convention of the retrospective section that frequently closes a travel narrative. In 'Retrospect' at the conclusion of *The Voyage of the Beagle*, for instance, Darwin acknowledges their presence. In these final pages he traces, as Lévi-Strauss was later to do, the 'clearer pattern' by identifying what images dominate and, therefore, what memories remain to give shape to the whole experience. By isolating the dominant images (for example, the plains of Patagonia, the wildness of the Fuegians, or the devastation after the Chilean earthquake), Darwin pays tribute to the memory that exists within the context of loss. He hopes that in the future these experiences will help him re-enter what time has left behind. These isolated images will hook on to the past and bring forward, closer to the present, the associations they carry with them. They will work both with and against oblivion. Like the notes and crates of specimens that he reassembles and arranges into the narrative, his naming of these images brackets segments of the past and prevents them from being swept entirely away by the current of forgetfulness.

FORGETFULNESS AND NOSTALGIA

The fact of forgetfulness that urges Darwin to bracket or mark what he sees does more than influence the course of his perspective. It also comments upon the character and consequences of the nostalgic moment.

Throughout his journey, Darwin's longing prompts him to think of the delicate life of nostalgia. He realizes that nostalgia depends upon forgetfulness as well as remembrance. Like a metaphor, this understanding runs beneath the surface of his text and its preoccupation with what survives. It is as if nostalgia roams between the tenor of death and the vehicle of life. Like Orpheus, nostalgia attempts to recover what darkness imprisons so that it might lead what is lost back towards the light of the living present. Nostalgia charms death with its bitter-sweet melodies (in Proust's idiom, with the phrase from Vinteuil's sonata[44]). But, as Orpheus learns, nostalgia can never completely resurrect what it releases. The past can never join the present. It must always remain several paces behind and eventually travel once more through the river of forgetfulness. When nostalgia turns to claim what it has raised, recognition fades. Briefly the released image inhabits consciousness, but soon the vividness weakens, and even though one might reach out like Orpheus, to hold it, the image turns to retread its path to the underworld of the unconscious. Nostalgia, therefore, continually repeats Orpheus's journey and, thus, knows a double death. The consequence for Darwin is that he understands that what resides in the regions of the past will necessarily die again – no matter how long he labors to retain it.

Even with this knowledge, though, Darwin must descend into the underworld of the mind if he is to find passage home. Just as Athena urged Odysseus to travel to Hades to confront the dead and recover, for a while, the presence of the beloved from his past, so does nostalgia require the same of Darwin. Neither Darwin nor Odysseus is allowed to forget the pain of remembering his origins. If Odysseus is to find his way home and outwit Scylla's jaws, he must meet his long-dead mother and friends. And so must Darwin periodically face the memories of his childhood, home, and friends. (I do not mean to imply that he must seek his mother; I simply suggest that he must recall the people and places of home.) These images keep his desire for England alive and ease his passage home. Significantly, nostalgia maintains both Odysseus's and Darwin's identity. It works against the 'idiocy' of insomnia that García Márquez describes in *One Hundred Years of Solitude*. There, of course, the sickness of insomnia causes people to lose their memories. Eventually, their recollection of childhood 'begins to be erased', and 'then the name and notion of things, and finally the identity of people and even the awareness' of their 'being' disappears.[45]

Forgetfulness is not always so destructive. Both Lévi-Strauss's and Darwin's experiences suggest that it can be constructive, beyond merely helping them pattern or structure their travels' particulars. In Darwin's case particularly, forgetfulness also produces an interval through which the individual can regard the past. Homesickness obviously needs this space so it might recognize the disparity between what is and what is not. It helps us, in Darwin's words, 'sympathize with ourselves in our present, in comparison to our former selves'.[46] In particular the spaces created by the periods of forgetfulness between nostalgic episodes make it possible to filter memory to reveal what is important and powerful. In this manner nostalgia purges memory, and, in a sense, rids it of its 'rogues' in the same way that species discard what is less than essential to their being when they move from past to future generations.[47] Darwin's nostalgia permits him, for instance, a few years after the voyage to disregard or minimize the colossus – seasickness – and write longingly to Captain Fitzroy (20 February 1840), 'However others may look back to the *Beagles* [*sic*] voyage, now that the small disagreeable parts are well nigh forgotten, I think it far the *most fortunate circumstance in my life* that the chance afforded by your offer of taking a naturalist fell on me – I often have the most vivid and delightful pictures of what I saw on board the *Beagle* pass before my eyes. – These recollections & what I learnt in Natural History I would not exchange for twice ten thousand a year.'[48] As a purge, though, nostalgia does not always rid memory of the dangerous or the violent. It does not, as some would claim, consistently reject the negative or cast the unwanted into oblivion. On the contrary, nostalgia occasionally clears away the quieter, edenic moments and surfaces the excitements associated with the more difficult, fearful, and threatening episodes – those that place the individual on the edge of disaster.[49] It honors what connects the individual to a sense of being. That is, nostalgia retains the thin line between the dead and the living, the forgetting and the remembering, in order to intensify experience and maintain the instinct for survival. Darwin's almost reverent attention to the riskier moments in *The Voyage of the Beagle* reflects this idiosyncrasy. After the voyage ends, he writes longingly of the times when he rode with the gauchos in hostile Indian territory and along wild mountain paths; he eagerly recalls the Fuegians' wildness and the exaggerated ruggedness of Tierra del Fuego; and he speaks in awe of the Chilean earthquake's fearful force and destruction. These experiences stimulate his mind in ways that the stability and habits of home cannot. They allow him to extend his understanding and to enlarge his point of reference.

Within the space between the past and the present, nostalgia's memory not only resurrects the dangerous, it also brings what had been peripheral into the center. The things to which Darwin, in Proust's idiom, had 'paid no attention', become important and what seemed significant disappears. In 'Retrospect', for instance, Darwin registers his astonishment that what eventually took 'so firm a hold' on his memory are the 'wretched' plains of Patagonia. It is not the 'more level, the greener and more fertile Pampas' that continue to pass before his eyes. He wonders why something that is marginal to the well-being of humanity should surpass such a serviceable and productive landscape and inhabit so great a portion of his consciousness. Looking back he understands that it is their enduring, boundless quality (the quality that defies oblivion or forgetfulness) that is more important to him than the 'civilized' character of the more fertile land. He explains that the Plains of Patagonia 'bear the stamp of having lasted, as they are now, for ages, and there appears no limit to their duration through future time'.[50] Darwin's experience is, once more, not far removed from Lévi-Strauss's. In *Tristes Tropiques*, combining Proust's preoccupations with Darwin's geological commentary, Lévi-Strauss describes what remains at the journey's end: 'time, the destroyer, has begun to pile up rubble. Sharp edges have been blunted and whole sections have collapsed: periods and places collide, are juxtaposed or are inverted, like strata displaced by the tremors on the crust of an ageing planet. Some insignificant detail belonging to the distant past may now stand out like a peak, while whole layers of my past have disappeared without a trace'.[51]

The periods of forgetfulness that distinguish and influence the nostalgic moment have yet other consequences. They also require the individual to regard experience from a distance. It is as if they offer the individual the view of one who stands at a mountain's crest. The landscape's particulars no longer splinter or arrest the larger field of vision. Instead, the details in their disappearing blend into a larger view so that, as Walter Benjamin suggests, 'the mysterious wholeness of the objects' becomes visible.[52] In other words, by reinserting objects into their former surroundings, nostalgia paradoxically restores the 'aura' to things remembered. Through nostalgia's perspective, the single butterfly isolated in a case absorbs into itself its former complicated and amazing habitat. Perhaps Darwin is therefore not always obligated to consider the single form of the orange tree or the mango and to regard his collection of specimens merely as orphaned pieces cut off from their previous surroundings. He may, with nostalgia's help, see them united into their larger landscape. Once more, he can, as he had done when he reached the crest of the Peuquenes ridge, look 'backwards' to see a glorious view.[53] At the end of his narrative, Darwin anticipates the quieter moments when liberated by forgetfulness and, consequently, freed from the myriads of fragments that confuse the eye, he will look upon each knowing its wholeness.[54] Each segment shall carry with it the map of home.

Of course, even though nostalgia can expand the point of reference, it can also restrict perspective. Because the longing for home sentimentalizes judgment by discarding the unwanted and inflating the desired, few trust its impulse or power. The critical and even analytical quality of Darwin's response to his own nostalgia, however, suggests that one should not be too quick to condemn nostalgia.[55] Admittedly, sections of Darwin's narrative easily slip into the skeptics' net. For instance, the generalizations about the glories of England with which he closes his narrative are not only sentimental but also self-laudatory. He speaks of the superiority of English ways and congratulates himself that 'I was born an Englishman'.[56] His nostalgia smooths imperialism's roughness. On the other hand, Darwin takes what he learns from nostalgia's custom of comparing the past with the present and of searching for vestiges of the past to help him in his work to 'revolutionize' and 'progress' the course of science. Comparison stimulates as well as stultifies, for Darwin's homesickness tenders him the opportunity to distance himself – to stand back and glance forward – and, thus, to break the habit of association so that he might not only long for home but also think about difference, change, and survival. His homesickness seems not to have curbed his critical abilities; instead, it seems to have spurred his sensitivity both to oblivion and to its attendant questions. The nostalgia that emerges from the tension between remembering and forgetting need not, therefore, always turn its subject's back to the future and bind him to a quest for what never can be fully recovered. Instead, if it chooses, it may use the spaces created by forgetfulness and the vividness of remembrance to create a context in which the individual may structure a criticism of the present. Darwin's example instructs that through nostalgia's paradoxical memory, the past need not close upon itself and upon those who look back to it with longing.

In the end, though, no matter how willingly Darwin's nostalgic impulse courts the critical eye, it cannot rid itself of the disturbing seed of forgetfulness that engenders longing. Darwin's engagement with his work through which he revises the history of the natural world can never obstruct this longing; it can only temper the pain of living intimately within a landscape where forgetfulness tugs at remembrance's sleeve. Darwin seems to recognize this reality when he writes about how his geological and natural studies barely enable him to carry the weight of his absence. In a letter to his sister Catherine, for instance, he explains, 'If it was not for these [invertebrate animals] & still more for geology, I would in short times make a bolt across the Atlantic to good old Shropshire.'[57] The sense of loss endures. No matter how vividly nostalgia restores by resurrecting the aura of the past and by revitalizing the present, there is no way to eradicate its engagement with what is irrevocably absent. That characteristic of its nature remains and can never be 'revised' or set aside.

Notes

1.   The quoted passage is from Darwin's *Autobiography* reprinted in *The Beagle Record: Selections from the Original Records and Written Accounts of the Voyage of H.M.S. Beagle*, ed. R.D. Keynes (Cambridge: Cambridge University Press, 1979) pp. 19–20. For examples of Darwin's sensitivity to the sublime, see *Charles Darwin's Beagle Diary*, ed. R.D. Keynes (Cambridge: Cambridge University Press, 1988), 30 December 1831 and 14 January 1832 (pp. 18–19), and see C. Darwin, *The Voyage of the Beagle*, ed. L. Engel (Garden City, New York: Doubleday, 1962) p. 499.

2.   *The Beagle Record*, p. 129.

3.   On 13 October 1834 Darwin wrote to his sister Caroline, 'I find being sick at stomach inclines one also to be homesick.' Ibid., p. 240.

4.   On 1 November 1832 Darwin wrote in his diary: 'A calm delightful day. – I know not the reason why such days always lead the mind to think of England and home. – It would seem as if the serenity of the air allowed the thoughts with greater ease to pass & repass the long interval.' See *Charles Darwin's Beagle Diary*, p. 113.

5.   *The Beagle Record*, pp. 229, 236, 296.

6.   F. Burkhardt and S. Smith, eds, *The Correspondence of Charles Darwin*, I: 1821–1830 (Cambridge: Cambridge University Press, 1985) p. 145.

7.   *The Beagle Record*, p. 54.

8.   Burkhardt and Smith, *The Correspondence of Charles Darwin*, I, p. 472.

9.   *The Beagle Record*, p. 155.

10. Ibid., p. 296.

11. Ibid., p. 155.
12. For examples of how Darwin's enthusiasm for the voyage alternated with his homesickness see his letters to W.D. Fox dated 19 September 1831 and May 1832 in Burkhardt and Smith, I, p. 163, pp. 232–3. Expressions of Darwin's indifference are few, but see *Charles Darwin's Beagle Diary* (11 December 1832 and 2 October 1836) pp. 12, 447.
13. Darwin, *The Voyage of the Beagle*, p. 498. In a letter dated 18 July 1836 to his sister Caroline, Darwin wrote, 'The next three months appear infinitely tedious & long.' See Burkhardt and Smith, *The Correspondence of Charles Darwin*, I, p. 501.
14. Ibid., p. 503.
15. Darwin, *The Voyage of the Beagle*, p. 337.
16. Ibid., p. 296.
17. *The Beagle Record*, pp. 184–5, pp. 223, 283.
18. Darwin, *The Voyage of the Beagle*, p. 21.
19. H.E. Gruber and P.H. Barrett, eds, *Metaphysics, Materialism, and the Evolution of Mind: Early Writings of Charles Darwin* (Chicago: University of Chicago Press, 1980) p. 141. See also P.H. Barrett, P.J. Gautrey, S. Herbert, D. Kohn, S. Smith, eds, *Charles Darwin's Notebooks, 1836–1844: Geology, Transmutation of Species, Metaphysical Enquiries* (Cambridge: Cambridge University Press, 1987).
20. For a lengthy account of the Fuegians' return, see *The Beagle Record*, pp. 108–9, 116–17. On 6 March 1834, after revisiting Jeremy Button, Darwin wrote in his diary, 'I hope & have little doubt he will be as happy as if he had never left his country; which is much more than I formerly thought.' See *Charles Darwin's Beagle Diary*, p. 227.
21. Such is Darwin's sense of the power and the necessity of memory that even after the voyage is over, he continues to reflect upon them. For instance, apparently motivated by the longing that had caused him to cling to bygone moments with family and friends, Darwin, upon his return to England, records the surviving moments of his childhood and writes his 'autobiography' – a collection of early memories that 'flash across' his consciousness and inform his questions about the origins of his own character and predispositions. In a similar mode he becomes interested in genealogy and starts to research his 'ancient' family's pedigree. This fascination also occasions a series of metaphysical notebooks in which he investigates the unconscious and remarks upon the surprisingly enduring character of certain memories. In these notebooks Darwin remarks on 'the vast power of memory' to connect the individual to such essential 'instincts' as 'parental affection' and 'love of virtue'. Man's 'very existence', Darwin emphasizes, requires this memory – a perspective that catches the reflection of his own reliance upon resurrected images of home to help him endure his five year's absence. See Gruber and Barrett, *Metaphysics, Materialism, and the Evolution of Mind*, p. 134.
22. Burkhardt and Smith, *The Correspondence of Charles Darwin*, I, p. 493.
23. Homer, *The Odyssey*, trans. A. Cook (New York: Norton, 1967) I: 9, line 197.
24. Gillian Beer in *Darwin's Plots: Evolutionary Narrative in Darwin, George Eliot and Nineteenth Century Fiction* (London: Routledge, 1983) p. 88

also remarks on Darwin's sensitivity to forgetfulness. She writes, 'Just as determinism requires that we accept the idea of unconsciousness and oblivion, so Darwinian theory requires that we accept forgetfulness and the vanishing of matter.'

25. *The Beagle Record*, p. 130.
26. Burkhardt and Smith, *The Correspondence of Charles Darwin*, I, p. 495.
27. G. G. Marquez, *One Hundred Years of Solitude*, trans. G. Rabassa (New York: Avon, 1970) p. 94.
28. See *The Notebooks of Samuel Taylor Coleridge*, ed. K. Coburn (New York: Pantheon Books, 1957) #1495 (September 1803).
29. In *Darwin and the Novelists: Patterns of Science in Victorian Fiction* (Cambridge, MA: Harvard University Press, 1988) pp. 16–17, George Levine comments on Darwin's sense of the mutability surrounding him:

in Darwin's world *everything* is always or potentially changing, and nothing can be understood without its history. Species, which had been conceived as permanent, transform into other species or are extinguished. The earth and all of its local ecological conditions are shifting. Traditionally, the more things change, the less 'real' – that is ideal – they are, the more corrupt and corrupting. But in submitting all things to time, Darwin challenges the ideals of a permanent substratum of nature and of permanent categories of thought.

30. *The Beagle Record*, p. 77.
31. *The Voyage of the Beagle*, pp. 140–1.
32. Ibid., p. 195.
33. Ibid., p. 303.
34. Ibid., p. 306.
35. Ibid., pp. 101–2.
36. Ibid., p. 136.
37. Ibid., p. 250.
38. Burkhardt and Smith,*The Correspondence of Charles Darwin*, II, pp. 356, 359.
39. Darwin, *The Voyage of the Beagle*, p. 302.
40. Burkhardt and Smith, *The Correspondence of Charles Darwin*, I, p. 506.
41. *The Beagle Record*, p. 89.
42. Burkhardt and Smith, *The Correspondence of Charles Darwin*, I, p. 368.
43. C. Lévi-Strauss, *Tristes Tropiques*, trans. J.and D. Weightman (New York: Atheneum, 1974) pp. 43–4. It is interesting that Darwin, after observing his father's elderly patients, noted how often a memory would 'spring up' after 'long intervals of forgetfulness'. See Barrett *et al.*, *Charles Darwin's Notebooks*, pp. 530–3.
44. M. Proust, *Remembrance of Things Past*, trans. C.K. Scott Moncrieff and T. Kilmartin, I (London: Penguin, 1988) p. 258.
45. Marquez, *One Hundred Years of Solitude*, p. 50.
46. C. Darwin, *The Expression of Emotions in Man and Animals*, 1872 (London: Julian Friedman, 1979) p. 217.

47. I have borrowed the term 'rogues' from *The Origin of the Species*. Darwin adopted the term to help him describe and account for the principle of selection.

48. Burkhardt and Smith, *The Correspondence of Charles Darwin*, II, p. 255. In his diary written during the voyage (5 and 6 May 1832), Darwin wrote that he looked forward to 'quiet retirement' – a period that 'can call back the recollection of childhood & times past, where all that was unpleasant is forgotten'. See *The Beagle Record*, p. 54.

49. In his autobiographical fragments (August 1838) Darwin recognizes, perhaps in the tradition of the sublime, that he is nostalgic for the childhood experiences connected with 'fear'.

50. Darwin, *The Voyage of the Beagle*, p. 501.

51. Ibid., p. 44.

52. W. Benjamin, 'The Work of Art in the Age of Mechanical Reproduction', *Illuminations*, ed. H. Arendt, trans. H. Zohn (New York: Schoken, 1969) pp. 221–3.

53. Darwin, *The Voyage of the Beagle*, p. 324.

54. That quiet Darwin desired was not so immediate. Shortly after Darwin returned, he wrote to W. D. Fox (6 November 1836), 'It is quite ridiculous, what an immensely long period it appears to me, since landing at Falmouth. The fact is I have talked and laughed enough for years instead of weeks, so my memory is quite confounded with the noise.' See Burkhardt and Smith, *The Correspondence of Charles Darwin*, I, p. 517.

55. Frederic Jameson in 'Walter Benjamin, or Nostalgia', *Salmagundi* (Fall 1969 – Winter 1970) p. 68 suggests, 'But if nostalgia as a political motivation is most frequently associated with fascism, there is no reason why a nostalgia conscious of itself, a lucid and remorseless dissatisfaction with the present on the grounds of some remembered plenitude, cannot furnish as adequate a revolutionary stimulus as any other: the example of Benjamin is there to prove it.'

56. Darwin, *The Voyage of the Beagle*, pp. 431, 502. Darwin wrote to his sister Catherine (14 February 1836), 'It is necessary to leave England, & see distant Colonies of various nations, to know what wonderful people the English are.' See *The Beagle Record*, p. 349.

57. Ibid., p. 139.

2

The Last of England and the Representation of Longing

'The Last of England! O'er the sea, my dear,
Our homes to seek amid Australian fields.
Us, not our million-acred island yields
The space to dwell in. Thrust out. Forced to hear
Low ribaldry from sots, and share rough cheer
From rudely nurtured men. The hope youth builds
Of fair renown, bartered for that which shields
Only the back, and half-formed lands that rear
The dust-storm blistering up the grasses wild.
There learning skills not, nor the poets dream,
Nor aught so loved as children shall we see.'
She grips his listless hand and clasps her child;
Through rainbow tears she sees a sunnier gleam.
She cannot see a void, where he will be.

Ford Madox Brown (1865)

One question that emerges from the nostalgic moment is how is it possible adequately to represent the longing that invariably accompanies the experience – more specifically, what kinds of images satisfactorily signify a yearning for something that is irrevocably absent? In order to address this matter, it is, perhaps, useful to turn to the genre of emigration painting popular in mid-nineteenth-century Britain and examine its attempts to depict the suffering of those who, either voluntarily or involuntarily, departed from their homes for North America, Australia, and New Zealand. The manner in which these artists, particularly Ford Madox Brown in *The Last of England* (1855), portrayed their subjects' exile reveals the possibilities and the limitations inherent in their task. In particular, their canvases draw attention to how difficult it is to bypass sentimentality and find a genuine means of expressing loss. Moreover, they illustrate the temptation to let the fascination with detail overwhelm the fact of absence and, thus, compromise the character of nostalgia's memory that, as I have discussed in the previous chapter, requires a forgetting as well as a remembering.

THE GENRE OF EMIGRATION PAINTING AND *THE LAST OF ENGLAND*

Predictably, because of the sentimental nature of Victorian genre painting, canvases depicting an emigrant's departure are replete with tender images reflecting the soothing, but illusory, myths of nation, home, and hearth. With titles like *Parting Words, Farewell to Home, The First Break in the Family, Farewell to Emigrants,* and *Leaving Home,* these works focus upon the heartbreak of relinquishing a familiar way of life.[1] Severed from the supposed continuity of home, their subjects pose somewhere between belonging and exile, for they look back at what they are leaving and anticipate the uncertainty awaiting them in an alien land.

As sentimental witnesses to their subjects' enduring moments of departure, these artists often idealized the people, the dwellings, and the landscape of home. With the exception of a few painters like Sir Hubert von Herkomer (*Pressing to the West*), they tended not to concentrate upon the harsh conditions that were forcing people to break away against their will. Instead, they focused upon the sorrow of leaving.[2] Paintings such as James Collinson's *Answering the Emigrant's Letter* (1850), Abraham Solomon's *Second-Class – The Departure* (1854), Richard Redgrave's *The Emigrants' Last Sight of Home* (1858), John Watson Nicol's *Lochaber No More* (1863), Thomas Faed's *The Last of the Clan* (1865), and Robert Herdman's *Landless and Homeless – Farewell to the Glen* (1887) depict protracted scenes of farewell that evoke memories of pastoral innocence and personal heroism. These paintings, consequently, tend to obfuscate the economic and political realities that had already dispossessed people. In a sense, because of their appeal to an idyllic past, many of these works are patriotic and display a certain affinity to propaganda art. In particular, they anticipate posters displayed in Britain during World War II. Redgrave's *The Emigrants' Last Sight of Home* (Figure 1), for instance, bears an uncanny resemblance to one of Frank Newbould's wartime posters entitled *Your Britain, Fight for it Now, The South Downs* (Figure 2). In both pieces the artists arrange their almost identical compositions so that a man faces home and sees a place where the pure, expansive beauty of the rolling hills blends with the comfort of the grove and the dwellings nestled within the peaceful countryside. Through these idyllic images, Redgrave and Newbould call upon their viewers' longing for the innocence of the past and draw them into a form of nostalgia and nationalism made even more potent by the threat of imminent loss.

Of all these mid-century works devoted to the subject of emigration, the one that has, perhaps, retained the most prominent place in the public's imagination is Ford Madox Brown's *The Last of England* (Figure 3). This is the painting that seems to be reproduced more than any other, and is, of course, the one most people are able to name. The composition is familiar. A husband and wife sit brooding in the stern of a ship. Silently they depart the land they will probably never see again. A baby sleeps sheltered under her mother's shawl. Behind them and held together within the painting's oval frame is a group of emigrants who register various reactions to their plight. And just behind them is a cabin boy who casually selects vegetables hanging from the boat's side. Beyond them all is a glimpse of the open sea and a corner of the white cliffs of Dover. Brown's description of the painting for his 1865 catalogue offers a more complete explication. Although long, it is worth recalling, for it refers to details that otherwise might elude the viewer's eye:

> This picture is in the strictest sense historical. It treats of the great emigration movement which attained its culminating point in 1852. The educated are bound to their country by quite other ties than the illiterate man, whose chief consideration is food and physical comfort. I have, therefore, in order to present the parting scene in its fullest tragic development, singled out a couple from the middle classes, high enough, through education and refinement, to appreciate all they are now giving up, and yet depressed enough in means, to have to put up with the discomforts and humiliations incident to a vessel 'all one class'. The husband broods bitterly over blighted hopes and severance from all he has been striving for. The young wife's grief is of a less cantankerous sort, probably confined to the sorrowing of parting with a few friends of early years. The circle of her love moves with her.
>
> The husband is shielding his wife from the sea spray with an umbrella. Next to them in the background, an honest family of the green-grocer kind, father (mother lost), eldest daughter, and younger children, makes the best of things with tobacco-pipe

and apples, etc., etc. Still further back a reprobate shakes his fist with curses at the land of his birth, as though that were answerable for *his* want of success; his old mother reproves him for his foul-mouthed profanity, while a boon companion, with flushed countenance, and got up in nautical togs for the voyage, signifies drunken approbation. The cabbages slung round the stern of the vessel indicate, to the practiced eye a lengthy voyage; but for this their introduction would be objectless. A cabin-boy, too used to 'leaving his native land', to see occasion for much sentiment in it, is selecting vegetables for the dinner out of a boatful.

The painting, begun in 1852, was finished more than nine years ago [1855]. To insure the peculiar look of *light all round*, which objects have on a dull day at sea, it was painted for the most part in the open air on dull days, and when the flesh was being painted, on cold days. Absolutely without regard to the art of any period or country, I have tried to render this scene as it would appear. The minuteness of detail which would be visible under such conditions of broad day-light, I have thought necessary to imitate, as bringing the pathos of the subject more home to the beholder.[3]

In obvious ways the composition of this painting conforms to the conceits of the emigration genre, for like its companions *The Last of England* dwells upon the point of departure when the people are caught between the unknown (the sea and their destination) and home (the white cliffs of Dover), and it focuses upon the moment when the distance between the emigrants and their native country widens. In addition, it too ennobles its principals (the husband and wife) who, depending on one's tolerance for the convention, stoically register their losses and reveal an appreciation for what they are having to leave behind.

However, for all these similarities that easily place Brown's painting within the commonplaces of this genre, there are important differences. Brown, for instance, refuses to idealize the working classes. Although he reserves some space in his canvas for 'an honest family of the green-grocer kind', he makes more room for the harsh faces of drunkenness and anger that loom behind the family grouping. More significantly, though, Brown modifies the genre by altering the perspective of departure. Instead of depicting a farewell scene in which what is about to be lost remains in view, Brown paints one in which, contrary to the promise of his painting's title, the subjects appear to have no view of England. The white cliffs of Dover, the only glimpse of England available in the painting, are behind them, out of sight. Consequently, they are not like Nicol's clansman who leans on the ship's balustrade and shares with the painting's viewer the receding sight of his precious native glen. Brown's painting refuses the principals such a reference. They face, instead, an anonymous observer and stare into a kind of blankness. Unlike the emigrants whose family and friends bend towards them with gestures of caring and farewell in Collinson's, Solomon's, Redgrave's, Faed's, and Herdman's paintings, Brown's husband and wife sit isolated and out of reach. There is no possibility for exchange, for reciprocity. A series of circles – faces, bonnets, the umbrella, and the vessel's ropes – work from the outside in to enclose and impede their perspective. Like the frame of the painting, these repeating circles constrict his principals' vision by blocking the peripheral, by excluding the larger context.

In this respect *The Last of England* is, perhaps, a more disturbing work than Redgrave's *The Emigrants' Last Sight of Home* and its provocative rendering of an idyllic England. In Redgrave's painting the emigrant still has a point of reference, for he stands before and, like the observer, sweeps his eye over the clear and full prospect of the bucolic landscape he is leaving. The villagers who gather in groups on the hills to wave farewell are a reassuring presence, although, admittedly, a dispersing one, by which the man with his wife and children can still measure and understand himself.[4] For the extended moment of the painting, his neighbors replicate his physical being and legitimize his identity. The man and wife in Brown's painting, however, have no such confirming mirror. Their eyes, particularly the husband's, come flat up against the canvas's surface that blocks reflection. They see only the invisible remnants of memory.

STEREOSCOPES, AFTERIMAGES, AND THE EXPERIENCE OF EXILE

These eyes that cannot see reflection are at the center of *The Last of England*. Conspicuous and disorienting, they set a disturbing tone that helps Brown represent the experience of exile. The principals' eyes, particularly the husband's, are disconcerting, for they are each abnormally detached from one another. (This detail is especially explicit in one of the cartoons for the painting. [See Figure 4].) In their vividness they sit as distinct entities on either side of these figures' faces. Brown, who habitually commenced his work by marking an 'x' where the eyes should go, painted these as if summoning the image of the stereoscope (an instrument that quantifies the operation of binocular vision) to serve as a metaphor representing their irregularity. Reflecting his century's interest in physiological optics, he painted the husband's and wife's eyes as if depicting the isolated images composing the two sides of the stereoscopic slide.[5] One expects them – these images, these eyes – as through a stereoscope, to converge and compose a single picture; however, in Brown's painting each one stares out, sees independently of the other, and waits in vain for the integrated image. Brown does not offer his principals a synthesizing lens. The painting takes its cue from this delay and simulates the consequent distortions of a broken stereoscope.

One symptom of this failed binocular vision is that in spite of the couple's clasped hands, the harsher images on the painting's 'masculine' left do not easily blend with or complement the quieter 'feminine' aura of the painting's right side. The cluster of boisterous individuals who are directly behind the husband and play out the excesses of his brooding and 'blighted hopes' contradict the openness and freshness that rise behind the wife's figure. The ship's muddled crowd, the soft colors of the sea and cliffs of home, the husband's lowered darkening eyes, and the wife's raised and brighter gaze fail to come together. As a result, the painting separates into two, almost contradictory, entities that reflect the principals' want of a synthetic center. Cut off from home, these exiles find it difficult to blend what they see, for as yet, there is no lens of meaning to fuse these images and let them slip into one another.

The painting's fragmented details are another symptom of this lack. As if the exile's unintegrated eyes had composed the picture, incomplete images of figures clutter the canvas. Looking at *The Last of England* is similar to regarding the pieces of an imperfect jigsaw puzzle, for the parts are disjointed. Instead of seeing whole bodies, the viewer notices its segments: a portion of an arm or a back, a bit of scarf, the sleeve of a jacket and the brim of a bonnet. The same is true for the objects. One sees, for instance, a piece of pipe or a fraction of a boat. Most disturbing is the fact that no face in the background is complete. Even in the more fully worked principal figures this sense of fragmentation persists. The hands of the man, woman, and sheltered baby seem cut off and stuck on. They don't give the impression of belonging, for their origins hide mysteriously beneath the folds of material draping the couple's body.

A further source for this sense of detachment is Brown's method of composing his paintings. Brown's detailed diary reveals an artist who appears to have concentrated upon one particular at a time. There is little sense of his working over a whole canvas so that each part relates to a larger context. His tendency is to work each element until it is right. For instance, when Brown was painting *Geoffrey Chaucer Reading the 'Legend of Custance' to Edward III and his Court at the Palace of Sheen, on the Anniversary of the Black Prince's Forty-fifth Birthday* (1851), he seems to have been preoccupied with collecting and sketching pieces of clothing and pairs of legs and hands. The painting, therefore, emerges as a montage, as an assemblage of draped cloth and borrowed limbs. A selection from his diary offers an insight into this method:

> drawing the draperies for Wicliff [sic].... Maitland came drew a study of his legs for John of Gaunt.... Went to see John Bromley & to make a scetch [sic] of the hand of his little girl for the female in the painting.... Laid in the head & feet of Wicliff.... Yates came & I made a drawing of his head for Chaucer. Afternoon drew at the head of Chaucer till Miss Ashley came, when I painted in the head of the female & left off.[6]

This technique of 'laying in' the particulars is also at work in *The Last of England*. Entries in Brown's October 1854 diary show him concentrating upon segments of the canvas, one piece at a time. Over a series of days, he records that he 'Worked at Emmas [sic] head' [Emma is Brown's wife], 'worked at my own head in the same – had a baby to put in the infants [sic] hand', placed 'the shawl on the lay figure [a wooden model]', 'began the shepheards [sic] plaid shawl', and 'worked on the tarpauling over the Ladies' [sic] knees in the last of England (3 hours)'.[7]

Because of this method of building up his paintings, Brown's canvases tend, as did many of the Pre-Raphaelites', too definitively to isolate one detail from another. Lacking continuity their particulars do not extend into shadow. Although Brown's intention is to complete each detail so it looks as realistic as possible (while working on the canvas, for instance, he placed the lay figure, draped in the wife's shawl, on its side, outside so that he might paint its fringes blowing in the wind), the results lack conviction, for nothing flutters and nothing touches. Like a piece of forged metal, the wife's scarlet ribbon seems wedged into the composition. Like all the other separated, fixed, and halted details in the painting, it stands in the frame and replicates yet another kind of visual distortion. This time, though, it is not the disorienting want of binocular vision; it is, instead, the absence of any temporal vision, the presence of which the nineteenth-century theorist W. J. Schelling thought essential to the art of seeing. In *The Ages of the World*, Schelling explains this basic principle: 'In the external world everyone sees more or less the same thing, and yet not everyone can express it. In order to complete itself, each thing runs through certain moments – a series of processes following one another, in which the later always involves the earlier, brings each thing to maturity.'[8] None of this overlapping or carrying over, however, is visible in *The Last of England*. Details rarely 'involve' something that comes before or after them; consequently, no 'afterimages' are present to bind one segment to another. It is as if one segment of the picture is to be seen and then forgotten as soon as the eye moves on to the next carefully wrought particular.

Just as the broken stereoscope can serve as a metaphor for the emigrants' disorientation, this lack of afterimage can help make more tangible what the Victorians popularly termed the 'curse of emigration' – the exile's sense of being cut off from the continuum of history. Through its disconnected pieces *The Last of England* replicates a world in which details fail to link together. It unintentionally reproduces the experience of the exile who belongs to no place and who will land in a country where he or she has no past. Through this canvas the emigrant travels into the fragmentary landscape of the new world, to a place where the particulars of the surroundings will seem disconnected, where details cannot complete themselves, for they are severed from the afterimages of memory.

THE 'INSPECTIVE FORCE' AND THE LOSS OF IMAGE

When Brown described *The Last of England*, he explained that he proposed to bring 'the pathos of the subject more home to the beholder'. If one considers the various visual distortions and their commentary upon the principals' plight, one can say Brown succeeded. But if one keeps looking, various contradictory elements within the work come forward to confuse his purpose and raise questions concerning the difficulties of representing the 'fullest tragic development' of these emigrants and their exile.

To begin with Brown compromises his intention by refusing to let his principals go. Through a telescopic lens that crowds the rounded particulars into the oval canvas, he holds the husband and wife close to the observing eye. As if imprisoning and secluding them in Jeremy Bentham's Panopticon – a prison scheme designed, in part, to prevent the emigration of criminals to Australia[9] – Brown places his figures within the solitary cell of his canvas so that they are continuously visible to the observer; they, however, like the prisoners, can never return the gaze of those who examine and watch over them. Through the painting's 'inspective force' these figures are always available not only to Brown but also to the visitor/viewer who is free to come anonymously and, as in the Panopticon, to walk the observation galleries and turn 'an invisible eye' on the inmates – in Bentham's design, the prison guards and visitors were able to look at the prisoner through a round hole cut in a piece of cloth.

As part of this unwillingness to let go and, perhaps, as an expression of his desire to interrupt the voyage, Brown attended closely to the painting's particulars. Almost compulsively he amassed details that effectively hold on to rather than release the figures from their unfortunate circumstances. Entries in Brown's diary, for instance, reveal an un-self-conscious preoccupation with the minutiae of his figures' clothing. As if not only desiring to see his subjects in 'broad daylight'[10] but also wanting to see them as closely as possible so he may wrap himself in the protective folds of their clothing, he repeatedly became absorbed in the selecting, collecting, and creating of a wardrobe for his emigrants. At times this activity was extravagant. For instance, periodically during the years he worked on *The Last of England*, he devoted considerable attention to the woman's shawl so that he might accurately catch the intimate details of its texture and design. Brown was not interested in how it looked at a distance; he wanted the image of it at hand. As a result, Brown reworked his rendering of the shawl until his representation of it satisfied him. His diary entries reveal his tenacity. In 1854, for instance, he decided to paint the woman in Emma's shepherd plaid shawl instead of the large blue and green plaid one he had already sketched. This decision, Brown declared, 'is a serious affair'.[11] Later in October and December of the same year, he spent 'all day placing the shawl on the lay figure' and 'worked out in the open air at the shawl till 1/2 past 3'.[12] In 1855, with relief, he announced that he had 'triumphantly stripped the lay figure & set the place somewhat to rights & restored poor Emma her shawl which she has done without the half of winter. The shawl is at length finished thank the powers above.'[13] But his wife was not to retrieve her shawl for long, because late in December Brown was once more outdoors working on the shawl and redraping the lay figure.

In a similar manner, Brown represented the faces of his family and assembled them within the painting's frame. The husband's face and hands are careful copies of Brown's own – he drew them by looking at their mirror image; the wife's face is Emma's; the detailed portrait of the child eating the apple is their daughter Lucy, and the baby's minutely painted fingers are their son's. Through these closely watched particulars he offered himself and his family, at least, the reassurance of the painting's reflection, a confirmation that its principals cannot enjoy. Through his efforts the image of his family will not disappear from view or from the narrative of the white cliffs.

It is interesting to note that when Brown was working on *The Last of England*, he periodically felt despondent and thought of emigrating to India. Worries about money were causing Brown, along with friends like Henry Holman Hunt (who in the 1850s thought of going to Australia to raise cattle), to consider leaving England and settling elsewhere. As a result, the painting, perhaps, reveals some evidence of Brown's identifying with his subjects' exile. For instance, as already noted, more than ever he appears to succumb to his practice of dwelling on intricate details and giving in to his impulse to 'go through to the extremity' in order to arrest or possess his immediate surroundings.

This need to guard against a sense of imminent loss, though, has its roots in another occasion. Brown began thinking about *The Last of England* soon after he, along with Henry Holman Hunt, Dante Gabriel Rossetti, and William Rossetti, had seen Thomas Woolner, Bernhard Smith, and Edward Latrobe Bateman off for Australia.[14] On a 'bleak' 24 July 1852 they sailed from Gravesend on the ship *Windsor*. Frustrated by a lack of recognition and money, Woolner had decided to join numerous others in finding his fortune in the 1852 gold rush[15] – it is Woolner's pipe that emerges from behind the husband's back in *The Last of England*. While he was wearily pursuing empty promises in the gold field, Woolner kept a journal. Throughout its pages, he periodically described the desecration of the landscape surrounding him. To make this perception more vivid he often concentrated upon the holes in the landscape – the chasms of nothingness. In one entry he writes about the gaping spaces, left by the diggers, that ruin the land and yield little profit:

> I never saw anything more desolate than the first sight of Mt. Alexander was to me: it was what one might suppose the earth would appear after the day of judgment has emptied all the graves. I saw holes with grass and wild flowers growing on their borders. The whole thing gave me one of the saddest impressions I ever felt – the carcasses of labor – the earthly shells of hard endeavour, often fruitlessly, and sometimes success proved a curse.[16]

At other times he focused upon the 'dark and dangerous rivers' that contain 'holes of fearful depth, their bottoms covered with nets of snags and logs – trees fallen from the side and washed down the stream, rushes and tangles of strong weeds'.[17] As reminders of loss, these dark spaces lurked among Woolner's intermittent enthusiasms, especially after he witnessed the death of his friend Henry Pinchin who was sucked down into one of the treacherous rivers. In his journal Woolner records that he 'saw Pinchin's face rise to the surface for a second...and saw it no more'.[18] This utter loss of image was, of course, disturbing, especially when it coupled in his mind with the thought that he 'shall never see England again'[19] so that even in 'moments most pleasant', the possibility of not returning home sent 'a shiver thro' me more foully horrible than anything I ever felt – almost like a brief gap giving a glimpse of hell'.[20] It is interesting to note that after Woolner gave up prospecting and for a short while settled in Melbourne to resume his sculpturing, he requested that his PRB friends send self portraits so that he might hang them in his studio.[21] The ostensible reason was to attract customers; a subjective motive, perhaps, was to eradicate the void left by the face that had disappeared. In the context of Woolner's discomfort, one should also remark on the fact that Brown felt uneasy with open areas – the holes – in his painting. When, for instance, Brown enlarged the frame of *The Last of England*, he began immediately, in his words, 'filling up' the empty spaces.[22] Preferring the full light of the details and their colors to the shadows of loss, he left no portion vacant.

Throughout the painting Brown continues to contradict his painting's title, for he not only keeps the figures close to the observing eye, allows no distance to come between him and his subjects, and lets no space remain open but also continuously moves toward home rather than away from it. The static details in the work contribute to this sense of reversal. Most of all the wife's predominant, stiff 'red madder' scarf that pushes horizontally across the canvas with an almost phallic force confuses the idea of departure. The scarf's rigid and sideways motion has little to do with the painting's nomadic subject, for the scarf binds the wife's power to the husband and suggests to the viewer that the more vital energy in the picture is not in the leaving but in the relationship between the husband and wife.[23] It is the family's strength, supplied in part by the wife's sense of belonging to home (it is she who wears the red madder, otherwise known as English red), that suggests a tension between the family's integration or stability and the diffusion or disorientation of exile. That is to say, the painting concentrates on a narrowing family circle while pretending to depict the widening circumference of traveling to an unknown land. It moves inward and retains while feigning to go outward and let go. This counter-motion has its ally in Brown's belief that when he executed a painting, he worked toward home. According to his grandson Ford Madox Ford, even in the last evening of his life,

Madox Brown painted with his brush to the 'x' by his name. Below it, on the left-hand side, the picture was completely filled in; on the right it was completely blank – a waste of slightly yellowed canvas that gleamed in the dusky studio. He said: 'You see I have got to that "x." I am glad of it, for half the picture is done and it feels as if I were going home.'[24]

Because of the contradiction between the artist's method of working and his subject matter, *The Last of England* resists genuine feelings of loss, separation, and longing. Although there is, as I have suggested, a sense of disorientation, displacement, and fragmentation, and although there is a certain lingering pain or distress in the principals' faces, the canvas's images are not entirely convincing. This failure, though, seems not solely to be the consequence of Brown's unwillingness to let his figures slip out of sight (his refusal to release an image from view), nor is it the consequence of his impulse to protect what is visible from the realities of irrevocable loss. It seems, instead, to be a result of his confusing treatment of his subject matter. *The Last of England* does not easily yield itself to a representation of the deprivation and yearning of exile, nor does it subscribe to the finality implicit in its title, for its closely worked and vividly colored details temper a sense of an ending. Abducted by the desire to depict what is present, Brown has difficulty acknowledging what is and will no longer be available. His painting cites presence, yet his subject requires absence.

This paradox is not only Brown's; it also belongs to his contemporaries' paintings of longing. In John Everett Millais' *Mariana* (1851) and William Morris's *Queen Guenevere* (1858), for instance, the women's lithe bodies stretch or rise in sexual yearning for an absent lover. But, as if compensating for these lovers' absence, each of these works avails itself of the ready details: the stained glass windows, the embroidered cloth, the knots in the floorboards, the embossed wallpaper, the religious objects on the altar, and the design of the belt. As in *The Last of England*, these closely worked particulars frustrate the artist's supposed intention by immersing the viewer within a fully worked, ornamental setting that holds and momentarily satisfies the eye. Millais and Morris have created a counter text to their intended subject. They have caught their viewers in the sin of seeing that obfuscates the idea of absence. So much rests on their paintings' surfaces that it is impossible to consider what is beyond or beneath their rich textures. There is no transparency.

One might argue that Redgrave's *The Emigrants' Last Sight of Home* is an exception, for within its frame are both those who are longing and that which is yearned for but soon not to be in sight. When one looks at the painting, one feels, as did Ruskin, a nostalgia for the landscape left behind, for its 'beautiful distance'.[25] The shape of the trees, the paths worn through the fields, the shadows passing over the hills, and the greens are images that revive idealistic memories of a place that subconsciously is always home for the one who has left England. In this respect Redgrave's painting seems more powerful than Brown's. The viewer can almost stand next to the father who turns one last time to set eyes on his village. In spite of this advantage, however, the painting does not completely succeed in representing the coming separation, for once more the work's meticulousness interferes. The painting's finely wrought particulars confuse the perspective and the representation of absence by making everything fully and easily available. Redgrave barely discriminates among the work's foreground, middle ground, and background. Except, of course, for the differences in size or proportion, the dwellings on top of the hill are almost as distinct to the eye as the folds of the child's shawl, and the leaves of the remotest tree are practically as visible as the man's extended arms. This same exaggerated attention to detail also works against representing the pathos of the emigrating family. In the manner of Brown, Millais, and Morris, Redgrave overdresses his foreground figures and dwells too long on the details of their clothing.[26] As a result, their humanity disappears; the people become mere lay figures for his drapery. The folds of cloth veil rather than reveal the details of thought in their minds' fabric. In the end the painting represents itself rather than what is internal to its subject. Socrates' observation that the image must not reproduce all the qualities of that which it is imitating if it is to be an image seems appropriate here. His thought implies that if one wants to approach the truth of one's subject, one must not 'duplicate' everything, for the painfully accurate and fully-named image does not necessarily portray its subject. One needs imperfection, shadow, and absence if one is to draw closer to a more genuine representation. One needs the chance to imagine the invisible – a chance, of course, which this group of paintings denies its viewers.[27]

IMAGES OF EXILE AND LONGING

At this point it is, perhaps, appropriate to turn to Ovid's the *Tristia* (A.D. 8–12). As one of the most poignant commentaries on exile, its verses offer some insight into the images attending longing and absence, and help explain why the representation of these experiences can be fraught with difficulty.[28]

Ovid's thirty-year exile in Tomis, away from his home, his wife, his daughters, and his native tongue made him, of course, painfully aware of his dependency on images of remembrance, for only they could yield him a presence in his absence.[29] Nothing else could bring him closer to home, not even his pleading 'for wings' so that 'the yielding air might give way before my rapid flight', and he 'might on a sudden behold the sweet soil of my native land, the faces in my lonely home, my loyal friends, and – foremost of all – the dear features of my wife'.[30] [*nunc ego iactandas optarem sumere pennas,/ sive tuas, Perseu. Daedale, sive tuas:/ ut tenera nostris cedente volatibus aura/ aspicerem patriae dulce repente solum,/ desertaeque domus vultus, memoresque sodales,/ caraque praecipue coniugis ora meae* (III. viii 5–10).] There was a sweet sadness in glancing at the images residing in his memory. Even though they frustrated his desire to touch home, they honored his need to see it. In Book III Ovid describes one of these ambiguously comforting moments when his home and his wife appear before his mind's eye:

> *ante oculos errant domus, urbsque et forma locorum,/ acceduntque suis singula facta locis./ coniugis ante oculos, sicut praesentis, imago est./ illa meos casus ingravat, illa levat:/ ingravat hoc, quod abest; levat hoc, quod praestat amorem/ inpositumque sibi firma tuetur onus.* [Before my eyes flit my home, the city, the outline of places, the events too that happened in each place. Before my eyes is the image of my wife as though she were present. She makes my woes heavier, she makes them lighter – heavier by her absence, lighter by her gift of love and her steadfast bearing of the burden laid upon her.[31]]
>
> (III iv 57–62)

Later in the poem when Ovid complains he will not be in Rome to witness Augustus Caesar's triumphant return from Germany, he becomes more sensitive to the inadequacy of such vicarious interludes and distinguishes between images that reside within the mind's eye and those that belong to what he calls the 'real sights/ spectacles' [*vera tamen*] of Rome. In the following passage the poignancy of this disturbing difference shows through his transparent flattery, perhaps mockery,[32] of the one who has banished him.

> *haec ego summotus qua possum mente videbo;/ erepti nobis ius habet illa loci:/ illa per inmensas spatiatur libera terras,/ in caelum celeri pervenit illa fuga;/ illa meos oculos mediam deducit in urbem,/ inmunes tanti nec sinit esse boni;/ invenietque animus, qua currus spectet eburnos;/ sic certe in patria per breve tempus ero./ vera tamen capiet populus spectacula felix,/ laetaque erit praesens cum duce turba suo.* [All this (Augustus Caesar's triumphant reentry into Rome) I, an exile, shall see in my mind's eye – my only way; for my mind at least has a right to that place which has been torn from me. It travels free through measureless lands, it reaches the heaven in its swift course, it leads my eyes to the city's midst, not allowing them to be deprived of so great a blessing; and my mind will find a place to view the ivory car (the carriage in which Caesar rides) – thus at least for a brief space I shall be in my native land. Yet the real sight will belong to the happy people, the throng will rejoice in the presence of their own leader.

But as for me – in imagination only and with ears far away I shall have perforce to realize the joy, and there will scarce be one sent far from Latium to the opposite side of the world to tell it all to eager me.[33]]

(IV ii 57–66)

These images that Ovid recalls through his imagination are the bits and pieces that survive the translations of memory and forgetfulness. They are the segments that remain after Ovid has bidden farewell to his family – what is left of his being after his departure has metaphorically 'torn' his body apart and broken him in two: 'I was torn asunder as if I were leaving my limbs behind – a very half seemed broken from the body to which it belonged'[34] [*dividor haud aliter, quam si mea membra relinquam,/ et pars abrumpi corpore visa suo est* (I iii 73–4)]. His wife's features, his friends' tears, and the Roman streets are, like the severed limbs, silent and detached. The streets have no map; the face has no body. These images will never possess the ampleness of actual sight, and, by extension, they will never display the completeness of Brown's principal figures in *The Last of England*, for there is no 'other' (like the painter) or site of mediation to help Ovid fill in the gaps hollowed out by his exile from Rome.

Because he has nobody to help him mediate his losses, Ovid turns to language and, in a sense, asks it to be something other than itself. He seems to want language to push itself into the spaces that the 'torn' images expose, that the absence of 'real sights' reveals, and to take on the responsibilities of the icon. As if attempting to fill in the emptiness and to join the fragmented images, he asks language to move forward and, like an image, restore the site of what is lacking. As a result, letters, verses, elegies, hymns, and invocations become missives that transform words into the faces and the places of home. Through language he attempts to resurrect the past by naming/ depicting what is no longer available to the physical/living eye. Understandably, then, Ovid, living among the people of Tomis who do not use his speech, despairs when he is 'at a loss' for a word, a name, or a place and finds that 'there is none who can inform' him of it. He complains, 'Oft when I attempt some utterance – shameful confession! – words fail me: I have unlearned my powers of speech'[35] [*saepe aliquod quaero verbum nomenque locumque,/ nec quisquam est a quo certior esse queam./ dicere saepe aliquid conanti – turpe fateri! – verba mihi desunt dedidicique loqui* (III xiv 43–6)]. For the exile who yearns for home, language becomes a mirror through which he can glimpse a reflection of himself and his native land. Under these conditions language attempts to replicate image by casting off its symbolic use and slipping into an iconic mode. The impossibility of this transformation, though, adds to Ovid's sense of loss.

With its repeated references to fragmentation and absence Ovid's the *Tristia* reminds the reader how exile is utterly surrounded by emptiness and burdened by loss. To portray the experience without these attendants is to misrepresent it. For this reason the poem's verses help one better understand the difficulties a painter, like Brown, faces when he depicts his emigrants on a canvas that demands to be completed – that rejects emptiness and allows no separation – and, therefore, requires him to compromise his intention of representing his subjects' latent longing. The sense of distance and space that is forever interrupting the richness of Ovid's language and its efforts to diminish the irrevocable gap between Rome and Tomis is not available in Brown's work which succumbs to the temptation to close every single gap and complete what should be left open and half forgotten. In this respect Ovid's the *Tristia* stands as an instructive contrast to *The Last of England*.

This tension between the two necessities (the one to leave a space; another, to fill it) is not nearly as troublesome to the artist, however, as the fact that images associated with exile tend to exist outside the strict borders of chronological time. Passages in the *Tristia* remind one that these images travel according to the erratic rhythms of the mind. Simply put, they move to a subjective rather than to an objective time. They are not set to measured minutes; instead, they choreograph their shape according to the shifting borders of recollection. As a result, like Ovid on the night of his exile, these images cannot simply 'set forth'; they must vacillate between going and coming[36] so that in each section of the *Tristia*, they defy the progress of time and step back and forth across the threshold of the present. They do not fall into that straight narrative measure but, instead, vary according to the pulse of Ovid's desires and fears. For instance, on his voyage across the seas to Tomis (see Book I), Ovid continuously shifts his focus among the three points of time: in the present he observes the waves agitated by the high winds; he then considers his future, and simultaneously turns his thoughts back to his faithful friends and Rome. Like the sea's waves, images of arriving and returning, death and survival, retrospect and anticipation, hope and loss, swell and recede to disrupt the progress of the journey as it inevitably moves towards its destination. Throughout the *Tristia* the almost obsessive repetitiveness of Ovid's recollected images continuously pulls back time and crosses its advancing path.

For Brown and the other genre painters who rely on narrative and take their cue from a story that unfolds according to the telling minutes of chronological time (from beginning to end) – recall Brown's account of *The Last of England* which reads like an introduction to a story or a play – this shifting subjective mode of memory is not as readily available.[37] Brown's painting lacks the variable and vacillating perspective of Ovid's journey, for desiring to represent a moment – the emigrants' departure – that beats out of strict time, Brown, paradoxically, relies on images that belong to another order and, therefore, allows the defined, progressive arena of narrative to overwhelm the more malleable space of remembrance.

Because images that move within the boundaries of subjective time are constantly shifting, they, perhaps, mimic the experience of metamorphosis. Like the exile who is caught between the past and the future and must constantly shuffle his or her identity between various points of reference, these images keep recasting and transforming themselves into something other than what they once were. In their mutability they reflect a present that inevitably modifies remembrance and a past that, in turn, necessarily alters the present. To represent these transitional phases and metamorphoses in painting is, obviously, difficult. One of the more successful attempts, partially, of course, because of its subject matter, is Antonio del Pollaiuolo's *Apollo and Daphne* (Figure 5). This work catches the two principals between contrary states of being: between having and not having, motion and stillness, fear and triumph, possibility and frustration, air and earth (half of each figure has left the ground), and, of course, between human and organic form. As if freezing a moment in their pursuit/flight across the canvas, Pollaiuolo simultaneously depicts a past, a transforming present, and a future. Apollo's and Daphne's limbs extend to the left- and right-hand margins thus pointing at once to a prior time and to an imminent moment. Apollo's arms recall the history of his desire, yet his face acknowledges the frustration of the coming rejection. Similarly, Daphne's lower body recounts the past and her fleeing while her arms display her future and her refuge. Their vacillating and altering presence stands in contrast to the more static conventional backdrop.

In contrast, the principal figures in *The Last of England* do not replicate this mutability. In a sense, Brown's painting inverts

Pollaiuolo's, for its background, not the foreground, moves and changes. The hodge-podge of figures with their various gestures of acceptance and rebellion construct a tangle of bodies that seem to be in the midst of a metamorphosis – the parts are jumbled because they have not yet realized their new selves in the future of their exile. The husband and wife in the foreground, who take up most of the space, however, sit firmly in the present of their presence. Their stubborn stillness subdues what activity rages behind them and quells any sense of a lasting alteration. Their extended figures rebel against change. For the moment of the painting, the husband and wife are caught in some resolute now that almost disqualifies a past and future. If one may briefly and liberally borrow from Charles S. Peirce's theory of signs to consider the difference between these two sets of figures, one sees that the husband and wife in *The Last of England* frustrate the moment of exile by being trapped in what Peirce might refer to as their 'Secondness', their actuality.[38] They are caught by facts that exclude any kind of generality or subjectivity. Because of Brown's exorbitant attentiveness to the details of their clothing, they are stuck in a 'thisness' of fact that not only forgets possibility but also, significantly, neglects the painting's object. The sharply delineated particulars in the painting (for instance, the veins on the cabbage leaves), as I have suggested before, take on a life of their own; they cease to point to the pathos of emigration they are supposed to be 'declaring' or representing.[39] Brown's belief that by depicting 'the minuteness of detail' he is 'bringing the pathos of the subject home to the beholder' turns on itself. He creates signs that lead to nothing but themselves.

The Last of England, like many of its companion genre paintings, is too involved in either celebrating detail – making a fetish out of it – or protecting itself from the loss of image to be able to portray an ending that cannot be revised and an absence that cannot be revoked. Images that are present for their own sake overwhelm the sorrow of departing. The result is a disorienting portrait of a farewell that refuses to let go and to step out of chronological time. Brown's painting offers one a better understanding of how difficult it is to represent an emigration scene in a manner that bypasses sentiment and reaches a more genuine expression of absence and longing – in a manner that attends or points to, rather than neglects or forgets, its object.[40]

Notes

1. For a fuller listing of these emigration paintings, see S. P. Casteras, ' "Oh! Emigration! thou'rt the curse...": Victorian Images of Emigration Themes', *The Journal of Pre-Raphaelite Studies*, VI (November, 1985) 1–23. See also C. Wood, *Victorian Panorama: Paintings of Victorian Life* (London: Faber and Faber, 1976).
2. In this respect these paintings resemble many of the emigration poems appearing in journals during the late 1840s and early 1850s. One of these, 'Home-Sickness', appeared in *Household Words*, IX (18 March 154) 104–5. The opening stanza reads:

> Where I am, the halls are gilded,
>   Stored with pictures bright and rare;
> Strains of deep melodious music
>   Float upon the perfumed air: –
> Nothing stirs the dreary silence
>   Save the melancholy sea,
> Near the poor and humble cottage,
>   Where I fain would be!

3. *The Pre-Raphaelites*, The Tate Gallery (London: Penguin Books, 1984) p. 124.
4. This need to have something by which to measure and understand oneself is also reflected in an emigration poem entitled 'The Emigrant Bird' appearing in *Household Words*, II (28 September 1850) 12. The last verse reads:

> I cannot leave all home behind,
> My heart – my heart would surely break!
> Therefore, sweet birds, tho' now confined,
> 'Tis love that doth thy prison make:
> When waves around us cease to foam,
> Your captor's hand shall set you free;
> And you shall sing to me of home,
> In the far land across the sea.

5. For an interesting discussion of theories of optics in the nineteenth century, see J. Crary, *Techniques of the Observer: On Vision and Modernity in the Nineteenth Century* (Cambridge, MA: MIT Press, 1990). For a contemporary article on stereoscopes, see 'The Stereoscope', *Graham's Lady's and Gentleman's Magazine*, XLIII (October, 1853) 537–42.
6. V. Surtees, ed., *The Diary of Ford Madox Brown* (New Haven: Yale University Press, 1981) pp. 23–7.
7. Ibid., p. 106.
8. Crary, *Techniques of the Observer: On Vision and Modernity in the Nineteenth Century*, p. 99.
9. For a complete description of Jeremy Bentham's Panopticon, see *The Works of Jeremy Bentham*, ed. John Bowring. IV (New York: Russell & Russell, 1962) pp. 40–174.

10.   *The Pre-Raphaelites*, p. 124.
11.   Surtees, *The Diary of Ford Madox Brown*, p. 93.
12.   Ibid., p. 106.
13.   Ibid., p. 113.
14.   For accounts of Woolner's departure and his life in Australia see, for instance, G. H. Fleming, *That Ne'er Shall Meet Again* (London: Michael Joseph, 1971); A. Woolner, *Thomas Woolner, R.A. Sculptor and Poet: His Life in Letters* (New York: AMS Press, 1971); and W. E. Fredeman, *The P.R.B. Journal: William Michael Rossetti's Diary of the Pre-Raphaelite Brotherhood. 1849–1853* (Oxford: Clarendon Press, 1975).
15.   For an account of the gold rush, see E.W.D., 'Gold', *Australian Encyclopaedia*, IV (Michigan State University Press, 1958).
16.   Woolner, *Thomas Woolner, R.A. Sculptor and Poet: His Life in Letters*, p. 37.
17.   Ibid., p. 32.
18.   Ibid., p. 27.
19.   Ibid., pp. 26, 30.
20.   Ibid., p. 30.
21.   Fredeman, *The P.R.B. Journal: William Michael Rossetti's Diary of the Pre-Raphaelite Brotherhood, 1849–1853*, pp. 340–1.
22.   Surtees, *The Diary of Ford Madox Brown*, p. 151.
23.   I am indebted to Irving Massey, Professor of English, SUNY at Buffalo, for making this point in a discussion about *The Last of England*.
24.   F.M. Hueffer [Ford Madox Ford], *Memories and Impressions: A Study in Atmospheres* (Michigan: Scholarly Press, 1971) p. 227.
25.   Wood, *Victorian Panorama: Paintings of Victorian Life*, p. 222.
26.   While commenting upon *The Emigrants' Last Sight of Home*, a reviewer for *The Art Journal* (1859) stated that Redgrave threw himself into the figure painting 'with a fervency of devotion rarely witnessed'. As quoted in S. Casteras and R. Parkinson, *Richard Redgrave 1804–1888* (New Haven: Yale University Press, 1988) p. 138.
27.   For a discussion of Socrates' observation, see W.J.T. Mitchell, *Iconology: Image, Text, Ideology* (Chicago: The University of Chicago Press, 1986) p. 92.
28.   In the following discussion when I compare Ovid's *Tristia* to the emigration paintings, I am not suggesting that in this case there is the expected tension between these 'sister arts'; though, I am, perhaps, participating in a commonplace of the space–time debate that maintains that poetry, rather, than painting, is more suited for representing the motions of time – in this case, motions that acknowledge loss and forgetfulness.
29.   In his introduction to his translation of the *Tristia* (Athens, GA: University of Georgia Press, 1975) p. ix, L. R. Lind explains:

      Tomis [is] in Moesia, on the western coast of the Black Sea. The region is called Dobrudja and lies about sixty-five miles southwest of the closest mouth of the Danube river on the site of the modern Constantza, Rumania. The bleak and chilly climate; the barbarous inhabitants composed of Getes, Sarmatians, Bessi, Ciziges, and other tribes who continually threatened the border town of Tomis and the adjacent area with plunder and warfare; the complete lack of books and of people cultured enough to understand him and his poetry made Ovid's life a continual hell on earth. From A.D. 8, the date of his banishment, until his death sometime after the latest date which can be absolutely confirmed from his poems, the consulship of Graecinus in A.D. 16, Ovid remained in Tomis.

For a thorough discussion of the various reasons why Ovid was sent away from Rome, see J.C. Thibault, *The Mystery of Ovid's Exile.* (Berkeley: University of California Press, 1964).

30. A. L. Wheeler, trans., *Ovid with an English Translation: Tristia. Ex Ponto* (Cambridge, MA: Harvard University Press, 1959) p. 131.
31. Ibid., p. 119.
32. L. R. Lind points out that 'It is possible . . . to interpret many passages of the *Tristia* as well as of the *Epistulae* as in reality veiled innuendoes and covert mockery of the sort which appears frequently elsewhere in Ovid's poems.' See Lind, *Tristia*, p. xii.
33. Wheeler, *Ovid with an English Translation: Tristia. Ex Ponto*, p. 171.
34. Ibid., p. 25.
35. Ibid., p. 155.
36. Ibid., pp. 23–5.
37. Stephen Owen in *Remembrances: The Experience of the Past in Classical Chinese Literature* (Cambridge, MA: Harvard University Press, 1986) p. 102 remarks:

A memory is not a story; a memory may be the occasion for much brooding and reflection, but a memory is not thought in the ordinary sense. They say memory is something like a visual image in the mind, but if it is, it is not the same as an image in our eyes. An image in our eyes has a background of detail and continuity with the living world; in our memory this background blurs, and certain forms rise up, forms in which are concentrated story and significance and unique problems of value.

38. For a discussion of 'Secondness', see C.S. Peirce, 'The Principles of Phenomenology', *The Philosophy of Peirce: Selected Writings*, ed. J. Buchler (London: Routledge & Kegan Paul, 1956).
39. Ibid., pp. 111–13.
40. Peirce discusses the relationship between the sign and its object in 'Logic as Semiotic: The Theory of Signs' in *The Philosophy of Peirce: Selected Writings*.

3

R.L. Stevenson's Nationalism and the Dualities of Exile

I heard the pulse of the besieging sea
Throb far away all night. I heard the wind
Fly crying and convulse tumultuous palms.
I rose and strolled. The isle was all bright sand,
And failing fans and shadows of the palm;
The heaven all moon and wind and the blind vault;
The keenest planet slain, for Venus slept.
The King, my neighbour, with his host of wives,
Slept in the precinct of the palisade;
Where single, in the wind, under the moon,
Among the slumbering cabins, blazed a fire,
Sole street-lamp and the only sentinel.
To other lands and nights my fancy turned –
To London first, and chiefly to your house,
The many-pillared and the well-beloved.
There yearning fancy lighted; there again
In the upper room I lay, and heard far off
The unsleeping city murmur like a shell;
The muffled tramp of the Museum guard
Once more went by me; I beheld again
Lamps vainly brighten the dispeopled street...

R. L. Stevenson, 'To
S. C. [Sidney Colvin]', lines 1–21

Of course, not all those who sailed away from the shores of England to live a life in exile left unwillingly. Robert Louis Stevenson is one notable example. When he first went to America, for instance, he did so by choice. This circumstance, however, did not prevent his feeling at once hopeful and homesick, and did not stop him from alternating between wanting to continue his journey and wishing to return

54

home. This vacillation was to remain with him and complement what was already for him an acute sensitivity to the antithetical character of experience – his inclination to remark upon his own contrary impulses and to dwell between contentment and longing, approval and disapproval, collectivity and individuality, the present and the past.[1] Because of this orientation, Stevenson readily acknowledged the Janus-like glances of the nostalgic moment and simultaneously engaged what is and what was or recalled what had been both painful and blissful, terrifying and golden. At times, though, Stevenson seems to have wanted to break away from this perspective by succumbing to the abstracting and contracting powers of longing that for the moment allowed him to transcend his contrary impulses and to lean upon expressions of patriotism. This submission, however, never lasted long, for Stevenson soon qualified the consequent synthesis by returning his attention to those ambiguities that all too easily reasserted themselves. Stevenson's exile, his nostalgia for Scotland, and his intermittent nationalism offer poignant examples of an engagement with a yearning that never completely escapes a consciousness of duality.[2] Longing is never simply savored as a sweet sadness; it is fraught with disturbing ambiguity.

THE DUALITIES OF STEVENSON'S NOSTALGIA FOR SCOTLAND

In August 1879 Stevenson, under the pseudonym of Robert Stephenson, set sail for America to join Fanny Osbourne, the American woman he had met a few years earlier in France and who was later to become his wife. Shadowed by uncertainty (Fanny was not yet divorced) and compromised by secrecy (he had not told his parents he was going), Stevenson's departure was fraught with difficulties.[3] It had, however, scarce the anxiety or the sense of finality that accompanied a majority of the passengers' leave taking. His ship, the *Devonia*, was carrying emigrants from Scotland, Ireland, England, Scandinavia, Germany, and Russia who were fleeing their homeland out of necessity rather than desire. For them, particularly those 183 passengers in steerage who, in Stevenson's words, 'had been unable to prevail against circumstances' at home,[4] the possibility of return was minuscule. Stevenson, on the other hand, knew that he could always go back to Scotland – he had 'second cabin' status. He could, therefore, afford to sing 'Auld Lang Syne', imagine the return voyage, and anticipate a reunion 'in the sanded inn, when those who had parted in the spring of youth should again drink a cup of kindness in their age'.[5] He was, as he admitted, an 'amateur emigrant'.

As a result of this experience, Stevenson wrote *The Amateur Emigrant*, a narrative of his passage from England to California. His account upsets the reassuring sentimentality of Ford Madox Brown's *The Last of England* by realistically dwelling upon the physical discomforts and the sense of disorientation that affected him and the other travelers, especially those in steerage, as they sailed across the ocean and, then, endured the arduous train ride across the plains.[6] One of the most poignant moments in Stevenson's narrative occurs on the long journey from New York to California when he and his fellow passengers notice other emigrant trains going east, back to the origins of their travels across the land. The warning cries of the passengers from the passing trains disturb him:

> as we continued to steam westward toward the land of gold, we were continually passing other emigrant trains upon the journey east; and these were as crowded as our own. Had all these return voyagers made a fortune in the mines? Were they all bound for Paris, and to be in Rome by Easter? It would seem not, for, whenever we met them, the passengers ran on the platform and cried to us through the windows, in a kind of wailing chorus, to 'Come back.' On the plains of Nebraska, in the mountains of Wyoming, it was still the same cry, and dismal to my heart, 'Come back!'[7]

About seven years later when Stevenson had reconciled with his parents and had returned, temporarily, to Scotland, he composed a passage in *Kidnapped* that, in some respects, recalls this earlier episode. It occurs when the ferry-boat carrying David Balfour pulls alongside an emigrant ship bound for the American colonies. David and the other passengers listen to the anguished pleas and farewells of the emigrants:

> In the mouth of Loch Aline we found a great seagoing ship at anchor... there began to come to our ears a great sound of mourning, the people on board and those on shore crying and lamenting one to another so as to pierce the heart.... We put the ferry-boat alongside, and the exiles leaned over the bulwarks, weeping and

reaching out their hands to my fellow-passengers, among whom they counted some near friends. How long this might have gone on I do not know, for they seemed to have no sense of time: but at last the captain of the ship, who seemed near beside himself (and no great wonder) in the midst of this crying and confusion, came to the side and begged us to depart.[8]

What recurs in the two quoted passages is not merely the emigrants' lamenting; it is also the striking image of the passing vessels traveling in opposite directions, one away from home; the other, back toward it. These intersecting antithetical images are significant, for they portray the dualities inherent in Stevenson's own exile and, subsequently, in his nostalgia for family, friends, and Scotland. They emerge as a metaphor for his continuous attention to the contrary nature of experience. Stevenson was always to be the passenger looking at the train or the boat going the other way. His life played upon the platform of these contradictions.

Stevenson's longing for Scotland is especially circumscribed by inversions and oppositions. Pride and mockery, admiration and deprecation permeated his commentary so that he alternately abhorred and respected, for instance, the Victorian gentility of Edinburgh, and simultaneously esteemed and ridiculed the Scots dialect.[9] Even when he recalled the splendor of the distant Pentland Hills, he did not forget Scotland's bleakness. Memories of the gust-blown rain lashing against the window tempered his enthusiasm for the surrounding landscape, summoned oxymorons, and caused him to regard Scotland as a 'blessed, beastly place'.[10] Cold, 'desolate recollections' of his youth mingled with the remembered pleasures of the hills and the purple moorlands.[11] Later, when Stevenson's past was haunting him more unremittingly than ever, negative images still occasionally qualified his yearning for home. For instance, in an October 1893 letter to Sidney Colvin, about the possibility of leaving Samoa to visit Britain, Stevenson wondered whether he could 'ever stand Europe again?' Wryly he queried, 'did she [Fanny] appreciate that if we were in London, we should be *actually jostled* on the street?' and, he added, punning on both the Samoan and the Scots dialects, that there would be 'nobody in the whole of Britain who knew how to take *ava* like a gentleman'.[12] *Ava* is the Samoan dialect for Kava (a potent liquor from the Sandwich Islands) and in Scots is the abbreviated phrase for 'of all' or 'at all' (as in 'That wus no like a gentleman *ava*'). Perhaps struck by the knowledge that these dialects send the meaning of even a single word in two directions at once, Stevenson, concluded his letter with "Tis funny to be thus of two civilisations.' The pun and its dependency upon linguistic dualities parallel the continuous cross-referencing of his own mind and illuminate the double vision that was inextricably his.

The negative remarks in the letter to Colvin, of course, did not tarry long. Soon the alternating currents of Stevenson's mood changed, and once again, he was writing longingly to his friend about the streets in Edinburgh and of his wish to be back among the hills of Penrith. As those familiar with Stevenson's biography know, these oscillating desires were partially the consequence of his chronically poor health. Suffering from a susceptibility to cold weather ('this damned weather weighs on me like curse'[13]) and from severe bronchial infections, Stevenson felt it necessary to escape from Scotland and seek a more hospitable climate. Like many of his contemporaries he went where the air was pure. In 1880, for instance, he went to Davos (Switzerland); after six months he returned to Scotland but finding he could not endure its cold, damp weather, returned to Davos and stayed until April 1881. He was later ordered South and moved to Hyères (France), and then, again because of poor health traveled to Saranac Lake (New York), to San Francisco, and finally to Samoa, where he lived until his death on 3 December 1894.

Stevenson's physical vulnerability gave him no easy exile, for he often felt guilty leaving Scotland. His illnesses offered him a means of explaining his absence, but did not eradicate the sense that he was abandoning his country and friends. His letters, like the one he wrote in January 1890 to his English friend Lady Taylor, are full of apologies:

> I do feel as if I was a coward and a traitor to desert my friends; only, my dear lady, you know what a miserable corrhyzal (is that how it is spelt?) creature I was at home; and here I have some real health, I can walk, I can ride, I can stand some exposure, I am up with the sun, I have a real enjoyment of the world and of myself; it would be hard to go back again to England and to bed; and I think it would be very silly. I am sure it would; and yet I feel shame, and I know I am not writing like myself.[14]

Over three years later, in May 1893, and still feeling apologetic, he wrote to S. R. Crockett with a bitter, pragmatic briskness that attempts to mask and contradict the sentiments of his longing:

I shall never take that walk by the Fisher's Tryst and Glencorse; I shall never see Auld Reekie; I shall never set my foot again upon the heather. Here I am until I die, and here will I be buried. The word is out and the doom written. Or, if I do come [back to Scotland], it will be a voyage to a further goal, and in fact a suicide....[15]

As an adult Stevenson had periodically attempted to resettle in Scotland. He had once more listened to the sweet, familiar sounds of a Pitlochry river 'singing loud and low in different steps of its career, now pouring over miniature crags, now fretting itself to death in a maze of rocky stairs and pots'.[16] But inevitably he had become ill as he did a year or so after he had heard the river and fallen victim again to the dreary weather.[17] Stevenson grumbled about his fate to William Ernest Henley (?4 July 1882). In the letter his thoughts alternate between going and coming, staying and remaining, and wanting and rejecting the land of his birth:

> I believe we shall have to leave this place [Stobo Manse]; it is low, damp, and *mauchy*; the rain it raineth every day; and the dam glass does tol-de-rol-de-riddle.
> Yet it's a bonny bit; I wish I could live in it, but doubt. I wish I was well away somewhere else. I feel like flight some days honour bright.[18]

Stevenson's desire to flee the land he wished to return to, though, is not simply the consequence of his need to find a suitable climate. As his biographers point out, it was also the residue of his awkward relationship with his parents.[19] As a young man Stevenson had been at odds with his mother and father over his choice of profession (he had not wanted to be an engineer or a lawyer), his youthful escapades, his 'Bohemianism', and his religious and political views – for a while he had proclaimed himself to be an agnostic and a socialist. Ultimately the quarrels dissipated. But even then Stevenson never felt as comfortable in Scotland as he would have cared to. His attachment to home was always to be qualified by what he perceived to be the 'old and rigid circle' of Edinburgh society that taught him 'to distrust his own fresh instincts'.[20]

Stevenson's ambiguous affection for Scotland was also affected by what he called 'my old gipsy nature'[21] – what his stepson, Lloyd Osbourne, recognized as Stevenson's desire 'to be off' and proclaim,

'*Vive la vie sauvage!*'.[22] Stevenson fancied himself as belonging to 'a race of gipsies' who loved change for its own sake.[23] To read his biography is to deal with a figure who is forever packing and leaving. For instance, soon after he had carried out his filial duty by being admitted to the Scottish Bar, he began a series of journeys that had as much to do with his love of adventure as with his requiring a warmer climate. In 1875 he joined his cousin Robert Alan Stevenson in France; a year later he and Walter Simpson paddled in their canoe through the canals of France (*An Inland Voyage*) – they had already been on lengthy walking tours together – and, in 1878, accompanied by his donkey Modestine, he walked 120 miles in the Cévennes (*Travels with a Donkey*). About ten years later after intermittent journeys to France, Switzerland, America, and Britain, Stevenson was still not content to dwell in the same place. In 1888 and in 1889, on board the *Casco* and the *Equator*, he set out on a series of South Sea voyages (*In the South Seas*), and in 1890, although he had bought land in Samoa, cruised aboard the *Janet Nicoll* to the Gilbert Islands. Even when these voyages were perilous and he was, for the moment, 'very glad to be done with them', Stevenson wanted 'to get to sea again ere long'.[24]

During these travels, of course, thoughts of home intermittently tugged at his desire for adventure, confused his sense of direction, and continued to place him between the polarities of hope and regret, curiosity and comfort, contentment and despair. In a letter to Edmund Gosse (8 October 1879), written shortly after arriving in California, Stevenson refers to one such disorienting moment:

> My head went round and looks another way now; for when I found myself over here in a new land, and all the past uprooted with one tug, and I neither glad nor sorry, I got my last lesson about mankind; I mean my latest lesson for of course I do not know what surprises there are yet in store for me. But that I could have so felt astonished me beyond description. There is a wonderful callousness in human nature, which enables us to live. I had no feeling one way or the other, from New York to California, until, at Dutch Flat, a mining camp in the Sierra, I heard a cock crowing with a home voice; and then I fell to hope and regret both in the same moment.[25]

Sounds of home were frequently to syncopate his longing 'to rise and roam' and to keep shifting his points of reference. Sailing to

America he had listened sympathetically to the emigrants in steerage sing, 'O why left I my hame' and to a sick man complain, 'O why did ever I come upon this miserable voyage?',[26] and in California he had heard the Scots bray of Mr. M'Eckron that 'touched' him 'home' and briefly upset his purpose (*The Silverado Squatters*),[27] but at the same time he had pressed forward to his destination. Like the elderly lady who on board the *Devonia* kept her watch to Glasgow time, Stevenson traveled to America conscious of the minutes ticking at home, but in his bags had carried a volume of George Bancroft's *History of the United States*.[28] The narratives of his past and future, the known and the unknown, the going and the returning, shared the same berth. Stevenson could not, as much as he tried, travel out of his country and himself;[29] he had trouble fully identifying with the traveler 'who shakes off the dust of one stage before hurrying forth upon another'.[30] Like a fine powder his past clung to the vestments of his being. It was an almost impossible task to encounter the new and the present on their own terms, for images of former times too easily pushed their way into his mind's eye and divided his attention. He could not, for instance, gaze upon the running water near Saranac Lake without noticing that the surrounding hills lacked the heather of the Highlands.[31]

Eventually permanently exiled in Samoa by health and by choice, Stevenson continued to live between the past and the present. As if acknowledging this condition he imported thirty-seven cases of furniture and belongings from his houses in Bournemouth and Edinburgh and placed them in Vailima, his home in Samoa. The chairs, tables, and silver services from Skerryvore and 17 Heriot Row stood as incongruously in the light of the tropical sun as did the Samoan servants who, under Stevenson's orders, on Sundays and other holidays, dressed in striped blazers and Royal Stewart Tartan skirts (an adaptation of the Samoan *lava-lavas*). Perhaps one of the most striking representations of this bifurcation is a group photograph of his family and staff at Vailima. Everyone except Stevenson's mother, Margaret Stevenson, turns towards the camera and wears the loose clothing appropriate for the tropical climate. His mother, however, sits facing sideways as if responding to another sort of eye or point of reference. She poses in the mode of old-world portraiture and dresses in the tightly buttoned, black high-collared style of nineteenth-century Edinburgh. Within a single frame these differing postures and styles of attire make visible the contrary impulses playing within Stevenson's mind and vying continuously for his approval. In a sense the photograph with its incongruities illustrates how the past can never be brought fully into the present, especially for the nostalgic individual. It must always be seen at an angle. It can never face one directly.

The image of Stevenson's mother is striking for its stark, sharply-angled singleness. Like the velvet curtain hanging on the window of the Vailima study door, it is at odds with its surroundings and reminds one that the concentric, confirming circles of an expanding frame of reference are not always necessarily available for those who are exiled. Václav Havel's sanguine paradigm of home as a small circle that, as one grows from childhood to adulthood, becomes embedded within other and larger frames of reference does not function here where experiences do not easily nestle into one another.[32] Rather than revolving around a single point of reference, the photographic images of the tartan skirts, the bare torsos, the uncrossed arms of the servants, the buttoned collars and the laced widow's cap circle in unattached spheres that exacerbate difference, discontinuity, and duality.

It is this split orientation of opposites, of course, that helps structure Stevenson's fiction. Throughout his novels the longing for home, the traditions of the past, and the seeking of a new self through adventure and the unrehearsed reverberate and cross paths. Stevenson's protagonists are always moving in contrary directions, facing forward and turning around, departing and arriving, almost simultaneously. Jim Hawkins, the young boy in *Treasure Island*, leaves home thinking only of adventure, except for the brief moment when he says goodbye to his mother and the Admiral Benbow Inn. He cries when he sees the boy who is to take his place – who is to carry on his old self. He mourns the loss of what once was, yet yearns to sail with the Squire and the Doctor. The familiarity of the inn cannot compete with the promise of the map and the prospect of the 'primitive'. However, as much as the novel's episodes take him away from Scotland and reshape his identity (he grows almost into a man), the experiences of the voyage eventually lead him back home. Stevenson does not want the boy to be left, like the pirates, stranded, cut off, isolated on a faraway island.

Similarly *Kidnapped* begins with departure and ends with a return. Eager to better himself now that both his parents are dead, David Balfour departs from Essendean. He is impatient with the kindly Mr Campbell who embraces him 'very hard' and hands him a gift of lily water for memory's sake.[33] When David turns to watch the gentleman cry goodbye, he guiltily realizes that he is relieved to be rid of the quiet countryside and of what he knows of home. The paradox, of course, is that he is about to launch upon a quest for his inheritance. He is turning his back on the landscape of home to recover it. And when he is with Alan Breck, these contrary rhythms resonate even more convincingly. The two work their way through the bogs, heather, shelters, nights, and forests of the highlands and lowlands of Scotland – one traveling toward and the other, away from his land. Like the warring bagpipes, the two move in opposite directions together in order to discover Scotland and to find a synthetic harmony.

So intricate are these antithetical gestures of arrival and departure, of acceptance and rejection in *The Master of Ballantrae* that Stevenson summoned two outsiders, Ephraim Mackeller and the Chevalier de Burke, to tell the story and choreograph its doubling movements. *The Master of Ballantrae* is a tale of inversions that makes exiles of those who remain at home and substitutes shadows of the dead for vestiges of the living. It is also a tale of duality, for throughout the narrative, the Master's comings and goings catch everyone he touches including himself, in a duel between a longing for what once was and a desire to move on and escape the past. Stevenson's 'puppets' stand in an uncomfortable space between love and repulsion, King James and King George. Like Miss Alison, the wife of Mr Henry but the intended of the Master, their loyalties and their passions are divided. For them the old Scottish ballads are simultaneously graceful and manipulative. Like Stevenson listening to the sentimental songs on board the *Devonia*, the characters alternatively lean toward them, listen sorrowfully to them, and reject them for the pathos that leaches their memory.

As intricate as the inversions and criss-crossing in these novels are, however, rarely does any one of them leave the reader in confusion. In spite of the continuous alternating, intertwining, and doubling of events and people, a synthetic filament runs through the text to bind these dualities. This strand is, perhaps, a paradigm for a certain kind of nostalgia that is able to overcome the dualities that normally attend the experience of longing. Like metaphor that recognizes what is present and what is absent from the eye, and thereby, discovers some spontaneous continuity between the two elements, the experience of nostalgia can occasionally bring the conflicting present and past together. It does not always have to trap consciousness between two conflicting points of reference, for just as the so-called 'vehicle' in metaphor refers to what lies outside the boundaries of the described and points away from the named ('the tenor') yet functions to create a single, echoing-reverberating meaning, so too can the distracting present in the nostalgic moment help to secure a single text – one that grows out of the opposition between what was and is. In this context, nostalgia emerges as a figure that can simultaneously acknowledge and dismiss difference or otherness. The result for Stevenson is that his novels reflect a kind of unity and that he in Samoa is not always obligated to think it incongruous to mix his images and compare the sound of the tree frog in the tropical forest to the ringing of the northern sleigh bells.[34]

NOSTALGIA AND THE EXPERIENCE OF NATIONALISM

Because of its capability to eradicate contradiction, nostalgia can also occasion a context for nationalism. Through its synthesizing power of abstraction, Stevenson's longing for Scotland sometimes produced the illusion of wholeness that condensed time and dissolved duality. His subsequent patriotism reflects this possibility. When, for instance, Stevenson was away from Scotland, his yearning for the people and the landscape of home frequently turned into composite expressions of nationalism that abridged or abstracted rather than separated experience.[35] He discovered he could acknowledge and appreciate what, at home, he had felt compelled to modify. As he admitted in a letter (1 August 1872) to his mother, 'I am grown most unsufferably national, you see. I fancy it is a punishment for my want of it at ordinary times.'[36] At these moments Stevenson disregarded his customary contrapuntal criticism of Scotland, turned his back on the contradictions embedded in his longing – the need to attach himself to, yet escape from, his native country – and embraced his nation without qualification so that there were no stars anywhere so lovely as Edinburgh street lamps, no regiment more superb than a Highland one, no people more convivial and liberal than the Scotch, no person more 'Scotty Scot' than himself, no place more conscious of its legends and history, no stream more alive with sound and color, and no poet more divine than a Scottish one. What had been divisive temporarily ceased to be so. In spite of its two languages, many dialects, innumerable forms of piety, and countless local patriotisms and prejudices, Scotland emerged as a unified entity – deep down it was one nation. A man from Glasgow may seem a foreigner, and a man from Barra to be 'more than half a foreigner', but away 'in some far country', a 'ready- made affection' joined the two.[37] Under these conditions Scotland's fabricated traditions bore the aura of truth and its quarreling tongues agreed. Through the filter of distance and the abstracting powers of nostalgia, the country drew together; it became a nation, and Stevenson, a nationalist.

Stevenson once compared this phenomenon to the composite photographs that the nineteenth-century scientist Francis Galton prepared so that he might reach the essential, unifying image of a type (Galton, for instance, placed portraits of the criminally insane over one another in order to isolate or let emerge the dominating facial features of the group).[38] In his essay 'Pastoral' in *Memories and Portraits*, Stevenson suggests that nostalgia's memory functions in a similar manner, for it also amasses the various features of Scotland's image and combines them to create a unified portrait that illuminates the nation's essence and leaves but 'a ghost of a trace of individual peculiarities'.[39] In the opening of his essay, Stevenson compares this layering of his memories to the effect of Galton's photographs:

> To leave home in early life is to be stunned and quickened with novelties; but when years have come, it only casts a more endearing light upon the past. As in those composite photographs of Mr. Galton's, the image of each new sitter brings out but the more clearly the central features of the race; when once youth has flown, each new impression only deepens the sense of nationality and the desire of native places.[40]

Although Stevenson was by no means intent, like many of Galton's followers, upon improving a race by breeding only those whose physiology displayed the desired features, he was interested, through his writing, in isolating and setting forth what is essentially Scottish. He wanted to place his own composite portraits of his nation before his readers. Stimulated by his longing for home, he abstracted the elements that constitute and propagate the David Balfours and Alan Brecks, delineated the leading lines and features of his country's landscape, and dwelt upon the unifying factors of its nationhood. Moreover, during the years he lived in Samoa, he also, it seems, tried to bring this nationalism to life and to reconstitute the Scottishness of home. As a result, even though Stevenson was critical of how the rivalries among the German, American, and British interests on the islands had forced the inhabitants to make cultural compromises, he formed, with little hesitation, his own immediate colonial community that, in part, took its structure from the Scottish paradigm. Consequently, at Vailima Stevenson became the Scottish 'laird' who lived in 'feudal splendor',[41] who led his clan, and, as Ian Bell suggests, 'took his duties as arbiter, provider, magistrate, and spiritual leader seriously'.[42] His stepson recalls, for instance, that Stevenson required 'absolute obedience' to his orders, posted proclamations, printed notices 'to correct petty irregularities', and defined 'the responsibility and authority of each member of the household'. In addition, when there were breaches of discipline, Stevenson imposed money fines, and if the offence were serious, held 'a regular court martial'.[43] The patriarchal Scot he had criticized at home – the magistrate or the providing father – and his ancestral pride were reborn within the boundaries of his South Sea estate.[44] It was, perhaps, this desire to honor his Scottishness that made Stevenson all the more sympathetic to the Samoans who did not want their history or their land compromised and that caused him to support those, like Mataafa the rebel king, who believed that Samoa should belong to the Samoans.[45]

At times, it seems, Stevenson's nationalism also prompted him to think of himself as embodying the composite portrait of the Scot. When he was away from Scotland, he spoke of himself in terms of his 'Scotch Body' and his 'Scottish eyes'.[46] And when he was content, it was often because he was enjoying a period of good health or sensing the vitality of his own Scotch body. Stevenson describes one such euphoric moment in an 1893 letter to Sidney Colvin:

> It pours with rain from the westward, very unusual kind of weather; I was standing out on the little verandah [at Vailima] in front of my room this morning, and there went through me or over me a heave of extraordinary and apparently baseless emotion. I literally staggered. And then the explanation came, and I knew I had found a frame of mind and body that belonged to Scotland, and particularly to the neighbourhood of Callander.[47]

At moments like this Stevenson felt less driven to return to his homeland. There was no need, for he carried Scotland within him. His body remembered the past. Stevenson could write, as he did to W. Craibe Angus (April 1891), 'I believe Fergusson lives in me.'[48]

Stevenson's wandering was also part of his conforming to the composite portrait of a Scot. His continual departing and absences identified him with his nation by linking him to the Highland chieftains who fled their homes in fear of their lives and to the 'Wandering Willies' of the ballads who carried what is lost within themselves and their memories. Part of being a Scot was to be living in exile, for better or worse. The meaning of its burden fluctuated. At sea, exile was no calamity, but at Vailima when Stevenson was feeling unwell, it was, naturally, distressing. In April 1894 he wrote to Frances Sitwell: 'I cannot make out to be anything but raspingly, harrowingly sad; so I will close and not affect levity which I cannot feel. Do not altogether forget me. Keep a corner of your memory for the exile.'[49]

As much as he cherished the identification with his forbearers, though, Stevenson was not completely comfortable with either his own or others' expressions of nationalism. Typically one train of thought crossed another and once more caught him in the net of contradiction and modification. Consequently, Stevenson, in spite of his nostalgia, often disliked the romancing about Scottish scenery and manners that too readily intruded upon his sensibility, and felt compelled to criticize, if not discredit, those, like Burns, whom others deified as gods of Scottish nationalism.[50] Most of all, even though he cherished the idea of the aboriginal memory that resides in his countrymen, he felt a certain distaste at the thought of being trapped by the past and of being caught in the repeating patterns of inheritance. Stevenson's speculation about what qualities he might have inherited from his mother's father, the 'old minister', is, therefore, accompanied by nearly as much anxiety as respect for the elderly gentleman. Longingly and somewhat nervously he writes, 'he moves in my blood, and whispers words to me, and sits efficient in the very knot and centre of my being'.[51] The protagonist in the short story 'Olalla' reflects and exaggerates this anxiety when he also considers the past that lives without invitation within himself. Fascinated, yet terrified, he looks into an ancient mirror and recognizes 'the filament' of his 'descent and the bonds that knit' him to his family. And amazed he gazes at a portrait of Olalla's ancestor in which he discovers that the woman he loves bares a resemblance to her:

Never before had I so realised the miracle of the continued race, the creation and re-creation, the weaving and changing and handing down of fleshly elements. That a child should be born of its mother, that it should grow and clothe itself (we know not how) with humanity, and put on inherited looks, and turn its head with the manner of one ascendant, and offer its hand with the gesture of another, are wonders dulled for us by repetition.[52]

Olalla herself is trapped by her heredity; against her will she must be a vampire. She has no singular self. She will always belong to others. Begging to leave so she won't destroy her lover, Olalla despairs:

> What is mine, then, and what am I? If not a curve in this poor body of mine (which you love, and for the sake of which you dotingly dream that you love me), not a gesture that I can frame, not a tone of my voice, not any look from my eyes, no, not even now when I speak to him I love, but has belonged to others?...The hands of the dead are in my bosom; they move me, they pluck me, they guide me: I am a puppet at their command; and I but re-inform features and attributes that have long been laid aside from evil in the quiet of the grave.[53]

On the one hand Stevenson prized the images of Galton's composite photographs for their power to identify an essence – their ability to preserve a type; on the other, he resisted the portrait of Olalla's ancestors for reminding him of how the present is a prisoner of the past. His wish to be both a part of a nation or a clan and to seek his own individuality are at odds. These contradictory impulses join the antithetical forces circling his consciousness and accompanying his longing. Stevenson cannot completely escape their presence; therefore, the synthetic moments that his nationalism affords cannot last long. Duality soon reasserts itself and becomes the defining condition of his exile.

Notes

1. In the most recent biography, *Robert Louis Stevenson: A Biography*, (New York: Random House, 1994) Frank McLynn, like many others who have written about Stevenson's life, presents Stevenson as a 'radically divided man'.
2. Stevenson's biographers often comment upon his mixed feelings towards his native land. See D. Daiches, 'Stevenson and Scotland', *Stevenson and Victorian Scotland*, ed. J. Calder (Edinburgh: Edinburgh University Press, 1981) and I. Bell, *Dreams of Exile. Robert Louis Stevenson: A Biography* (New York: Henry Holt, 1992). In his biography, Bell refers to Stevenson's tendency to look both ways at once, of his Janus-like perspective. See also McLynn, *Robert Louis Stevenson: A Biography* pp. 47–50 for a discussion of Stevenson's ambiguous attitude towards Edinburgh. Richard Holmes in 'On the Enchanted Hill', *The New York Review of Books* (8 June 1995) 14–18 also refers to Stevenson's tendency to alternate between 'journeys and homecomings'.
3. In 'Stevenson and Scotland', p. 45, Daiches explains that when Stevenson first sailed for America, he did so 'without telling his parents and against the advice of friends. Only Charles Baxter and William Ernest Henley were entrusted with his American address'. For an account of Stevenson's departure, see McLynn, *Robert Louis Stevenson: A Biography* p. 146.
4. R. L. Stevenson, *The Amateur Emigrant*, introd. J. Raban (London: The Hogarth Press, 1984) p. 15.
5. Ibid., p. 20.
6. It is interesting to note that the realism of *The Amateur Emigrant* distressed Stevenson's father and friends. For this reason, the book was first published with excisions in 1895 and was not published in its complete form until 1966.
7. Stevenson, *The Amateur Emigrant*, pp. 128–9.
8. R. L. Stevenson, *Kidnapped* (New York: Bantam Books, 1982) pp. 105–6.
9. Daiches, 'Stevenson and Scotland', p. 11.
10. Ibid., p. 19.
11. B. Booth and E. Mehew, eds., *The Letters of Robert Louis Stevenson 1854–1894*, II (New Haven: Yale University Press, 1994, 1995) p. 130.
12. Ibid., VIII, p. 185.
13. Ibid, II, p. 80.
14. Ibid., VI, p. 352. Stevenson became friends with Sir Henry and Lady Taylor when he and Fanny were living in Bournemouth (1885–1887).
15. Ibid., VIII, p. 75.
16. Ibid., III, pp. 188–9. The June 1881 letter to Sidney Colvin reads:

> We have a lovely spot here: a little green glen with a burn, a wonderful burn, gold and green and snow-white, singing loud and low in different steps of its career, now pouring over miniature crags, now fretting itself to death in a maze of rocky stairs and pots; never was so sweet a river. Behind, great purple moorlands reach-

ing to Ben Vrackie. Hunger lives here, alone with larks and sheep. Sweet spot, sweet spot.

17.   On one occasion Stevenson complained about the Scottish weather in a 7 November 1874 letter to Katharine De Mattos. Ibid., II, pp. 80–1:

> Edinburgh is much changed for the worse (*ah oui Madame, c'est encore possible*) by the absence of Bob [Stevenson's cousin, Robert Stevenson]; and this damned weather weighs on me like a curse. Yesterday, or the day before, there came so black a rain squall that I was frightened – what a child would call frightened, you know, for want of a better word – although in reality it has nothing to do with fright. I lit the gas and sat cowering in my chair, until it went away again.

On another occasion Stevenson's wife, Fanny Osbourne, remarked, humorously and disparagingly, on the Scottish tolerance for bad weather. See Mrs. R. Stevenson, 'Prefatory Note', *Treasure Island* (London: William Heinemann, 1924), p. xix:

> It was a season of rain and chill weather that we spent in the cottage of the late Miss M'Gregor, though the townspeople called the cold, steady, penetrating drizzle 'just misting'. In Scotland a fair day appears to mean fairly wet. 'It is quite fair, now' they will say, when you can hardly distinguish the houses across the street.

18.   Booth and Mehew, *The Letters of Robert Louis Stevenson*, III, p. 338.
19.   Holmes in 'On the Enchanted Hill', *The New York Review of Books* (8 June 1995) 15 comments on the sense of duality and split loyalties resulting from Stevenson's conflict with the Victorian values of his parents. In addition, McLynn's recent biography pays particular attention to Stevenson's conflict with his parents. See McLynn, *Robert Louis Stevenson: A Biography*, pp. 58–66.
20.   Stevenson, *The Amateur Emigrant*, p. 81.
21.   Booth and Mehew, *The Letters of Robert Louis Stevenson*, III, p. 161.
22.   L. Osbourne, *An Intimate Portrait of R.L.S.* (New York: Charles Scribner's Sons, 1924) p. 72. In addition, *c.* 12 March 1881 Stevenson wrote from Davos to Sidney Colvin:

> My dear Colvin, My health is not just what it should be; I have lost weight, pulse, respiration etc., and gained nothing in the way of my old bellows. But these last few days, with tonic, cod-liver oil, better wine (there is some better now) and perpetual beef-tea, I think I have progressed. To say truth I have been here a little overlong. I was reckoning up; and since I have known you, already quite a while, I have not, I believe remained so long in any one place as here in Davos. That tells on my old gipsy nature; like a violin hung up, I begin to lose what music there was in me; and with the music, I do not know what besides, or do not know what to call it, but

something radically part of life, a rhythm, perhaps, in one's old and so brutally overridden nerves, or perhaps a kind of variety of blood that the heart has come to look for.

See Booth and Mehew, *The Letters of Robert Louis Stevenson*, III, p. 161.

23. Stevenson, *The Amateur Emigrant*, p. 129.
24. Booth and Mehew, *The Letters of Robert Louis Stevenson*, VI, p. 256. The biography that seems to give the most vivid sense of Stevenson's continuous traveling is McLynn's *Robert Louis Stevenson: A Biography*. In the new edition of the Stevenson letters, there is detailed information about the various cruises Stevenson made on board the *Casco*, the *Equator*, and the *Janet Nicoll*. See Booth and Mehew, *The Letters of Robert Louis Stevenson.*, VI, pp. 205, 242–3, 324–5.
25. Ibid., III, p. 16.
26. Stevenson, *The Amateur Emigrant*, pp. 25–6.
27. R. L. Stevenson, *Travels with a Donkey, An Inland Voyage, The Silverado Squatters*, introd. T. Royle (London: J. M. Dent, 1904) p. 215.
28. Stevenson, *The Amateur Emigrant*, pp. 10, 93.
29. Stevenson, *Travels with a Donkey, An Inland Voyage, The Silverado Squatters*, p. 73.
30. Ibid., p. 153.
31. Booth and Mehew, *The Letters of Robert Louis Stevenson*, VI, p. 25.
32. Havel discusses this paradigm in 'On Home', *The New York Review of Books* (5 December 1991) p. 49.
33. Stevenson, *Kidnapped*, p. 4.
34. Booth and Mehew, *The Letters of Robert Louis Stevenson*, VII, p. 12.
35. In *Cultural Institutions of the Novel*, eds. D. Lynch and W. B. Warner (Durham: Duke University Press, 1996) p. 203. Katie Trumpener mentions that the Scots who emigrated to Canada experienced a long-distance nationalism. Far from home, people who had quarreled with one another discovered, through their nostalgia, a joint national identification.
36. Booth and Mehew, *The Letters of Robert Louis Stevenson*, I, p. 238.
37. Stevenson, *Travels with a Donkey, An Inland Voyage, The Silverado Squatters*, pp. 216–17.
38. In *Inquiries into Human Faculty and its Development* (London: J.M. Dent, 1928) pp. 5–7, Francis Galton explains:

The general expression of a face is the sum of a multitude of small details, which are never in such rapid succession that we seem to perceive them all at a single glance. If any one of them disagrees with the recollected traits of a known face, the eye is quick at observing it, and dwells upon the difference. One small discordance overweighs a multitude of similarities and suggests a general unlikeness; just as a single syllable in a sentence pronounced with a foreign accent makes one cease to look upon the speaker as a countryman. . . . The effect of composite portraiture is to bring into evidence all the traits in which there is agreement, and to leave but a ghost of a trace of individual peculiarities.

Galton describes how he made his composite pictures:

> As a means of getting over the difficulty of procuring really representative faces.... (1) I collected photographic portraits of different persons, all of whom had been photographed in the same aspect (say full face), and under the same conditions of light and shade.... (2) I reduced their portraits...to the same size.... (3) I superimposed the portraits like the successive leaves of a book, so that the features of each portrait lay...in front of those of the one behind it.... Thus I obtained a book, each page of which contained a separate portrait, and all the portraits lay exactly in front of one another. (4) I fastened the book against the wall in such a way that I could turn over the pages in succession.... (5) I focused my camera on the book.... (6) I began photographing, taking one page after the other in succession without moving the camera....

39. Galton, *Inquiries into Human Faculty and its Development*, p. 7.
40. R. L. Stevenson, *Memories and Portraits* (New York: Charles Scribner's Sons, 1897) p. 90.
41. L. Osbourne, *An Intimate Portrait of R. L. S.*, p. 129.
42. Bell, *Dreams of Exile. Robert Louis Stevenson: A Biography*, p. 251.
43. I. Strong and L. Osbourne, *Memories of Vailima* (New York: Charles Scribner's Sons, 1902) pp. 136–9.
44. In a 5 September 1893 letter to George Meredith, Stevenson ironically boasted about 'living patriarchally': 'My health is vastly restored, and I am now living patriarchally in the place six hundred feet above the sea on the shoulder of a mountain of 1500.' See Booth and Mehew, *The Letters of Robert Louis Stevenson*, VIII, p. 163.
45. When Stevenson was living in Samoa, he actively defended the cause of Mataafa, the rebel chief, who resisted the attempts of the Germans to colonize his island. He opposed a puppet king installed by the Germans. Stevenson helped Mataafa by giving him advice and by visiting him at his armed camp. When eventually the chief was imprisoned, Stevenson saw to it that he and his followers received adequate food and water. See Bell, *Dreams of Exile. Robert Louis Stevenson: A Biography*, pp. 257–8. For a detailed account of Stevenson's engagement with the cause of Mataafa, see McLynn, *Robert Louis Stevenson: A Biography*, pp. 421–36, 461–4.
46. Stevenson, *Travels with a Donkey, An Inland Voyage, The Silverado Squatters*, p. 178.
47. Booth and Mehew, *The Letters of Robert Louis Stevenson*, VIII, p. 91.
48. Ibid., VII, p. 110.
49. Ibid., VIII, p. 283.
50. Bell, *Dreams of Exile. Robert Louis Stevenson: A Biography*, p. 125.
51. Stevenson, *Memories and Portraits*, p. 114.
52. R. L. Stevenson, *Robert Louis Stevenson: The Body Snatcher and Other Stories*, ed. J. Meyers (New York: New American Library, 1988) p. 126.
53. Ibid., pp. 140–1.

4

The 'shaking, uncertain ground' of Elizabeth Gaskell's Narratives

> It was a pleasant place that early home!
> The brook went singing by, leaving its foam
> Among the flags and blue forget-me-not;
> And in a nook, above that shelter'd spot,
> For ages stood a gnarled hawthorne-tree,
> And if you pass'd in spring-time, you might see
> The knotted trunk all coronal'd with flowers,
> That every breeze shook down in fragrant showers.
> E. Gaskell, 'Sketches Among the Poor', lines 47–54

> a large railway hotel has driven away the orchard and gooseberry
> bushes which two years before flourished in its place.
> 'Dumbledowndeary', *Household Words* (19 June 1852)

> The landscape is never inert, people engage with it, re-work it, appro-
> priate and contest it. It is part of the way in which identities are
> created and disputed, whether as individual, group, or nation–state.
> B. Bender, *Landscape: Politics and Perspectives*

The experience of exile, of course, does not belong solely to people
who leave their native land; it also touches the lives of those who
suffer displacement at home. Elizabeth Gaskell's fiction addresses
this form of exclusion, for her narratives inhabit a landscape of
change that disorients the location of the self and affects the familiar
understanding of time and place.[1] Until they bump into Gaskell's
impatience with their naiveté, the nostalgic moments that her characters experience in her writing journey among these shifting contours.

To comprehend more fully the nature of this exile – this displacement – and its attendant, nostalgia, one needs to consider the ways
in which Gaskell moves her characters through intersecting spheres

of time, removes them from the protective circumference of the collective memory, sends them in search of a refuge, and then requires them to imagine alternative ways of mapping their environment – a task made more complex by the coming of the railroads and the laying down of new tracks upon the land. By concentrating upon the landscape of memory in her stories and upon the intrusion of the railway in her fiction, one can understand better 'the shaking, uncertain ground' of her narratives.

NOSTALGIA: THE SITES AND PLACES OF MEMORY

When one reads Gaskell's fiction, one enters narratives about how the past accompanies, intersects with, and occasionally overwhelms the present moment. What once had been alive and tangible stalks her texts so that gestures and images from another time are seldom out of sight. Gaskell rarely tucks away the past. She is not like the displaced aristocrat, Monsieur de Chalabre, who, after he has lost his title and property to the French Revolution, sequesters a pencil drawing of the château Chalabre – the only remnant of his past – in the tiny dressing-room of his English cottage ('My French Master').[2] Gaskell, instead, opens these doors wide and keeps the appanages of former days fully in view: in Alice Wilson's Manchester cellar (*Mary Barton*) she displays dried flowers and herbs, relics of a bygone pastoral life, in *Cranford* she unfurls Miss Matty's red silk umbrella, a survivor of her family's history, and in *Sylvia's Lovers* she hangs the Corneys' patchwork curtains, 'the united efforts of some former generations'.[3] These are the remnants in which the nostalgic memory roots itself. But events and objects from the past do more than leave traces. As those familiar with Gaskell's fiction know, they also come forward to create episodes of disturbing and humorous incongruity in which Gaskell makes it clear that differences between the old and new ways are insuperable. This reality embeds Gaskell's characters within a nonsynchronic landscape – within an environment that allows Squire Hamley's watch, 'given him by his father when watches were watches long ago' to read 6:15 p.m. and his elder son's, set to the more recent clock of the Horse Guards in Whitehall, to show 6:00 p.m.[4] Nostalgia, of course, emerges from this disparity and attempts to compensate for the subsequent discontinuity. It mourns the loss of a collective memory that glosses over change and differences in time by repeatedly moving the past into a seamless present, and offers, through a shared set of rituals, the illusion of belonging to a communal identity where remembrance occurs among people, not within the solitary individual's mind. Gaskell's yearning for Cranford belongs to this nostalgia.

Although, in her absence, Gaskell might have been nostalgic for the society of Cranford – for her own memories of her early years in Knutsford – the ladies who live there are not, for they are securely enclosed within its well-defined and mutually comprehended boundaries. In their society, 'Everybody lived in the same house, and wore pretty nearly the same well-preserved' clothes.[5] In short, they belong to a world of collective memory where repeated events and ceremonies (such as the annual gathering to honor Mrs Forrester's wedding day and the teas at Miss Betty Barker's) and shared codes (their mutual sense of propriety and 'elegant economy') affirm and keep their identity intact, even when the present in the form of commerce, trade, and steam invades their territory and the passing of time creates incongruities. Their ceremonies and rules, their 'acts of transfer' that make remembering possible, gently, yet firmly, carry the past continuously forward;[6] these rituals soften and smooth out the effects of change so that, for instance, Captain Brown, who breaks their rules and represents a more modern age or progress, may be admitted from the periphery into the center of their society – without rupturing its core. The ladies may open up their circle, for it will easily close again because the habits of their past seal with approval what they do in the present and validate their sense of themselves.[7]

What is available for Miss Matty, Miss Jenkyns, Mrs Betty Barker, Miss Pole, and Mrs Jamieson, though, is not necessarily in place for most of Gaskell's protagonists whom Gaskell removes from the custody of collective memory. By cutting her characters loose, she forces her protagonists to seek an identity, more or less alone, as individuals manoeuvering outside a defined circle, in and about shifting spheres of influence and expectation.[8] They are thrown back on themselves – for the most part reminiscence occurs within their own thoughts, not with others.

Some who have commented on Gaskell's fiction have noted that her main characters are orphans. Libbie Marsh, Mary Barton, Ruth Hilton, Molly Gibson, and Margaret Hale begin their lives in the novels as displaced persons. Having lost her father and mother, Libbie Marsh moves to Manchester where she must live alone separated from what had been familiar; similarly Ruth Hilton has to move from her rural dwelling to endure life as an 'orphan apprentice'; having lost their mothers, Mary Barton and Molly Gibson are exiled from their home-space; and cut off from the country town of her youth, Margaret Hale must learn to find her way through the alien industrial city of Milton. Wrenched from shared intonations, customs, expectations, and associations of their past, they start out as isolated figures, separated from communal remembrance. They have to forge a life for themselves within a context of scattered memory – scattered because there is no longer a familiar, spatial entity to synthesize and retain such details.[9] It is, of course, this dislocation that evokes their nostalgia.

Even though Gaskell was sometimes impatient with the sentiment (she often celebrated 'the real progress we have made since those times'[10]), and even though she periodically questioned its validity (she undercut the longing for an arcadian past by reminding her readers that such an idyll is a lie), she well understood the impulse to yearn for a time and a place that seems to compensate for and soothe the rough incongruities of the present. Gaskell might have agreed with the writer of the poem 'Now' that appeared in a 26 November 1853 issue of *Household Words* who counseled the reader not to get caught in the chains of the past, and have sympathized with the author of 'The Present' (*Household Words* 13 October 1855) who advised 'Do not crouch to-day, and worship/ The old Past, whose life is fled', even though she herself longed to be 'off into the deep grassy solitudes of the country'.[11] She too had had to leave her childhood country town and reorient herself in the 'great manufacturing town' of Manchester.[12] And Gaskell might have insisted that one ought 'to give thanks for living in the present' – an assertion that finds its voice in all the 'But's' that briskly qualify expressions of nostalgia[13] – yet she felt drawn towards the imaginative forgetfulness of longing that purifies and simplifies the past. She, therefore, understands Monsieur de Chalabre's desire to return to his château, Margaret Hale's, Ruth Hilton's, and Sylvia Robson's need to go back to their childhood spaces; she comprehends Sylvia's wish to be with the old servant from Haytersbank Farm, and assents to Nest Gwynn's request to walk back to the well, the site of her beautiful and romantic past – the place where Edward Williams had 'overtaken her' ('The Well of Pen-Morfa'); moreover, with a knowing sympathy she repeats Cousin Phillis's futile closing words: 'Then – we will go back to the peace of the old days. I know we shall; I can, and I will.'[14] In these moments nostalgia is more than a rhetorical device to evoke and make more vivid the grittiness, and in Nest's case, the lameness, of the present; it is also a genuine impulse to discover refuge from the vicissitudes of time and to nestle in an environment where one's being is confirmed rather than always doubted. It is a way of closing the question of identity.

Gaskell's depiction of this impulse, though, is not entirely free of the commonplace or of clichés. For instance, Gaskell plays with the city/country dichotomy so pervasive in the history of the imagination.[15] Consequently, in her novels and stories, in spite of her subtle reminders that Alice Wilson's country home was not necessarily blissful,[16] the focus of her characters' longing tends to be on the rural scenes, the spaces of innocence, purity, virtue, and peace, rather than on the busy, chaotic, noisy, corrupt city. And at the center of her idyllic interludes and natural scenes are maternal figures who, in the context of the nostalgic moment, provide the desired stability: Mary Barton's mother offers tender words of comfort, Ruth Hilton's sits by the fire, and Sylvia Robson's fronts the setting sun so she may search 'through its blinding ray for a sight of her child'.[17] As if posing for the commonplaces of the genre artist's canvas, in these moments they function as a fixed domestic presence that counterbalances the instabilities produced by the buffeting present. In this role they emerge as the all too familiar caretakers of imagined communities in which identity and social relations remain intact.[18]

Another convention of the nostalgic imagination in nineteenth-century England is, of course, the pastoral image of the cottage or farmhouse, structures that continue to be used as symbols of simplicity and peace by those dissatisfied with contemporary culture.[19] In her fiction Gaskell also occasionally utilizes this trope; at times she borrows from the poetry of George Crabbe and, at others, approaches the sentimentality of such poems as 'A Cottage Memory' (*Household Words* 14 September 1850) that describes 'The white little cottage with nest-crowned eaves,/ Peeping out half the year from an ambush of leaves.' But, once more she periodically qualifies such expressions with a stern impatience so that the pastoral and the anti-pastoral co-exist.[20] Gaskell's corrective remarks are most noticeable in *North and South*. Through the words and experiences of Margaret Hale, Gaskell reminds her public that a yearning for the picturesque cottage and its idyllic surroundings is naive. She informs Bessy that 'there's a deal to bear there' and that people, especially the laborers who are out in all weathers, suffer from debilitating rheumatism.

And she reminds Mr Lennox that not all is sunshine: 'we have rain and our leaves do fall, and get sodden'.[21] When Margaret herself returns to Helstone, she abruptly learns that not everything is as her longing had imagined. Chaos, cruelty, and change inhabit what she had thought a refuge. It is as if Gaskell forces Margaret to look at the puddles, the dungheaps, and the filthy, messy interior of the Corneys' farmhouse in *Sylvia's Lovers*. When Gaskell describes this particular dwelling, she has no nostalgic illusions about its picturesqueness. The gardens are not replete with ornamental blossoms or sweet-smelling flowers. They are composed of cabbage beds and potato grounds. Like the author of 'Pinchback's Cottage' in a 22 March 1862 issue of *All the Year Round*, she was capable of distinguishing between what he calls the 'stage English cottage' and 'the real English cottage'. The stage one is 'over-dressed with painted roses' and has little resemblance to poor Pinchback's cottage in Downshire where there are no flowers, 'but a good deal too much of dung-heap; it is not a bower of roses; it is a nest of rheumatism and a den of ague and low fever'.[22]

Yet Gaskell's corrections to the idyll are milder than those of her more critical contemporaries. Her writing does not bear the weight of the stark realities and details recorded in the reports of the Medical Officer of Health or of the Commission on the Employment of Children, Young Persons and Women in Agriculture. Nor does it compare with Richard Heath's articles on rural England. Heath was among many to be alarmed by these 'dirty hovels' and to exclaim, 'Picturesque and harmonious from the artist's point of view, these cottages are in most respects a scandal to England.' In 'The Cottage Homes of England' (*Leisure Hour* 1870), he quotes from an 1863–4 report written by a sanitary inspector to the city of Norwich. The details and the emphasis in his selection have little resemblance to Gaskell's picturesque, decaying, irregular, and straggling cottages.[23] Gaskell tends to slide over the worst, saving that for her description of the rooms and cellars of the Manchester mill workers.[24] Those passages come closer to the inspector's statement about cottage life:

A stranger cannot enter the village without being struck with surprise at its wretched and desolate condition. Look where he may, he sees little else but thatched roofs – old, rotten and shapeless – full of holes and overgrown with weeds; windows sometimes patched with rags, and sometimes plastered over with clay; the walls, which are nearly all of clay, full of cracks and crannies;

and sheds and outhouses – where there are any – looking as if they had been overthrown very early in the present century, and left in the hopeless confusion in which they fell.[25]

Perhaps Gaskell's elisions with regard to the offensive realities of her cottages and farmhouses reflect an unwillingness, on her part, to let go completely of the idyll and of the picturesque. Indulging the nostalgic impulse, Gaskell, at times, preferred to recall the fragrance of their surroundings and remark upon the charm of their old-fashioned inconveniences. When writing to her friend Eliza Fox on 29 May 1849, she expressed her delight with

> a very pretty, really old fashioned cottage, at Shottery, the village where Shakespeare's wife lived in her maiden days, near S. on Avon; a cottage where one's head was literally in danger of being bumped by the low doors, and where the windows were casements: where the rooms were all entered by a step up, or a step down: where the scents through the open hall door were all of sweet briar and lilacs and lilies of the valley: where we slept, with our windows open to hear the nightingales ... and where the very shadows in the drawing room had a green tinge from the leafy trees which over hung the windows. Cd. there be a greater contrast to dear charming, dingy dirty Panton Square? (The Gaskell home was a mile and a half 'from the *very* middle of Manchester').[26]

In her fiction during moments similar to these, Gaskell puts herself in the position of Margaret Hale who wants to stop 'for a minute or two' so she can sketch the picturesque yet decaying cottages haunting her imagination.[27] She becomes the artist who paints brief interludes of tranquility and sweetness that she can keep with her – sketching is a way of extending the past into the present. And like the mermaid who holds up a mirror to the homesick sailor, faraway at sea, and lets him gaze at 'the little cottage near Aber in Wales ... as plain as ever he saw it in life, and his wife standing outside, shading her eyes as if she were looking for him',[28] Gaskell provides images of refuge. She offers the displaced still places that guard the older values and connect the yearning viewer to the illusion of the communal memory.

In these pictures Gaskell often shows gardens bordered with sweet briar and fraxinelle, and filled with old-fashioned herbs planted long ago, blue forget-me-nots, tall white lilies, noisettes, golden celandine, and primroses – the very act of naming becomes a gesture of longing; she draws attention to the creeping scented roses, the ivy that climbs the outer walls, the gnarled hawthorne tree, the straggling honeysuckle, the many- speckled fowls, the sweet-balmy air that clings to the clothes, and the pretty green lanes. In the domestic mode of nostalgia, she places before the dwellings a comforting mother clutching ripe damsons in her apron and a wistful mother standing in the doorway of her moorland cottage.[29] Within these pictures, Gaskell's images of rural life almost resemble those that congregate and clutter to form the cottage and farmhouse paintings done later by Helen Allingham (1848–1926).[30] Allingham's watercolors of these dwellings in Surrey, Kent, and the Isle of Wight also offer elided, idyllic views of rural life (Figure 6). Through her paintings one approaches the cottage from a dirt path which takes the viewer through an open gate and to a profusely flowering garden that grows up to the doorway, presses against the walls covered with crawling roses and clinging ivy, and leads the eye up to the thatched roof (perhaps the only part of the painting that admits any mark of distress). Smoke curls reassuringly from the chimney. Standing at the gate is a young woman or mother, dressed in an old-fashioned bonnet and in a brightly starched white pinafore, holding a round-cheeked child. Before the gate ducks, cats, doves, chickens, sparrows, rabbits – images of domesticity – forage without harm. Over all the painting a diffuse, equable light intensifies the colors. No shadow crosses the paper: no mud, no rain, no winter, no misery, no ill-health. As the critic for an 1888 issue of *Art Journal* remarked, 'In Mrs Allingham's art there is no trace of sympathy with the stern realism to which we have grown accustomed in the works of many modern painters. For her there would be little attraction of a pictorial kind in the marks of grime and toil on rugged hands and bronzed faces.'[31] John Ruskin would have agreed, for much as he admired Allingham's watercolors, he found fault with their 'prettinesses'. In his Academy Notes (1875), he remarks on both Allingham's and Kate Greenaway's paintings: 'both Miss Kate and Mrs. Allingham might do better duty to their day, and better honour to their art, if they would paint, as verily, some of these poor country people in faraway places, rather than the high-bred prettinesses, or fond imaginations, which are the best they have given us yet for antidote to the misery of London'.[32]

In spite of her own images' fleeting resemblance to Allingham's, Gaskell too might have concurred with the *Art Journal* critic, for she was never to linger long in pastoral scenes that lie. She could not subscribe indefinitely to Allingham's illusions. With their primary attention to surface and to a light that diffuses difference, Allingham's paintings destroy any sense of depth or even the possibility of despair. Without shadow there is no dimension other than an overreaching, almost rigid, brightness that obliterates both memory and history. This emptiness turns Allingham's pictures into stage sets for a drama that has neither plot nor character. Gaskell could not write with the Chinese White of Allingham's palate, nor could she always, as did Allingham, bring the freshly laundered props out of the cupboard of her imagination,[33] or keep placing sketches of professional models (done in her studio or garden) into the blank spaces of her text. As frequently as she emphasized the beauty of her young protagonists, Gaskell was also eager to expose their foibles – to soil their pinafores – and to explore the subtleties and intricacies of their humanity and their history. She attempted to release them from the set poses of Allingham's studio nostalgia. Furthermore, she was not intent upon isolating her idyllic scenes. When Allingham painted her watercolors, she removed anything that distracted the eye from her idealized subject: she never included outbuildings, extensions, neighboring cottages, distant roofs and towers. Allingham concentrated exclusively on the single dwelling. Gaskell did the opposite. Like her novels with their interlocking stories and overlapping perspectives, her farmhouses and cottages are very much attached to, summoned by, and compromised by the communities, near and far, around them. In this respect they are, perhaps, linked to the memory of place rather than to the site of memory. As Edward S. Casey suggests, the memory of place calls for an inclusive sense of space, where the landscape has a context – is situated – and where the individual, the figure in the landscape, has a recollection of having been there, of being 'slowed down, stopped, or in some other way caught-in- place'.[34] Sites of memory, on the other hand, have no such dimension; they are not connected to a wider orbit. They possess no points of attachment. Instead, separated from their origin, they freeze a detached moment. Ironically, it seems, these sites of memory negate their subject – they erase the memory of what they are supposed to commemorate. Such is the state of Allingham's cottages and farmhouses. Even with her attention to place, these isolated structures are not ultimately satisfying to the viewer, for they lack the sense of multiple dimensions. Gaskell's, however, are made to extend beyond a protective border and to expose their thresholds to what lies elsewhere. Like the idyllic farmhouse in *Cousin Phillis*, they are touched and altered by the various spheres of time: the produce of the past (the last Ribstone Pippin), the needs of the present (the recent arrival of the penny post), and the seasons and tracks of the future (the coming of the train). To survey this property is to see people walk through it, to take note of these intersections of images and events, and simultaneously to hear the faraway rumble of carts and to imagine the whistle of the approaching train. This pastoral spot, this refuge, consequently, cannot remain intact; it is necessarily vulnerable to change. Therefore, when Gaskell sketches her cottages, she, like Margaret Hale, acknowledges that they will alter, decay, tumble down, and eventually disappear in the same way as at the end of *Sylvia's Lovers*, the 'memory of man fades away' and only a few people can recall the 'tradition of the man who died in a cottage somewhere about this spot'.[35]

Allingham was only occasionally sensitive to her subjects' vulnerability. Commenting, for instance, on her painting of Tennyson's estate and surroundings, she notes that the content of her *Farringford Dairy and Home Farm* would look quite different a number of years later, for in 'This last year, or two Mrs. Diment's growing family of fowls (not to speak of guinea-fowls and peacocks) have picked away most of the grass and hedge near the gate.'[36] But rather than reflect or anticipate the fact of alteration, for the most part in her pictures she chose to overlook it. Enveloping her cottages and farmhouses in an unchanging past, she helped propagate the pastoral myth of Happy England. She not only isolated these dwellings by cutting them off from their surroundings but also made repairs to them. She became a conserver. According to Ina Taylor, Allingham rendered her cottages as she thought they could have looked: 'Those cottages which Helen believed had once possessed thatched roofs, she "re-thatched", and those missing the old windows, she restored by copying frames she kept in her studio.'[37] It seems, therefore, that Allingham's nostalgia differs considerably from Gaskell's. Allingham's sequesters images from alteration and memory – she frames them in a fixed, unviolated moment of imagined history – but Gaskell's demands alteration and a place in what Jenny Uglow identifies as 'the shifting and sliding planes of time'.[38] Figures like Alice Wilson and Mary Barton might want to transform their childhood spaces into *sites* of memory, detached and released from the necessity of time and from the industrialized world, but Gaskell does not. Her nostalgia significantly differs from theirs, for it insists that such sites become places of memory attached to an unstable landscape. In the larger picture of her fiction, she cannot protect these sites from what exists outside their fragile boundaries. Helstone must change and so must Margaret Hale's perception of it. Gaskell is not a writer who is afraid to risk history. She does not depict her landscapes at 'the expense of historical understanding'.[39]

THE SHIFTING LANDSCAPE

Just why Gaskell has this perspective, rather than Allingham's, becomes easier to comprehend if one recognizes that the geography of her fiction is never a stable one. Its scenery belongs to a general topography of change; therefore, the nostalgic desire to identify and mark a still place is not as readily satisfied as her characters might wish. Gaskell's settings are never inert; they continually shift and register alteration and, thereby, refute the popular idea of an unchanging rural past.[40] Characters in her novels and stories move through a landscape in which road systems, train tracks, and the penny post not only vary the appearance of the land but also alter the relation of one place to another. Commerce recasts social structures, drainage and deforestation modify the shape of the countryside, the tentacles of the industrial cities reach into their surrounding counties, new buildings replace older ones, and villages evolve into manufacturing towns – as Gaskell observed, 'even in small towns, scarcely removed from villages, the phases of society are rapidly changing; and much will appear strange, which yet occurred only in the generation immediately preceding ours' ('The Last Generation in England').[41] Her characters live where the old maps or landmarks have been disturbed or are being destroyed. The result is that the kindly Mr Bell, upon his return to the place of his birth, loses his way – 'aye, among the very piles of warehouses that are built upon my father's orchard', and Margaret Hale forfeits her orientation when she departs from her childhood home where there was a stone wall with 'gray and yellow lichens that marked it like a map'.[42] When she moves to Milton, she must discover new patterns among the town's innumerable streets. Not only has the collective memory been broken up but also the landmarks by which individuals had located themselves.

Margaret's dilemma is, of course, one that confounds many other characters in Gaskell's fiction. Forever changing their home-places, they must constantly negotiate – re-map – these most intimate of spaces. For instance, Paul, the narrator of *Cousin Phillis*, moves from his childhood town to lodgings in Eltham, then finds a place at Hope Farm ('I knew my room, like a son in the house'[43]), and eventually returns to Birmingham. Each time he must learn to locate the landmarks – the contours of expectation – that chart these spaces. In the same story Mr Holdsworth abruptly swerves from place to place, country to country (from Italy to Canada), each time setting down fresh sets of tracks; even the Reverend Holman who is firmly rooted in the county of his ancestors surveys his fields so that he can better understand the changes that will soon alter their profile. Phillis's world is not a static one.[44] Neither is Mary Barton's environment. There people have to shift between the clearly delineated Green Heys Fields and the streets of Manchester where 'The keen east wind' sometimes rises and makes the 'Houses, sky, people, and every thing' look 'as if a gigantic brush had washed them all over with a dark shade of Indian ink.'[45] Then there are the characters like Ruth Hilton whose life can never rest but must drift from Fordham, to London, to North Wales, to Eccleston and Abermouth. Confused and lost like a child 'who gets a few pieces of a dissected map', she wanders until 'a glimpse of the whole unity is shown' her – until Mr Benson can help her chart the course of her conduct.[46] In *Sylvia's Lovers* the shifting sites of home stand next to the blue trackless water of the sea. The Parish church, the market place, the bridge, the cemetery, the ruins of the monastery, the stone fences, and the steps leading up to the cliffs do not hold Monkshaven and its surroundings still, but are there to measure difference. These landmarks see Sylvia Robson move from the open moors of Haytersbank to the back room of Philip Hepburn's shop in town where she must leave off her morning dress and 'don a stiff and stately gown'.[47] They observe Philip leaving the town in disgrace, and when he returns, look upon his disfigured face searching among the irregular roofs for his own home. They also remain to monitor the decay of Haytersbank Farm and watch as it falls into a rusted disuse.

Finally, in *Wives and Daughters*, there is Molly Gibson, who, even though she never leaves the country town of Hollingford, must in her own way cope with changing places. She moves back and forth in the social and physical topography of her own home, of Lord and

Lady Cumnor's Collistone Park (she gets lost in its grounds), and of Hamley Hall. In addition, she must deal with the disorienting changes in habits, ornamentation, and furnishings that her stepmother imposes at home: the arrangement of her mother's room – a map of Molly's past – gets destroyed under the new Mrs Gibson's renovating hand. Not even the natural world is immune. Caught in the inevitable progress of evolutionary change, the land on the estates gets drained, the old shepherd dies, and the wasps dispossess the bees by entering their hives and eating up their honey.

Within this shifting context there is no single way to orient oneself; there is necessarily more than one way to find a place and give directions. For instance, when Ruth Hilton's seducer asks Ruth how to reach her childhood home, she replies: 'just over the bridge, and up the hill where the elm-trees meet overhead and make a green shade; and then comes the dear old Grange, that I shall never see again'[48] – a response that is familiar to anyone who has asked directions in the countryside and has received an answer that relies upon local, living markers validated by the subjective memory. But when Philip Hepburn tries to instruct Sylvia Robson about how to locate places beyond Haytersbank, he relies upon abstract entities such as the 'four quarters' of the globe and measured quantities like 'how many inhabitants is in each'.[49] These two sets of directions belong to different kinds of maps: one that is inscribed upon the surface and one that reflects the process of memory.

One rarely finds the ordered and classified map in Gaskell's fiction, for that would imply a static landscape; it suggests a globe covered with fixed symbols that hold one's surroundings still. Obviously, Philip's geography lesson to Sylvia depends upon these inscriptions. And so does Mr Holdsworth's theodolite that records, measures, and abstracts the contours of the fields surrounding Hope Farm (*Cousin Phillis*). But neither Philip's atlas nor Mr Holdsworth's instrument represents the entire space of Gaskell's settings where one discovers, instead, many more maps that draw upon the process of memory – in the manner of Ruth's directions to Milham Grange. Characters know where they are according to what has taken place in the past. Forgotten places and moments help create a landscape not *of* memory but *as* memory. This distinction between these two kinds of landscape occurs in Susanne Küchler's study of mapping in New Ireland (Melanesia) in which she contrasts 'the western conceptualisation of landscape as inscribed surface from which social and cultural relations can be read off, with the

New Irelanders' understanding of landscape as process'.[50] She explains that 'Every man and woman can trace the trees of former gardens which were started by them and the trees of gardens in which they used merely to have a plot. What appear to be just trees among trees in secondary forest figure as memoriae *loci* that can be used to retrace relationships of considerable time-depth since rights to former garden land are passed down the generations.'[51] In *Sylvia's Lovers* Philip Hepburn participates in this form of mapping. When, for instance, he returns from London and goes to Haytersbank to see Sylvia Robson, he first catches a glimpse of her standing in her garden. He recalls the history of the garden, 'placed long ago by some tenant of the farm on a southern slope; walled in with rough moorland stones; planted with berry-bushes for use, and southernwood and sweet-briar for sweetness of smell' and remembers how he had once helped Sylvia 'with the arrangement of this garden; laying out his few spare pence in hen-and-chicken daisies at one time, in flower-seeds at another; again in a rose-tree pot. He knew how his unaccustomed hands had laboured with the spade at forming a little primitive bridge over the beck in the hollow before winter streams should make it too deep for fording...but now it was months and years since he had been' there.[52] The garden is a memory template forever being transformed. Similarly, in *Ruth* the narrator cannot locate the larch tree outside Ruth Hilton's workhouse without reminiscing: 'Poor old larch! the time had been when it had stood in a pleasant lawn, with the tender grass creeping caressingly up to its very trunk; but now the lawn was divided into yards and squalid back premises, and the larch was pent up and girded about with flag-stones.'[53] The nostalgic memory creates the narrator's map.

Gaskell reveals her dependence on this kind of mapping when she introduces her stories and novels with descriptions of places that display the tangible presence of their former years. She opens *Ruth* by locating her protagonist's workplace within a building that carries its past within its walls. She talks about houses 'too solidly grand to submit to alteration' so that people are 'occasionally surprised, after passing through a commonplace-looking shop, to find themselves at the foot of a grand carved oaken staircase, lighted by a window of stained glass, storied all over with armorial bearings'.[54] Ruth herself sews in a room in which the wallpaper reveals not only the room's former elegance but also a memory of her own idyllic past: 'visions of other sister-flowers that grew, and blossomed, and withered away in her early home'[55] – a dwelling that the narrator speaks of as a cluster of memories: 'a house of afterthoughts; building materials were plentiful in the neighbourhood, and every successive owner had found a necessity for some addition or projection'.[56] And when Gaskell introduces the story of 'Morton Hall', she begins by conforming to the demands of the inscribing map but quickly shifts her perspective and inserts her description into a map of remembrance: 'Morton Hall is situated about five miles from the centre of Drumble. It stands on the outskirts of a village, which when the Hall was built, was probably as large as Drumble in those days; and even I can remember when there was a long piece of rather lonely road, with high hedges on either side, between Morton village and Drumble. Now, it is all street, and Morton seems but a suburb of the great town near. Our farm stood where Liverpool Street runs now.'[57] Later she refers to the street 'they are going to build right through the rooms through which Alice Carr [the protagonist of the story] was dragged in her agony and despair'.[58] Recollection with its subsequent transformations, not the solid lines of an atlas, compose this narrator's map.

As a rule Gaskell's protagonists are not familiar with conventional maps. Mary Barton might have seen 'a terrestrial globe' and, at one time, known 'where to find France and the continents on a map', but she does not consider turning to a map so that she can help Alice Wilson locate South America.[59] She does not, as does Reverend Holman, bring out 'a large old-fashioned atlas' to find the country's exact placement.[60] What she calls her 'ignorance' is, in a sense, no different from Alice Wilson's vague understanding of where South America is ('at t'other side of the sun, they tell me'[61]), nor, perhaps, is it unlike Sylvia Robson's resistance to geography lessons, for in each case there is no traditional geography; there is, instead, a kind of anti-geography – an orientation that is very different from that proposed by Philip Hepburn when he wants his cousin Sylvia to find Greenland in the pages of an atlas. Because their lives are subject to a continuing series of alterations and, perhaps, because they themselves are no longer supported by the codes belonging to a collective memory, their perspective refuses to draw upon firmly fixed, classified, ordered, and inscribed spaces. Dwelling on a shifting land rather than within steadily delineated borders, Gaskell's protagonists experience the fluctuations and temporality of their circumstances and must, therefore, devise their own sense of how one place, one time, and one person relate to another. These figures cannot rely on conventional maps but neither can they situate themselves solely within a landscape of recollection and nostalgia. They have to become their own cartographers.[62]

In the opening of *Wives and Daughters*, Gaskell acknowledges this necessity and this impulse. She first situates Molly Gibson by responding to a conventional question posed by geography: in what country is this town? 'In a country there was a shire, and in that shire there was a town, and in that town there was a house, and in that house there was a room, and in that room there was a bed, and in that bed there lay a little girl.'[63] But as quickly as she can, Gaskell pushes this map away by making Molly bound out of her bed and open the window to survey the landscape for herself – to look out and over the garden, the meadow, and the little town of Hollingford. A new map begins with Molly, not with an external referent marking the text for her. This gesture continues throughout the novel so that whenever Molly enters new territory (for example, Lord and Lady Cumnor's and Squire Hamley's estates), she first of all goes to the window to see what was to be seen. And so do others: Libbie Marsh gazes out of the window and climbs to the top of the grassy knoll to gain a fuller view of her new environment – of Manchester 'far away in the blue plain' ('Libbie Marsh's Three Eras');[64] from her cottage window Lizzie Leigh stares long and wistfully over the grey moors ('Lizzie Leigh'), and Ruth Hilton repeatedly places her forehead against the window pane or wanders from window to window to see 'the far-away hilly line of the horizon'.[65]

In these acts of looking out, these figures extend the boundaries of their immediate surroundings so they can revise the traditionally prescribed enclosures and locate themselves within a larger sphere that, with its undulating horizons, allows for change, absorbs change into itself, or compensates for it. They can also accommodate their own need to let their personal geography overwhelm the fixed linearity of inscribed spaces. Within this map, Ruth Hilton can add her remembrance of the wilder Welsh landscape to the carefully delineated, domesticated space of the Eccleston parsonage. In this way, even though Ruth has entered the boundaries of Mr Benson's threshold, she can continue to 'look abroad over the still and quiet town – over the grey stone walls, and chimneys, and old high-pointed roofs' to the distant scene of her passion.[66] Both experiences are part of her geography. This more inclusive map had already been hers when, as an orphan seamstress she had pressed her forehead against the cold glass of her workplace window and gazed into the larger landscape of the winter's night – an act of seeing that through her imagination appends the contours of home to her immediate restricted surroundings. Ruth tries to be the cartographer who does not deny or shut out what is left behind; she attempts to map the past with the present. Similarly, Lizzie Leigh, although confined to her moorland cottage, peers through her window to undefined places across the moor where her daughter might be. Her determined eyes pierce the stern, authoritative spaces of home and help her reach beyond its inscribed enclosures. Her map includes the near and the far, the living and the lost, the known and the unknown. Sylvia Robson is also this kind of cartographer, for she constantly pushes against the dark, confining barriers of her life to gaze upon the free open spaces that take her to the memory of Charley Kincaid. Under the great dome of sky, hers is a landscape of fields bounded only by loose stone fences.

In a different mode these expanded and fluctuating spaces also belong to Maggie Browne (*The Moorland Cottage*) and Margaret Hale (*North and South*). Through their larger maps, these individuals cope with the difficulties of home. Within these more ample areas, they gain a broader perspective that distinguishes them from their contemporaries. Margaret, who makes a point of leaving her own home to learn about the mill workers' lives and who throws the window wide open so she can see and hear the rage of the angry strikers, is constantly widening her field of vision by this and other acts. Her view extends beyond the more restricted prospects of both the workers and the factory owners. And so does Maggie's. She is always seen going out of doors or walking beyond the gate of her moorland cottage to the wide and open moor, and, oriented by its 'swelling expanse', she sees more deeply than those who have travelled 'half over Europe'.[67] This perspective helps her deal with the rigid conventions of her hierarchical environment. It is interesting to note that her orientation is not dissimilar from what Gaskell claimed was Charlotte Brontë's. In her biography, Gaskell emphasizes how Charlotte, like her sisters, stretched her imagination beyond the walls of the Haworth Parsonage, out over the moors that 'swelled' about her to an horizon that melted 'away into aërial tints'.[68] Preferring this larger prospect that breaks through the barriers of convention, Charlotte found fault with Jane Austen's fiction for its lack of open country: 'no fresh air, no blue hill, no bonny beck'. She proclaimed, 'I should hardly like to live with her ladies and gentlemen, in their elegant but confined houses.'[69]

THE RAILROADS AND THE CARTOGRAPHY OF CHANGE

No matter, though, how assiduously or consciously Gaskell's characters survey and chart their lives – through convention, memory, revision, or expansion – few are immune to the effect the railroads have upon the shifting landscape and upon the way people interact with their surroundings. Reflecting the mid-nineteenth-century preoccupation with railroads,[70] Gaskell engineered her fiction so that their presence orients her narratives and emerges to serve as both a significant emblem of change and yet another source of nostalgia. In many of her works, trains advance across the text to impinge upon people's lives and superimpose another order of classification – another kind of map. In their journeys, these trains reshape the contours of the land, redefine time, memory, and distance, realign relationships, and, as in the example of Captain Brown's death in *Cranford*, abruptly alter the routines of life.

In nineteenth-century periodicals it is not uncommon to find an author using a railway journey as a means of entering a discourse. Consequently, an article about Cassiobury, an estate outside of Birmingham, begins with the essayist's settling into a train carriage and 'flying along, some twenty-five miles an hour' to his destination [Watford Station].[71] A decade later in *Household Words* an essay on market gardens opens with the author looking out from his train window onto a plot of cabbages, onions, celery, asparagus, and rhubarb.[72] And in the next volume Charles Dickens commences his account of the Preston Strike at the moment he passes through the doors of the Preston railroad station and enters the manufacturing town, made still and smokeless by the strike.[73]

Trains are also a point of entry for Gaskell. For example, she introduces *Cranford* by informing her readers that the town is 'distant only twenty miles on a railroad'; she commences her biography of Charlotte Brontë by identifying the Leeds and Skipton railway line that takes one to Keighley, the town close to Haworth, and, of course, she tells the story of *Cousin Phillis* through Paul, who works for a railway engineer and whose father has 'devised several valuable improvements in railway machinery'.[74] At the beginning of *My Lady Ludlow*, the elderly narrator uses the image of the 'whizzing' train with its screaming whistle to comment upon the unfortunate differences between the present and the past – a disparity that motivates her nostalgia and her longing for people like Lady Ludlow. And in the opening of *Sylvia's Lovers*, Gaskell uses the fact of there being no railroads in Monkshaven to place her characters in time – a device she also exploits when she situates Molly and Cynthia in an era 'before railroads were, and before their con-sequences, the excursion- trains' took people up to London.[75]

In contemporary essays on the railroads, it was also not unusual for the author to recognize that the train can take passengers through areas alien to their experience. One example is in yet another number of *Household Words*. In 'What a London Curate Can Do if He Tries', the writer boards a train at the London station and passes through the poorer districts. From the compartment window he can peer into the apartments of all the upper-floor inhabitants between Fenchurch Street and the station in St. George's-in-the-East, for the railway line runs 'through the buildings, on a level with many of their roofs' and permits 'the passenger to look...into the dingy tenements of the Eastern region'.[76] When Gaskell offers her readers a glimpse of the damp, feverish cellars and the crowded dwellings in the Manchester of *Mary Barton* and *North and South*, like the London train, her fiction exposes what is often out of sight.

The railroad, though, does considerably more than transport the author and her readers into the text and serve as a metaphor for the privileged position from which one can view the unseen or the unbidden. It also propels Gaskell's characters into other zones of time and space, and, thereby, contributes to their sensitivity to change, exacerbating their nostalgia.[77] For example, the railway wrenches the Hales away from the gentle curves of Helstone and abruptly deposits them into the 'long, straight, hopeless streets' of Milton. In its journey, the train hastens, if not obliterates, their transition from the South to the North. As if aware of this con-sequence, Margaret Hale attempts to ease this sudden alteration by first spending a few days in a northern costal town that, although full of purposelike activity, offers some semblance of a transition from the quiet rural life to the bustle and noise of the industrial city. She, not the railroad, interrupts the cannonball motion of their journey to create an illusion of an intermediate zone. Such awful abruptness also characterizes Margaret and her brother Frederick's departure at the Outwood Train Station. At one moment Frederick is on the platform; at the next there is the 'whizz' of the approaching train, and he is gone – for good. The railway quickens the sequences of their lives, for it is responsible not only for their sudden leave taking but also for their swift and decisive reaction to the appearance of Leonards, the disreputable figure who recognizes the exiled Frederick. What had started out in the fields by the station to be a leisurely farewell between the sister and brother swerves into a different mode when the train appears. With minimal preparation one tenor of reference replaces the other when the train with its exact hour and minute intrudes upon the longer, approximate moments of their few days together. This rapid exchange of time also characterizes Mr Holdsworth's abrupt parting from Hope Farm and Hornby. With little warning he catches the night train to leave for Canada where another railroad line waits to be laid. Submitting to the demands of railroad time, he darts from place to place without a proper farewell. He soon forgets the quieter pace of the farmer's land. This suddenness of movement sharpens Phillis's keen yearning for him.

Mary Barton is another figure whose life succumbs to the way the railroad affects the hours and minutes of the day. When for the first time in her life she boards a train for Liverpool, the railroad hurls her out of her slower, familiar surroundings, sends her through tunnels, and exposes her to the anxious hurry and screams of the arriving trains. The train sweeps her past the objects and places of her life and with such velocity that she feels bewildered and exiled. She becomes homesick and experiences 'some of the same sentiment which gives pathos to the thoughts of the emigrant'.[78] It is this sort of reaction that Dr Gibson humorously anticipates when he affectionately chastises his daughter for saying that she never wants to leave Hollingford: 'Nonsense!... Why, you've all your travelling to do yet; and if these new-fangled railways spread, as they say they will, we shall all be spinning about the world; "sitting on tea-kettles," as Phoebe Browning calls it'[79] – a wonderfully comic allusion to cartoons, such as an 1830 hand-colored etching by Seymour Shortshanks (entitled *Locomotion: Walking by Steam, Riding by Steam, Flying by Steam*), depicting ladies precariously perched upon steam-propelled kettles and teapots.

With these rapid alterations of time comes the shrinking of distance. Pressed by speed, space diminishes so that people and places are in a closer proximity to one another. In *North and South* railway lines reduce the landscape between Oxford and Milton so that Mr Hale and Mr Bell can enjoy an easy accessibility. The wide gap that separates Philip Hepburn from Sylvia Robson, when he travels via land and steamship to London, is not part of Mr Hale's and Mr Bell's experience. Nor is the larger city some foreign territory outside the borders of their lives. Their sense of place is not what it is for those who live in Molly Gibson's village before the railways and for whom London is some alien, if not exotic, country.

Speed also affects the individual's perception of the landscape. A view from a railroad compartment is a fleeting, disappearing one so that, for example, from her compartment window Mary Barton 'loses sight' of her home – her surroundings fly by and disappear.[80] The train's swiftness elides and eradicates images, and, thereby, changes her sense of where she is. It is perhaps worth while to note that in her published letters, Gaskell devotes few words to what she sees out of the train window. Her correspondence is full of railway schedules, times of arrivals and departures, and routes, but not of what she spies on the way. The only occasion is when a train she was on comes to a halt, but significantly all she sees then is the railroad embankment that blocks any prospect. It is as if these railroad journeys obliterate not only images but also what landscape comes in between the departures and the arrivals.[81] They wipe out the landmarks that attach the individual to the collective memory. Mary Barton and the Hales go from one station to another, but virtually nothing exists on the way. The one prospect from the Hales's compartment window appears when the train slows down, and they approach Milton for the first time, but it is a kinetic view that orders and abstracts images into lines of streets and periodic patterns of obstruction: 'Quick they were whirled over long, straight, hopeless streets of regularly-built houses, all small and of brick. Here and there a great oblong many-windowed factory stood up, like a hen among her chickens, puffing out black "unparliamentary" smoke, and sufficiently accounting for the cloud which Margaret had taken to foretell rain.'[82]

This sort of perspective changes radically when Gaskell's characters walk among the streets, lanes, hills, and moors of England and Wales. To walk is to slow down and see, hear, smell, and feel their surroundings, and it is to gaze at what lies immediately before them as well as what is in the distance.[83] Gaskell might have agreed with the author of 'Out for a Walk' who in a 10 September 1853 issue of *Household Words* wrote that having missed the train at Wolverhampton he had to trudge 'ten, thirteen, or fifteen miles ... to Birmingham' and found it to be 'the most wonderful night walk in the country'.[84] He suggests that one does not really know a place – has not really traveled it – unless one has walked it. The narrator of 'The Well of Pen-Morfa' has done just this; she walks, lingers and dwells among the details of the prospect, both far and near, and tells the reader what she sees:

> There are rocks high above Pen-Morfa; they are the same that hang over Trê-Madoc, but near Pen-Morfa they sweep away, and are lost in the plain. Everywhere they are beautiful. The great, sharp ledges, which would otherwise look hard and cold, are adorned with the brightest-coloured moss, and the golden lichen. Close to, you see the scarlet leaves of the crane's bill, and the tufts of purple heather, which fill up every cleft and cranny; but, in the distance, you see only the general effect of infinite richness of colour, broken, here and there, by great masses of ivy. At the foot of these rocks come a rich, verdant meadow or two; and then you are at Pen-Morfa.[85]

Gaskell takes her reader into this story on foot, in the same manner as she leads her reader through *Ruth, Sylvia's Lovers, The Moorland Cottage*, and *Wives and Daughters*. In these works, set before the coming of the railways, movement is slower and there are interludes in which the walker stops to gaze upon the prospect and pauses to follow the course of a brook, to smell the scent of the gorse and the primrose, to climb the hill, to hear the hidden warblers, and to feel the wild thyme or the crackling of the hoarfrost under foot.

It is a recognition of this alternative that opens *The Biography of Charlotte Brontë*. Once Gaskell descends from her railway compartment after her train arrives in Keighley, she writes as if regaining her sight and her hearing. Passing through the town she describes the architectural details of the town's houses, takes a glimpse into their interiors, and overhears the 'hard' discordant tones of people's speech. On her way to Haworth in a horse-drawn vehicle, she travels four slow and deliberate miles along a country road. From her seat she describes the vegetation, the shrubs, the distant hills, and listens to the horse breathe more easily as it passes into the quiet little by-streets that lead to Haworth Parsonage. When she steps down, she enters a landscape of walkers. For Gaskell the world of the Brontës is one which the inhabitants know by foot. As pedestrians they observe wild creatures and understand the natural signs. Day after day, in all weathers, they tread the fluctuating, sweeping moors and amethyst-tinted hills. They absorb what is around them; the speed, noise, and enclosures of the train do not separate them from their senses or the landscape.[86] Charlotte Brontë's intermittent trips to London and her concerns about the family's share in rail-road stock seem strange within this perspective. And so do the moments when Anne and Charlotte rush to Keighley to catch the train to Leeds from where they are 'whirled up by the night train to London'.[87] The rapid switch from one mode to the other reflects Gaskell's sense of the shifts within the topography of people's lives. More generally, it mirrors her sensitivity to change that disorients the location of self and the understanding of time and place.

Although sensitive to the ways in which railroad travel alters a person's perception, Gaskell herself rarely complained about them – trains did expedite her need to 'change places' and find spaces in which to write (in her biography of Gaskell, Uglow entitles one chapter 'Changing Places'). She did, however, allow her characters to be critical and to echo the public's concerns about the railways. Consequently, her protagonists worry about railroad schedules (Margaret Hale fears missing her train back to Helstone) and being delayed (Gaskell draws attention to an anxious episode when Char-lotte Brontë has to make her way alone to her lodgings in London, for 'the train from Leeds to London, which should have reached Euston-square early in the afternoon was so much delayed'[88]). Her characters complain about the noise (the new tenant of the farm in *A Dark Night's Work* is relieved that he will not be perpetually troubled by the sound of trains coming directly by the house), and her narrators fret about the speed. Trains turn into projectiles that 'whirl', 'whizz', 'spin', and 'hurry' passengers from place to place. Moreover, by concentrating upon the trauma of railroad travel for Mary Barton, Margaret Hale, her mother, Cousin Phillis, and Ellinor Wilkins, Gaskell, herself, admits that railroad travel is a 'shock' to the individual's system. When Miss Munro (*A Dark Night's Work*) learns that the cutting of the new line of railroad from Hamley to the nearest railway station is responsible for the discovery of Mr Dun-ster's body, she also speaks of it as a 'shock'.[89]

In her fiction Gaskell likewise acknowledges the popular anxiety about railway collisions – a worry which she does not seem to share, for when Miss Munro criticizes the timorous Ellinor Wilkins for being fearful of traveling on the train, she takes the opportunity to correct the public's fears and register her irritation:

there was no greater danger in travelling by railroad than by coach, a little care about certain things was required, that was all, and the average number of deaths by accidents on railroads were not greater than the average number when people travelled by coach, if you took into consideration the far greater number of travellers.[90]

Gaskell's work includes none of the obligatory train collisions found in mid-nineteenth-century fiction or in contemporary cartoons like the one in an October 1853 issue of *Punch* showing a man arriving late for his train and cursing, 'Confound it! just too late! Another minute and I should have caught it', at the very moment the departing train, out of the man's sight, is colliding with another coming in the opposite direction. She does, however, devise her own version of this convention by transforming it into a metaphor of encounter, an adaptation that allows her, once more, to insist upon linking the railroad to the idea of change. For this reason her fiction often turns on the 'collisions' occasioned by the existence of the railroad.[91]

Under the blaze of the station's lights in *North and South* not only Leonards but also Mr Thornton (the mill owner who loves Margaret Hale) sees Margaret and her brother, Frederick, speaking affectionately to one another – a sighting, one recalls, that leads to a serious misunderstanding which significantly alters the relationship between Margaret and her admirer. In the context of the railroad, people collide. And it is, of course, a later accidental encounter between Mr Bell and Mr Thornton in a railway carriage that occasions the beginning of a resolution to this misunderstanding, for during their conversation Mr Bell informs his railroad companion that Margaret has a brother. Other moments in the novels and stories concern a different kind of collision. These occur when the train is instrumental in causing the private life to collide with the public sphere. What a character would like to remain unsaid or out of view gets exposed and thrust upon the ears and eyes of the public. The most obvious example is in *A Dark Night's Work* when the railway engineers cut a new line and dig up the body of the murdered Mr Dunster, an act that reveals to the public the secret Ellinor Wilkins, her father, and the servant Dixon have tried hard to bury. To save the wrongly accused Dixon (it was Ellinor's father who was responsible), Ellinor must rush by train back to her town and speak the truth out loud to the man she had lost because of her secret. This difficult encounter with her past and this collision between what she has held tightly within herself and what she must admit also occur in one of the most poignant episodes in *Mary Barton*, in which Mary hastens by train to defend Jem Wilson, wrongly accused of murdering the young Mr Carson. In the court of law, speaking in the hearing of all present, she says what she has up to this moment kept to herself – that she loves Jem Wilson: 'I love him now better than ever, though he has never known a word of it till this minute.'[92] Before an audience of strangers Mary Barton must make a public expression of a private feeling, something that Mr Bell tries to avoid when, after learning of Mr Hale's death, he throws himself back in his seat on the London train and tries to conceal his tears from his fellow passengers (*North and South*). In these episodes public and private thoughts meet and exchange places. The private becomes public. Like Alice traveling in a compartment with her back to the train's direction,[93] these protagonists are forced to reverse their usual way of looking at the order of things and to expose themselves to the opinions of strangers. The people in the court-room look at Mary Barton as if they are peering through the binoculars held by the train conductor (in the Tenniel illustration) who leans into Alice's carriage and inspects her. In a sense these characters are forced to violate Gaskell's own principle of storytelling which is to gauge the public sphere within the private. They have to turn upside down her practice of domesticating political issues – her preference to discuss the larger issues within the enclosures of home rather than on the public platform. As Rosemarie Bodenheimer notes in 'Private Grief and Public Acts in *Mary Barton*', the proper forum for grief and mourning in Gaskell's fiction is 'the familial and neighborly world', not places like the Liverpool Assizes.[94]

CONCLUSION

The railway is an appropriately prominent image within the boundaries of Gaskell's texts, for its presence helps emphasize her own preoccupation with mutability. The shocks, the collisions, and dislocations accompanying the railroad's forceful progress replicate and clarify similar unsettling realities within the landscape of her fiction and within her characters' variable and changing lives. Moving across shifting zones of time and space, and through areas crossed with incongruity and instability, the railway contributes to this unsettled geography. Like the beard of Alice's train companion that seems to melt away, images disappear. The railroad intrudes upon what few still points there are and damages the sites of memory. Like the person who writes about her childhood in a 25 May 1850 issue of *The Ladies Companion at Home and Abroad* and complains that the home of her early days is changed because the railroad with its 'whistle' and its 'roar' now passes by, Gaskell's characters too, at moments, 'long for the romance of those early days'.[95]

In a sense it is ironic that the train should come to play such a significant part in these narratives of change, for the railroad was eventually the means by which time was standardized (in the 1840s to coordinate the various train lines it became necessary to settle upon one agreed time). The train was supposed to mediate among the various spheres of measurement and resolve the differences between the Hamleys' watches and also Mr Benson's and Mr Bradshaw's (in *Ruth*, Mr Bradshaw complains that Mr Benson's watch is set to a different time). Moreover, the train was designed to set straight, unswerving lines across the landscape; it was supposed to regularize the uneven contours of the earth. As Wolfgang Schivelbusch explains, to lay tracks engineers found it necessary to make the ground even so that the lines would lie flat and secure.[96] In short, the train was built with the hope of ridding time and space of incongruity and variation. It was constructed as if it were supposed to be an inscribed map that orders and classifies the land. However, in Gaskell's fiction such attempts at conventional mapping fail, for the forces of change are stronger. The railroads are a victim of this reality, for the ground is too unsteady. In *Cousin Phillis* this irregularity puzzles Mr Holdsworth and his engineers. They have difficulty carrying their line over this 'shaking, uncertain ground'. Because of the Heathbridge moss, 'one end of the line' goes up 'as soon as the other' is 'weighted down' – there is no 'steady bottom'.[97] Gaskell's narratives belong to this 'shaking, uncertain ground' because their various maps, reflecting the process of memory, mark the sites and intersections of change and survey the places where the past and the present collide. Not even the steady lines of Gaskell's efficient writing hand can still the shifting landscape of her text – a place of intermingling spheres of time, incongruity, fractured and scattered memory, and revision. Not even nostalgia with its desire to find a refuge from these changes can hold the landscape still for long.

Notes

1. In her biography of Elizabeth Gaskell, Jenny Uglow speaks of Gaskell as someone 'preoccupied with the pressure of change'. See J. Uglow, *Elizabeth Gaskell: A Habit of Stories* (London: Faber and Faber, 1993) p. 4. She is among many critics (for instance, W. A. Craik, Angus Easson, Shelagh Hunter, John Lucas, Pam Morris, Mary Poovey, and Andrew Sanders) who remark upon this sensitivity. The critics, however, tend to emphasize and explore the nature of social, technological, and scientific changes recorded in Gaskell's fiction. Although I acknowledge these realities, I concentrate on the ways in which acts of remembrance and modes of perception are related to these changes.

2. E. Gaskell, *The Moorland Cottage and Other Stories*, introd. S. Lewis (Oxford: Oxford University Press, 1995) p. 220.

3. E. Gaskell, *Sylvia's Lovers*, introd. A. Sanders (Oxford: Oxford University Press, 1982) p. 135.

4. E. Gaskell, *Wives and Daughters*, introd. P. Morris (London: Penguin Books, 1996) p. 252.

5. E. Gaskell, *Cranford*, introd. E. P. Watson (Oxford: Oxford University Press, 1980) p. 13.

6. When Paul Connerton comments on the collective memory, he writes, 'the past and recollected knowledge of the past ... are conveyed and sustained by (more or less ritual) performances'. Later he refers to 'those acts of transfer that make remembering in common possible'. See P. Connerton, *How Societies Remember* (Cambridge: Cambridge University Press, 1989) pp. 4, 39.

7. David Lowenthal points out that 'The past validates present attitudes and action by affirming their resemblance to former ones. Previous usage seals with approval what is now done.' See D. Lowenthal, *The Past is a Foreign Country* (Cambridge: Cambridge University Press, 1985) p. 40.

8. John Lucas introduces his discussion of the nineteenth-century provincial novel by remarking that he is 'concerned with the nature of social change ... and ... its effects on individual lives, on patterns of living, on communities. Above all I am concerned with the processes of separation: what it means for a person to find himself ... struggling to retain an undivided sense of selfhood. And failing. For a sense of self isn't finally separable from a sense of community or family, and yet change enforces separation from both.' See J. Lucas, *Literature of Change: Studies in the Nineteenth-Century Provincial Novel* (Sussex: The Harvester Press, 1977) p. ix.

9. Connerton maintains that 'no collective memory can exist without a reference to a socially specific spatial framework.... We conserve our recollections by referring them to the milieu that surrounds us.' See Connerton, *How Societies Remember*, p. 37.

10. Gaskell, *Sylvia's Lovers*, p. 98. E. Holly Pike comments upon Gaskell's belief in progress and states that in her fiction, 'the religiously reformed and better educated modern world offers greater stability than a hierarchy uninformed by those values'. See E. H. Pike, *Family*

and Society in the Works of Elizabeth Gaskell (New York: Peter Lang, 1995) pp. 128–9.

11. J. A. V. Chapple and A. Pollard, eds, *The Letters of Mrs. Gaskell* (Cambridge, MA: Harvard University Press, 1967) p. 21.

12. Ibid., p. 14. See also E. L. Duthie, *The Themes of Elizabeth Gaskell* (Totowa, NJ: Rowman and Littlefield, 1980) pp. 14–24.

13. John Lucas writes: 'One recognizes her [Gaskell's] entry by a brisk nononsense air that comes over her prose, an insistence that the past is after all merely quaint and that we ought to give thanks for living in the present.' See Lucas, *Literature of Change: Studies in the Nineteenth-Century Provincial Novel*, p. 18.

14. E. Gaskell, *Cousin Phillis and Other Tales*, introd. A. Easson (Oxford: Oxford University Press, 1981) p. 354.

15. See R. Williams, *The Country and the City* (London: Chatto & Windus, 1973).

16. For an excellent discussion of the web of illusions that surround Alice Wilson's memories of her childhood experience, see C. Lansbury, *Elizabeth Gaskell: The Novel of Social Crisis* (New York: Barnes & Noble, 1975) p. 25.

17. Gaskell, *Sylvia's Lovers*, p. 61.

18. For a series of essays on the subject of nostalgia and gender, see J. Pickering and S. Kehde, eds, *Narratives of Nostalgia, Gender, and Nationalism* (New York: New York University Press, 1997).

19. Cottages and farmhouses remain a focal point for people's nostalgia in twentieth-century culture. It is, therefore, not unusual in 1997 to find a mail-order company like *Past Times* selling *Paradise Lost: Paintings of English Country Life and Landscape: 1850–1914*, a book that chronicles through paintings the romantic Arcadian idyll of Victorian country life. This nostalgia continues a sentiment already felt at the beginning of this century. See S. Dick, *The Cottage Homes of England* (New York: British Heritage, 1984) pp. 2, 22. Dick looks at Helen Allingham's pretty watercolors of picturesque cottages and remarks that in these shifting and transitory times it is lovely to be reminded of the dignified English cottages which reflect the true spirit of England and the 'toil simple and healthy under the open sky'.

20. For an article on this co-existence, see P. L. Brown, 'The Pastoral and Anti-Pastoral in Elizabeth Gaskell's *Cousin Phillis*', *The Victorian Newsletter* (fall 1992) 22–8.

21. E. Gaskell, *North and South*, introd. M. Dodsworth (Harmondsworth, Middlesex: Penguin Books, 1970) pp. 60, 182.

22. 'Pinchback's Cottage', *All the Year Round*, VII (22 March 1862) 31.

23. For idyllic descriptions of cottages and farmhouses, see E. Gaskell, *Mary Barton*, introd. S. Gill (Harmondsworth, Middlesex: Penguin Books, 1970) p. 40 and Gaskell, *Cousin Phillis and Other Tales*, pp. 269, 298.

24. For a discussion of how Elizabeth Gaskell uses the reports of the various committees investigating the conditions in the mill towns, see Stephen Gill's introduction to *Mary Barton*.

25. R. Heath, *The Victorian Peasant*, ed. K. Dockray (Gloucester: Alan Sutton, 1989) p. 42.

26. Chapple and Pollard, *The Letters of Mrs. Gaskell*, pp. 80–1.
27. Gaskell, *North and South*, p. 56.
28. Gaskell, *Mary Barton*, p. 200.
29. Gaskell, *Wives and Daughters*, p. 459; Gaskell, *The Moorland Cottage and Other Stories*, p. 33.
30. Helen Allingham studied at the Birmingham School of Design and eventually at the Royal Academy schools where she came under the influence of Frederick Walker. She also attended the Slade School where she worked alongside Kate Greenaway. The two became friends. In 1890 Allingham became the first woman to be elected to full membership into the Royal Watercolour Society. Through her marriage to the Irish poet William Allingham, she became a friend of the Tennysons – Tennyson used to enjoy pointing out picturesque cottages and scenes to her. Although Allingham does not seem to have known Elizabeth Gaskell, she moved in the same Unitarian circles. A plaque commemorating the death of Allingham is in the Rosslyn Hill Chapel in Hampstead.
31. I. Taylor, *Helen Allingham's England: An Idyllic View of Rural Life* (Exeter, Devon: Webb & Bower, 1990) p. 72.
32. E. T. Cook and A. Wedderburn, eds, *The Works of John Ruskin*, XIV (London: George Allen, 1904) p. 409.
33. Ina Taylor mentions that Allingham kept 'freshly laundered props' in 'the painting cupboard as women no longer wore them [bonnets and pinafores] in real life'. See I. Taylor, *Helen Allingham's England: An Idyllic View of Rural Life*, p. 68.
34. E. S. Casey, *Remembering: A Phenomenological Study* (Bloomington, Indiana: Indiana University Press, 1987) p. 198.
35. Gaskell, *Sylvia's Lovers*, p. 502.
36. A. Paterson, *The Homes of Tennyson* (New York: Haskell House, 1973) p. 50.
37. I. Taylor, *Helen Allingham's England: An Idyllic View of Rural Life*, p. 97.
38. Uglow, *Elizabeth Gaskell: A Habit of Stories*, p. 291.
39. The phrase is from E. K. Helsinger, *Rural Scenes and National Representations: Britain, 1815–1850* (Princeton: Princeton University Press, 1997) p. 7.
40. The myth of an unchanging rural landscape is a tenacious one. Recent books on the history of the British landscape are still having to refute it. See, for instance, A. Everitt, *Landscape and Community in England* (London: The Humbledon Press, 1985), F. M. L. Thompson, 'Towns, Industry, and the Victorian Landscape', *The English Landscape: Past, Present, and Future*, ed. S. R. J. Woodell (Oxford: Oxford University Press, 1985), and Christopher Taylor, *Village and Farmstead: A History of Rural Settlement in England* (London: George Taylor, 1983).
41. Gaskell, *Cranford*, p. 161.
42. Gaskell, *North and South*, pp. 277, 467.
43. Gaskell, *Cousin Phillis and Other Tales*, p. 329.
44. In his introduction to *Cousin Phillis and Other Tales*, Angus Easson writes, 'And yet even within Phillis's world, life is not static.' See Gaskell, *Cousin Phillis and Other Tales*, p. xiii.

45. Gaskell, *Mary Barton*, p. 81.
46. E. Gaskell, *Ruth*, introd. A. Shelston (Oxford: Oxford University Press, 1985) p. 143.
47. Gaskell, *Sylvia's Lovers*, pp. 341–2.
48. Gaskell, *Ruth*, p. 42.
49. Gaskell, *Sylvia's Lovers*, p. 108.
50. B. Bender, ed. *Landscape: Politics and Perspectives* (Oxford: Berg, 1993) p. 11.
51. Ibid., p. 100.
52. Gaskell, *Sylvia's Lovers*, p. 231.
53. Gaskell, *Ruth*, p. 5.
54. Ibid., p. 3.
55. Ibid., p. 7.
56. Ibid., p. 45.
57. Gaskell, *The Moorland Cottage and Other Stories*, p. 168.
58. Ibid., p. 203.
59. Gaskell, *Mary Barton*, p. 71.
60. Gaskell, *Cousin Phillis and Other Tales*, p. 317.
61. Gaskell, *Mary Barton*, p. 71.
62. Kathleen M. Kirby suggests, 'A space persists only as long as the boundary creating it is deliberately maintained, and the spaces these boundaries encircle are subject to continual remodeling.' See K. M. Kirby, *Indifferent Boundaries: Spatial Concepts of Human Subjectivity* (New York: The Guilford Press, 1996) p. 18.
63. Gaskell, *Wives and Daughters*, p. 5.
64. E. Gaskell, *A Dark Night's Work and Other Stories*, introd. S. Lewis (Oxford: Oxford University Press, 1992) p. 183.
65. Gaskell, *Ruth*, p. 140.
66. Ibid., p. 140.
67. Gaskell, *The Moorland Cottage and Other Stories*, p. 56.
68. E. Gaskell, *The Life of Charlotte Brontë*, introd. A. Easson (Oxford: Oxford University Press, 1996) p. 257.
69. Ibid., p. 274.
70. This preoccupation is, perhaps, best reflected in the number of articles and cartoons on railroads in mid-nineteenth-century periodicals. For instance, in *Household Words*, between May, 1850 and July, 1856, there were numerous articles: 'The Railway Station' (4 May 1850), 'Railway Comfort' (3 August 1850), 'The Individuality of Locomotives' (21 September 1850), 'Railway Waifs and Strays' (28 December 1850), 'Railway Strikes' (11 January 1851), 'Excursion Trains' (5 July 1851), 'The Tax on Excursion Trains' (19 July 1851), 'Need Railway Travellers be Smashed' (29 November 1851), 'A Novelty in Railway Locomotion' (6 March 1852), 'Self-Acting Railway Signals' (12 March 1853), 'Iron Incidents' (31 December 1853), 'An Excursion Train, Before Steam' (30 September 1854), 'Ruined by Railways' (3 March 1855), 'Poetry on the Railway' (2 June 1855), 'By Rail to Parnassus' (16 June 1855), 'What Shall a Railway-Clerk Have for Dinner' (22 September 1855), 'An Excursion Train' (29 October 1855), 'The Railway Companion' (8 December 1855), 'Sick Railway Clerks' (19 April 1856), 'Railway

Dreaming' (10 May 1856), 'The Fairy Puff-Puff' (28 June 1856). *Household Words* was, of course the magazine in which much of Gaskell's fiction appeared.

71.   'Railway Rambles', *The Penny Magazine of the Society for the Diffusion of Useful Knowledge*, XXVII (August, 1842) 333–4.
72.   'Market Gardens', *Household Words*, VII (2 July 1853) 409.
73.   'Locked Out', *Household Words*, VIII (10 December 1853) 345.
74.   Gaskell, *Cousin Phillis and Other Tales*, p. 259.
75.   Gaskell, *Wives and Daughters*, p. 281.
76.   'What a London Curate Can Do if He Tries', *Household Words*, II (16 November 1850) 172.
77.   In the following discussion on how trains alter people's perception of time and space, I am indebted to Wolfgang Schivelbusch, *The Railway Journey: The Industrialization of Time and Space in the 19th Century* (Berkeley: University of California Press, 1986) and to James Buzard, *The Beaten Track: European Tourism, Literature and the Ways to 'Culture': 1800–1918* (Oxford: Oxford University Press, 1993).
78.   Gaskell, *Mary Barton*, pp. 343–4.
79.   Gaskell, *Wives and Daughters*, p. 562.
80.   Gaskell, *Mary Barton*, p. 343.
81.   Schivelbusch observes: 'on the one hand, the railroad opened up new spaces that were not easily accessible before; on the other, it did so by destroying space, namely the space between points.' See Schivelbusch, *The Railway Journey: The Industrialization of Time and Space in the 19th Century*, p. 37.
82.   Gaskell, *North and South*, p. 96.
83.   Buzard comments on the differences in pace and perception when people walk rather than take a train. He notes that it alters their sense of place, for everything they pass when they walk is more fully a place or alive to them. He quotes a passage from *Modern Painters* in which Ruskin proclaims:

> every yard of the changeful ground becomes precious and piquant; and the continual increase of hope, and of surrounding beauty, affords one of the most exquisite enjoyments possible to the healthy mind; besides that real knowledge is acquired by whatever it is the object of travelling to learn, and a certain sublimity given to all places, so attained, by the true sense of the spaces of earth that separate them. A man who really loves travelling would as soon consent to pack a day of such happiness into an hour of railroad, as one who loved eating would agree... to concentrate his dinner into a pill.

See Buzard, *The Beaten Track: European Tourism, Literature and the Ways to 'Culture': 1800–1918*, pp. 35–6.

84.   'Out for a Walk', *Household Words*, VII (10 September 1853) 25.
85.   Gaskell, *The Moorland Cottage and Other Stories*, p. 125.
86.   Once visiting a friend in the Lake country, Charlotte Brontë was taken in a carriage to see the region, but she found the trip disappointing,

for it alienated her from the scenery. In a 27 September 1850 letter to a friend, she complained: 'Decidedly I find it does not agree with me to prosecute the search of the picturesque in a carriage. A wagon, a spring-cart, even a post-chaise might do; but the carriage upsets everything. I longed to slip out unseen, and to run away by myself in amongst the hills and dales.' See Gaskell, *The Life of Charlotte Brontë*, p. 355.

87. Ibid., p. 282.
88. Ibid., p. 197.
89. Schivelbusch devotes a chapter in *The Railway Journey: The Industrialization of Time and Space in the 19th Century* to the experience of 'shock' in railroad travel.
90. Gaskell, *A Dark Night's Work and Other Stories*, pp. 118–19.
91. It is interesting to note that in her biography of Gaskell, Uglow speaks of the drama of *Sylvia's Lovers* as being 'the collision of opposites'. See Uglow, *Elizabeth Gaskell: A Habit of Stories*, p. 508.
92. Gaskell, *Mary Barton*, p. 390.
93. L. Carroll, *Alice Through the Looking-Glass* (London: Academy Editions, 1977), p. 30.
94. R. Bodenheimer, 'Private Griefs and Public Acts in *Mary Barton*', *Dickens Studies Annual*, IX (1981) 213–14.
95. 'Fancies of a Country Child', *The Ladies Companion at Home and Abroad* (25 May 1850) 347–8.
96. Schivelbusch, *The Railway Journey: The Industrialization of Time and Space in the 19th Century*, pp. 21–3.
97. Gaskell, *Cousin Phillis and Other Tales*, pp. 263, 275.

1. Richard Redgrave: *The Emigrants' Last Sight of Home.*

2. Frank Newbould: *Your Britain – Fight for it Now, the South Downs.*

3. Ford Madox Brown: *The Last of England*, 1855.

4. Ford Madox Brown: Cartoon for *The Last of England*, 1852.

5. Antonio del Pollaiuolo: *Apollo and Daphne*.

6. Helen Allingham: *Old Cottage at Pinner*.

7. Robert Louis Stevenson: *Game of Dibbs.*

8. Robert Louis Stevenson: untitled, from an 1863 letter to his parents.

9. Robert Louis Stevenson: *Sudden and Awful Catastrophe.*

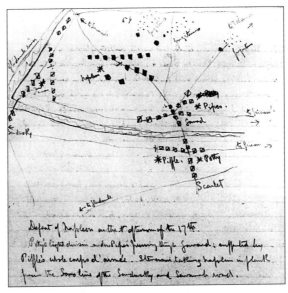

10. Robert Louis Stevenson: *Defeat of Napoleon on the afternoon of the 17th.*

11. William Raymond Smith after J. M. W. Turner: *Long-ships Lighthouse, Land's End*, etching.

12. William Raymond Smith after J. M. W. Turner: *Long-ships Lighthouse, Land's End*, engraver's proof (a).

13. J. M. W. Turner: *Shield's Lighthouse*, engraver's proof (b).

14. John Ruskin: *Turner's Earliest 'Nottingham'*.

15. John Ruskin: *Turner's Latest 'Nottingham'.*

16. John Horsburgh after J. M. W. Turner: *Bell Rock Lighthouse.*

Part II
Childhood Spaces

What a person wishes to recover is not so much the actual *place* where
he passed his childhood but his youth itself.

Kant, *Anthropology*, 1798

The places we have known do not belong only to the world of
space .... None of them was ever more than a thin slice, held between
the contiguous impressions that compose our life at that time; the
memory of a particular image is but regret for a particular moment;
and house, roads, avenues are as fugitive, alas, as the years.

Marcel Proust as quoted in Gregory McNamie's
review of Simon Schama's *Landscape and Memory*
(*The Nation* 22 May 1995)

5

The Landscape of *A Child's Garden of Verses*

> Most of us, looking back on young years, may remember seasons of a light, aërial translucency and elasticity and perfect freedom; the body had not yet become the prison-house of the soul, but was its vehicle and implement, like a creature of thought, and altogether pliant to its bidding.
>
> Thomas Carlyle, 'Characteristics' (1831)

Whenever Robert Louis Stevenson wished to be released from the dualities inherent in the experience of the present, he often turned his attention to the absorbing spaces of his childhood and attempted to re-enter their flexible and synthetic landscape. Nostalgic for this prospect, he not only re-engaged the play, the vicarious violence, and the places of his early years but also began composing *A Child's Garden of Verses* (1885).[1] These poems offered him a sanctuary that was more durable and satisfying than that afforded by his nationalism, for they were his means of writing toward home and reclaiming, momentarily, what was no longer fully available to him. These verses helped him walk back into the spaces of his early years and recover what Carlyle termed the 'elasticity' of childhood.

STEVENSON'S LONGING FOR CHILDHOOD

Like one who closely watches passing trains traveling in opposite directions, Stevenson constantly altered his focus and turned his head from one compartment of his life to another. As an adult he kept shifting between childhood and maturity and could not, therefore, regard himself as a 'constant'.[2] He was never simply his chronological age. Referring to himself in a letter to his cousin Robert Alan Stevenson, he explained, 'You are twenty, and forty, and five, and the next moment you are freezing at an imaginary eighty; you are never the plain forty- four that you should be by

107

dates.'[3] Because of this perspective, Stevenson had difficulty in portraying an adult without making some reference to a childish feature or characteristic in the person. Sensitive to the child that lives within the adult, he referred to himself as a grown man who feels 'weary and timid in this big, jostling city' and wants to run to his nurse,[4] and, at another time, described his aging and infirm grand-father as a person who sits 'with perfect simplicity, like a child's, munching a "barley-sugar kiss"'.[5] The child adhered to the adult as the shadow sticks to the young boy in the poems 'My Shadow' and 'Shadow March' (*A Child's Garden of Verses*). Whether it was before or after him, or for the moment invisible, this second self was always in some way attached to the person. Consequently, in Stevenson's fiction protagonists move effortlessly back and forth between child-hood and adulthood. At one moment the young narrator of *Treasure Island* speaks of himself as 'only a boy', but at another adopts the persona of an adult and imperiously commands, 'I've come aboard to take possession of this ship, Mr. Hands; and you'll please regard me as your captain until further notice.'[6] Similarly, David Balfour and Alan Breck alternate between 'the rude, silly speech of a boy of ten'[7] and the measured phrases of maturity. Their vacillating responses to each other and to themselves reflect the giddiness of their shifting identities.

Stevenson's sensitivity to these fluctuations resulted not only from his recognizing the child within himself and others but also from his yearning for that segment of his life. Reading through Stevenson's prose and poetry one soon realizes that his nostalgia for Scotland was not nearly as pressing as his longing for his early years there. Even though Stevenson spoke of his childhood as 'a very mixed experience, full of fever, nightmare, insomnia, painful days and interminable nights',[8] he also remembered the happier moments that combined with the difficult to make his childhood a more intense time than the present. As an adult he wanted to relive that intensity.

Stevenson's attachment to children is an expression of this desire. When he watched them or when he was with them, he could see what he wanted to retrieve from his past and what he hoped still to find within himself. His letters that include passages about children echo this longing. For instance, from Mentone in 1874, Stevenson wrote to his mother about a Russian child of two and a half who was staying with her mother at his hotel: 'she speaks six languages. She and her sister (*aet.* 8) and May Johnstone (*aet.* 8) are the delight of my life. Last night I saw them all dancing – o it was jolly; kids are what is the matter with me.'[9] Like so many other young people, that child was 'ever interesting'.[10] Periodically Stevenson also wrote letters to children of his friends. In a letter to Thomas Archer, aged three, for example, Stevenson describes a few moments from his own boyhood and displays an unusually acute memory of what it was like to be Thomas's age. His words reveal his yearning for the games of his youth: 'I was the best player of hide-and-seek going; not a good runner, I was up to every shift and dodge, I could jink very well, I could crawl without any noise through leaves, I could hide under a carrot plant, it used to be my favourite boast that I always *walked* into the den.'[11]

Significantly, it is in this love of play that one finds the primary expression of Stevenson's attraction to children and childhood. Most of all he wanted to be back among his boyhood play. Longing to relive these moments he later devised elaborate war games with toy soldiers, designed maps, printed newspaper reports about the troops' daily movements, and with his willing stepson produced dramas, set up printing presses, and traveled into countries unknown to anyone but themselves. Accompanied by Lloyd Osbourne, Stevenson was able to continue the imaginative play he and his cousin Robert had enjoyed when they had been younger and had eagerly created the lands of Nosington and Encyclopaedia. In his essay 'Crabbed Age and Youth', Stevenson, barely disguising his identity, speaks of his wish to reclaim the games of his childhood and admits his reluctance to give up his playthings:

A child who had been remarkably fond of toys (and in particular of lead soldiers) found himself growing to the level of acknowledged boyhood without any abatement of this childish taste. He was thirteen; already he had been taunted for dallying overlong about the playbox; he had to blush if he was found among his lead soldiers; the shades of the prison-house were closing about him with a vengeance. There is nothing more difficult than to put the thoughts of children into the language of their elders; but this is the effect of his meditations at this juncture: 'Plainly', he said, 'I must give up my playthings in the meanwhile, since I am not in a position to secure myself against idle jeers. At the same time, I am sure that playthings are the very pick of life; all people give them up out of the same pusillanimous respect for those who are a little older; and if they do not return to them as soon as they can, it is only because they grow stupid and forget. I shall be wiser; I shall conform for a little to the ways of their foolish world; but so soon as I have made enough money, I shall retire and shut myself up among my playthings until the day I die.'[12]

Stevenson took his own advice, for, of course, his essays, fiction, and poems are expressions of this impulse to shut himself up with his toys. With their more elaborate versions of hide-and-seek, their dressed dramas, and their arenas of adventurous conflict, *Treasure Island, Kidnapped, The Master of Ballantrae,* and *St Ives,* for instance, kept the adult Stevenson 'halfway between the swing and the gate', and such poems as 'Pirate Story' and 'A Good Play' from *A Child's Garden of Verses* allowed him to hear 'a kind of childish treble note'.[13] It is as if he wrote the books and the verses he wished he could have picked up and read – the kind that would have let him re-engage his childhood play. In an 1884 letter to William Ernest Henley, Stevenson, who had just recovered from a serious illness, exclaimed, 'I want to hear swords clash. I want a book to begin in a good way; a book, I guess, like *Treasure Island,* alas! which I have never read, and cannot though I live to ninety. I would God that some one else had written it! By all that I can learn, it is the very book for my complaint.'[14]

THE LANDSCAPE OF *A CHILD'S GARDEN OF VERSES*

Stevenson's unwillingness to abandon the pleasures of play issues partly from his sense that a child's spatial orientation differs significantly from an adult's. The boundaries marking the experience of childhood bore no resemblance to those defining adulthood – to become an adult, therefore, was to exchange one kind of map for another and to step outside the child's realm. It was to lose a perspective that might release him from the disturbing dualities that split the attention of his adult life.

This division of worlds is, perhaps, nowhere more visible than in *A Child's Garden of Verses.* Here Stevenson becomes the cartographer poet who delineates a topography that essentially excludes adults. 'Grown ups' stand outside the contours of the child's space, beyond what the poems, with their geographical imagery, survey and map. Adults are outsiders who enter momentarily to put the child to bed. As voices from another 'estate', they intrude and call the child home to tea. They are mothers who listen to the patter of feet from another room. None, not even the kindly aunt ('Auntie's Skirts'), is fully part of the child's subjective and self-contained space. Like the nurse who appears to be 'very big', they do not even share the same scale ('My Kingdom'). The 'we' in the poems, therefore, refers almost exclusively to children, for they are the primary community. Just as the children Stevenson observed on board the *Devonia* found each other 'like dogs' and moved about 'all in a band, as thick as thieves at a fair' while their elders were 'still ceremoniously manoeuvering on the outskirts of acquaintance',[15] the young people in *A Child's Garden of Verses* spontaneously form and dissolve their own society that marginalizes the adult world. Like the child in 'Foreign Lands', the young boys and girls search for a 'higher tree' so they can see 'To where the grown-up river slips/ Into the sea among the ships'. To become an adult is to lose this point of view.

Although Stevenson acknowledged that a phantom of the child stalked the adult and could, at times, seem more real than the adult figure himself, he recognized, of course, that childhood was not fully recoverable. No matter how much he consciously tried to re-enter its domain and how often he tried to take hold of it, his boyhood was always to be somewhat elusive. He remarked that in his adulthood he had 'grown up and gone away' from what he once was. Enough remained, though, in memory and impulse, that Stevenson could isolate and long for what was lacking. He did not, of course, regret the passing of the child's terror of chastisement and the suffering that accompanied his frequent illnesses. He did, however, regret the absence of the child's spontaneity and the expansiveness of his imagination – Stevenson envied the child who does not have to travel to activate his mind, who requires merely the stage of his immediate surroundings and the props of the simplest, everyday objects to reach places that he knows only by name. Keenly aware of this loss in his adulthood, he instructed his name-child, at the end of *A Child's Garden of Verses*, to lay down his spelling lesson and 'go and play' ('To My Name-Child').

Even more significantly Stevenson deplored the absence of a certain elasticity of perception that is such an integral part of childhood. The child inhabits a malleable space. Like Princes Street (Edinburgh) that can either interminably extend itself and lead the spectator's eye 'right into the heart of the red sundown' or 'shrink' so that the street 'seems to lie underneath' one's feet,[16] the child is able to expand and contract his attention, yet never lose touch with himself. He keeps his name and his identity. His shadow moves, grows, and diminishes with him. With ease, the child journeys back and forth between modes of consciousness and varieties of terrain without the experience of difference that can complicate the adult experience. In a sense, perhaps, the child is able to realize or make facile the fantasy of empire and eradicate the anxieties attending its displacements.

The poems in *A Child's Garden of Verses* are about Stevenson's nostalgia for this flexibility. They follow the child as he journeys between what is near and far, as he moves from night to day, and as he swings within and beyond the borders of the garden wall, sails in and out of the harbors of home, and grows large or becomes small. In all these situations the child remains intact and secure. The dualities of home and distant skies, land and sea, trees and ships, neither divide him nor cause one part of his consciousness to regard the other as alien – as exiled. In his terrain, beds and books, darkness and light, meadows and seas, pillows and battlefields mingle to form the single subjective topography of his inner landscape. He is part of a larger perspective that collapses the distant and the contiguous and, simultaneously, expands the immediate into the distant – where the rain at the same moment falls 'on the umbrellas here' and 'on the ships at sea' ('Rain') and where the child senses, although he cannot see them, the presence of other children who, like him, go to bed, play, take their tea, and sing – in Japan, Spain, or India ('Foreign Lands', 'Singing', and 'The Sun Travels'). There is no layering, no schematic drawing of geological strata. The layers only separate when the adult intrudes with a voice that wrenches what is single apart; then, the child becomes self-conscious and in 'The Land of Story-Books' speaks of an otherness:

> So, when my nurse comes in for me,
> Home I return across the sea,
> And go to bed with backward looks
> At my dear land of Story-books.

This looking backwards is a way of perceiving imposed by those who feel the differences of time and place. It is a mode of seeing that belongs to the adult who has difficulty blending the absent and the present and holding what is near and far comfortably within his sight. Unlike the child in the swing, the adult cannot readily see outside and inside the boundaries of his life in one motion. The adult does not have the invisible sweeping eye; he must elicit a mediating object, like the map, to extend his perspective. Recognizing this necessity, Stevenson once recommended to Edmund Gosse (17 March 1884) that in his new office overlooking the Thames he should keep on his table 'a great map spread out'. Stevenson suggested that 'a chart is still better – it takes one further – the havens with their little anchors, the rocks, banks and soundings, are adorably marine'.[17] The child in the poems requires no such mediating object to collect into one space what is near and far, what can be seen and what is invisible. It is only later, as an adult, that Stevenson needs maps and charts to help him reclaim this suppleness of mind so he can compose his fiction.

Because they unite the dualities that leave the adult staring at the space separating the then and the now, the far and the near, the children in Stevenson's verses do not necessarily experience nostalgia – as in 'Where Go the Boats?' they look forwards, not backwards. The child's orientation is not, therefore, like that of Dr Jekyll or the Master of Ballantrae, for his self is not a divided house; it need not turn back to regard itself and stare at its own 'imperfect and divided countenance' (*Dr Jekyll and Mr Hyde*). The child blends the nights and days and the open and the secret that come between Dr Jekyll and Mr Hyde and cause Hyde, at one point, to look back through the space of his anguish and review his life from his infancy. The child is spared this pain, for he lives in an ever-revolving present – even when he says goodbye, the images he desires sparkle with a presence that keeps them alive. They are, in spite of the valediction, still there ('Farewell to the Farm'). Memory does not continually press against him. In this frame of mind, then, Stevenson's young child considers what it will be like to grow older and does not fear that he will have to recall what he once was ('Looking Forward'). On the contrary, he looks forward to being able to realize and to extend his desires – he will learn to take a ship out to sea ('My Ship and I'), and he will become the lamplighter ('The Lamplighter'). From his perspective his older self will actualize or confirm his being; it will neither oppose nor diminish it, for his circumference of sight will expand and allow him to see 'farther' ('Foreign Lands'). Continuity rather than interruption or retrospection measures the child's globe.

Stevenson's verses emerge from a longing for this circumstance. But as Stevenson realized, he and his nostalgia for the past cannot restructure what had been. One reason they fail is that the adult, unlike the more flexible child, cannot play properly – he has

difficulty accepting substitutes and, thus, can never fully entertain
the notion of recovery, for he feels cut off from the authentic or
legitimate experience. He is thus more than usually sensitive to
difference. The child in Stevenson's verses, on the other hand, is
constantly using one object for another – a bed for a boat – and that
suffices; it becomes the real thing. For him, in the world of play, the
shadow does as well as the substance ('Block City'):

> What are you able to build with your blocks?
> Castles and palaces, temples and docks.
> Rain may keep raining, and others go roam,
> But I can be happy and building at home.
>
> Let the sofa be mountains, the carpet be sea,
> There I'll establish a city for me:
> A kirk and a mill and a palace beside,
> And a harbour as well where my vessels may ride.

When the adult is an exile from this dominion, that possibility
disappears. As Stevenson complained, 'the mature mind...desires
the thing itself'.[18] The experience of nostalgia, perhaps, also contributes to the failure. Because it gathers bits and pieces from the
past and assembles fragments arising from the involuntary memory,
nostalgia merely offers vanishing glimpses of what was. This incompleteness denies the possibility of substitution by inscribing the
sense of loss or absence and, thereby, awakens a longing for the
fuller, more lasting picture. With the exception of its abstracting
powers, nostalgia usually confirms the presence of a divided self.
In a sense, it signifies the ultimate duality. Stevenson's child,
though, for whom the shadow is sufficient, does not have to struggle with memory's imperfections and demands. Moreover, because
nostalgia waits in the future, unbeckoned, the child can look out of a
moving train's window ('From a Railway Carriage') and without
anxiety see the sights fly by.[19] The poem's last line, 'Each a glimpse
and gone for ever!' can gaily rattle along with the train's repetitive
rhythm.

One reason that these passing glimpses are not threatening and
do not disquiet the child is that in the elastic space of Stevenson's
verses there is, for the child, always the possibility of return, of
recovery. No matter how far he roams, he can always go back.
Moving through a malleable map that stretches and shrinks, he

never really loses sight of where he is. Like Princes Street, home is always, somehow, available; everything is 'handy to home' ('Keepsake Mill'). The number of poems in A Child's Garden of Verses that convey this sense of security is noteworthy. The poems depict a child who wanders far and wide, yet returns to the safety of his room; who swings high but always comes back down; and who marches round the village and goes 'home again'. Like the cow, the child 'wanders' yet 'cannot stray' ('The Cow'). He moves in a landscape of recovery. In this terrain, the continuous movement of the 'old mill wheel' is the 'keepsake' that promises that 'we all shall come home' ('Keepsake Mill'). Through this land runs the river, the surface of which once disturbed by the wind, the 'Dipping marten', or the 'plumping trout', always returns to its former unruffled self:

> Patience, children, just a minute -
> See the spreading circles die;
> The stream and all in it
> Will clear by-and-by.
>   ('Looking-Glass River')

The verses' cycles of sleeping and rising, darkness and light are part of this reassuring rhythm of recovery. They revolve the child in a world of re-awakenings. One wonders, perhaps, if Stevenson's desire to travel was not partially a quest for a place where he might re-enter the orbit of the jet-black night and clear day – where he might, as he did on a train between Edinburgh and Chester, travel and feel reborn. Stevenson describes one such experience in a September 1874 letter to Frances Sitwell:

How a railway journey shakes and discomposes one mind and body! I grow blacker and blacker in humour as the day goes on, and when at last I am let out, and the continual oscillation ceases, and I have the fresh air about me, it is as though I were born again, and the sick fancies flee away from my mind like snows in spring.[20]

Obviously, for the ailing Stevenson to go out was not always to be able to come back. The myth of resurrection could not endure. The Master of Ballantrae might return from the dead twice, but not three times.[21]

THE SANCTUARY OF PLAY AND VICARIOUS VIOLENCE

Significantly, Stevenson's nostalgia for childhood includes more than a yearning for the expansive and supple imagination that placed him, as an Edinburgh child, in rooms 'full of orange and nutmeg trees' and in 'cold town gardens... alive with parrots and with lions'.[22] It is also, it should be recognized, a longing for the vicarious violence of play. Readers often notice that Stevenson's work is replete with violence, but the connection with childhood is not made clear. On the sharp brim of the gentle lines in *A Child's Garden of Verses* sits the disorderly figure of conflict that is somehow sustaining and exhilarating: amid the soft folds of the comforting counterpane hide regiments of soldiers ('The Land of Counterpane') and across the sweet pleasantness of the meadow charge frenzied cattle, galloping destructive winds, pillaging pirates and grenadiers ('Pirate Story', 'Marching Song'). When cities burn and squadrons charge ('Armies in the Fires'), there is a vitality, an edge, that seems always to have attracted Stevenson. Indeed, throughout his life the sounds of a ravaging west wind or the 'horror of creeping things'[23] stimulated him. In an 1873 letter, for instance, which Stevenson wrote to Frances Sitwell, one hears him responding buoyantly to the wild wind's rousing force:

It is a magnificent glimmering, moonlight night, with a wild, great west wind abroad, flapping above one like an immense banner and every now and again swooping furiously against my windows. The wind is too strong perhaps, and the trees are certainly too leafless for much of that wide rustle that we both remember; there is only a sharp angry sibilant hiss, like breath drawn with the strength of the elements, through shut teeth, that one hears between the gusts only.[24]

This is the wild wind that sounds again in 'Windy Nights' and 'The Wind' from *A Child's Garden of Verses* when the child listens to the trees 'crying aloud', feels the strong wind's call pushing against him, and hears its 'loud' song.

In a similar manner murder also animated his imagination. For instance, the soft, yet violent, figure of an 'undoubted assassin' doting on his sleeping children intrigued him.[25] In an 1889 letter to Sidney Colvin about the murderer, Stevenson savors the disturbing oppositions between 'savagery' and propriety, the presence of the innocents and the memory of the man's violent deed:

> The whites are a strange lot, many of them good kind pleasant fellows, others quite the lowest I have ever seen even in the slums of cities. I wish I had time to narrate to you the doings and character of three white murderers (more or less proven) I have met; one, the only undoubted assassin of the lot, quite gained my affection in his big home out of a wreck, with his New Hebrides wife in her savage turban of hair and yet a perfect lady, and his three adorable little girls in Rob Roy Macgregor dresses, dancing to the hand organ, performing circus on the floor with startling effects of nudity, and curling up together on a mat to sleep, three sizes, three attitudes, three Rob Roy dresses, and six little clenched fists: the murderer meanwhile brooding and gloating over his chicks, till your whole heart went out to him, and yet his crime on the face of it was dark: disembowelling in his own house, an old man of seventy and him drunk.[26]

When one thinks of the coupling of blazing cities, armies, and wicked shadows with the images of dimpling rivers, meadow flowers, and golden sand that quietly play within *A Child's Garden of Verses*, this later taste for violence seems not incongruous with childhood as he depicts it. It is not out of character, then, for Stevenson to write to 'the little girls in the cellar' – children at a London (Kilburn) school – and dwell on the 'very wild and dangerous' places in the Samoan landscape. He is also quick to point out to Charles Baxter a fence 'all messed with blood where a horse had come to grief',[27] to dwell upon perilous storms at sea, and to accentuate the dangers and the mysteries of the threatening unknown with which the forest paths are fraught.

Just as he had in childhood, Stevenson undoubtedly found a certain pleasure, if not comfort, in the idea of violence because the fantasy of its aggressiveness compensated for the chronic periods of inactivity when he was ill and for those moments when he was actually strapped motionless to the bed to prevent hemorrhaging.[28] As Jerome Buckley points out, Stevenson's interest in action was an expression of his despising his own weakness.[29] Stevenson feared being passive. To be violent was to engage his surroundings – to do battle with them. Thoughts of such activity offered him a kind of sanctuary from his poor health. He liked the idea of clashing swords; therefore, during times of inactivity he would ask, 'Shall we never shed blood?'[30] And he was pleased to think back to the times he had weeded the land around his Samoan estate and partaken in a 'silent battle' in which he inflicted a 'slow death' upon 'the contending forest' surrounding it.[31] As he had during his early years, he treasured the notion of being at sea and contending with the elements – these are the moment he relives through 'Pirate Story' and 'My Bed is a Boat'. That possibility was preferable to watching himself slowly grow weaker. It is interesting to note that when Stevenson reflected upon his sickness, he turned to his friends and confided that he wanted to die 'violently'. In an 1892 letter to Sidney Colvin, he wrote: 'If only I could secure a violent death, what a fine success! I wish to die in my boots; no more land of counterpane for me. To be drowned, to be shot, to be thrown from a horse – ay, to be hanged, rather than pass again through that slow dissolution.'[32]

As an adult Stevenson obviously never fully realized this fantasy nor grew to be, as he had once dreamed, 'the leader of a great horde of irregular cavalry, devastating whole valleys'.[33] He had to turn to his fiction to commit such acts. The blood that runs above and below deck in *Treasure Island* and *Kidnapped*, the fighting, dueling, beatings, and murders that accentuate his stories and even his travel pieces reflect this impulse. His words sharpen under the influence of the cutlass and the terror of a 'wildly beating heart' (*Treasure Island*). Their fury generates the rapidity of Stevenson's style and infuses a vitality that permeates his characters. David Balfour, for instance, is invigorated when he joins with Alan Breck in the protracted killing of the mutineers. After the fighting, surrounded by broken glass and 'a horrid mess of blood', he feels triumphant in spite of his distress and his beginning 'to sob and cry like any child',[34] for he has participated in a rite of passage that has taken him from a passive to a more vigorous relationship to his surroundings. Similarly in *The Master of Ballantrae*, the mild-mannered narrator, Mr Mackellar, is exhilarated and transformed when he discovers that he has the ability and the desire to do harm. Although he does not actually murder the Master, he comes close enough to gain self-respect and to sense his own empowerment.[35]

Fiction was one means by which Stevenson vicariously engaged the exhilaration of the idea of violence; another was, of course, through the games of his boyhood. More than anything else, perhaps, Stevenson was nostalgic for the childhood battles he describes in *A Child's Garden of Verses* and in his letters. In October 1893, for instance, he wrote to his cousin Henrietta Milne (*née* Traquair) and longingly remembered their play: 'you were sailing under the title of Princess Royal; I, after a furious contest, under that of Prince Alfred; and Willie, still a little sulky, as the Prince of Wales. We were all in a buck basket about halfway between the swing and the gate; and I can still see the Pirate Squadron heave in sight upon the weather brow.' Stevenson concluded, 'You were a capital fellow to play.'[36] It is, of course, this recollection that echoes in poems such as 'Pirate Story', 'Armies in the Fire', 'Young Night-Thought', 'The Land of Story-Books', 'Marching Song', and 'A Good Play' and that, for the moment, carries Stevenson back to a time when he could fully be part of the imagined skirmishes and campaigns. These games were part of his childhood garden's landscape.

Stevenson was especially nostalgic for the child's easy involvement in the fury and passionate bursts of activity – in the vicarious, yet absorbing, violence of play. Unlike the adult, the child enters the game's arena and acts out his part. His whole self is in the scene, and for a few moments he becomes the pirate or the soldier and realizes the figure's gestures. The adult, though, separated by memory, intellect, and conscience, only partially steps in. He is not committed to its battles. Caught between the silence of a spectator and the voice of a participant, he finds no easy utterance. Stevenson focuses upon this important distinction in his essay 'Child's Play':

the child, mind you, acts his parts. He does not merely repeat them to himself; he leaps, he runs, and sets the blood agog over all his body. And so his play breathes him; and he no sooner assumes a passion than he gives it vent. Alas! when we betake ourselves to our intellectual forms of play, sitting quietly by the fire or lying prone in bed, we rouse many hot feelings for which we can find no outlet.[37]

The adult, essentially, cannot act out the violence, for he performs within the obstructed gap between the character and himself; furthermore, he falls into the space between the then and the now – he cannot locate himself exclusively within the present of the game's circumference. Because he cannot help but 'stir up uncomfortable and sorrowful memories, and remind' himself 'sharply of old wounds',[38] it is impossible for him to exclude another time. The adult, therefore, carries the burden of reference that throttles the action and translates games into history. Consequently, when he attempts to take his part in play, he finds himself self-consciously repeating the lines rather than actively participating in the scene. He cannot break out of his twofold nature. This dilemma offers a commentary upon the experience of nostalgia. The adult who cannot fully enter the world of play is similar to the adult who longs for the past. To be yearning for something that is absent is also to be caught in the bondage of self-consciousness and to be trapped in the double vision of Janus. Such a posture makes a history out of the present. It remembers, yet barely touches what it desires; it can never fully revitalize what it hopes to recover – one leaves the ground one longs for as soon as one touches it. Paradoxically, nostalgia is prevented from ever properly resurrecting the past because it relies on a memory that depends upon comparison and a sense of otherness. It cannot fully recover what lies there, for like the adult who attempts to play, it cannot adequately move the limbs and quicken the voices of the absent. Nostalgia, it seems, is always attended by a reference to an 'other' that censors by qualifying the player's gestures and discourages by accepting no substitutes.

Even Stevenson, who continued to play war games with his stepson and who gave utterance to the child's voice in his verses, is not spared this circumstance. He understood that if he wanted to recover what he desired, he had to break away from these oscillating rhythms of dualism. One way was to participate in the act or the play of writing. Writing was a vicarious means of warring against a static life. It was what was left to a person who could no longer gather his 'allies' and attend to the games of childhood that codify or organize violence without inflicting harm. Writing allowed him to become the child in *A Child's Garden of Verses* and keep on beginning again. It permitted him to bypass duality by giving him a way of participating in the narrative's continuous present, for its sentences and characters, like the child, acted out the gestures and uttered the passions of play. As Stevenson once observed, 'Fiction is to the grown man what play is to the child.'[39] His characters, therefore, never have to repeat or remember something they have once said; they belong to an elastic map; they, even in their exile, are members of a community – the community of an everlasting now that transcends the split consciousness of memory.

Stevenson's experience suggests that nostalgia defeats itself except when it goes around itself to the text and keeps the writer and the reader, for the moment, revolving in a time and a space that is always fully available and, especially in Stevenson's case, needs no otherness, not even a third-person narrator, to explicate or qualify it. The writer becomes Jim Hawkins (*Treasure Island*); he enters his body and his mind, and that way finds his passage. Writing is the only way home. As Hyde notices, writing keeps what was in the present. Even though he cannot return to the form of Dr Jekyll, Mr Hyde can still write in Jekyll's own hand – that part of his 'original character' that remains to him.[40] It is this original hand that leads Stevenson back into the landscape of his boyhood, into his *A Child's Garden of Verses*.

Notes

1. Although many critics and biographers have remarked upon the fact of Stevenson's yearning for his childhood and have documented his engagement with the games, the play, the maps, and the interiors of his early years, none has dwelt upon the idiosyncratic nature of their 'typography', especially that which he describes in *A Child's Garden of Verses*.
2. R. L. Stevenson, *Virginibus Puerisque and Other Papers* (London: Chatto & Windus, 1905) p. 59.
3. B. Booth and E. Mehew, *The Letters of Robert Louis Stevenson 1854–1894*, VIII (New Haven: Yale University Press, 1994, 1995) p. 366.
4. Ibid., III, p. 33.
5. R. L. Stevenson, *Memories and Portraits* (New York: Charles Scribner's Sons, 1897) p. 112.
6. R. L. Stevenson, *Treasure Island* (London: William Heinemann, 1924) pp. 139, 156.
7. R. L. Stevenson, *Kidnapped* (New York: Bantam Books, 1982) p. 172.
8. Booth and Mehew, *The Letters of Robert Louis Stevenson 1854–1894*, V, p. 97.
9. Ibid., I, p. 429.
10. Ibid., I, p. 441.
11. Ibid., VI, p. 218.
12. Stevenson, *Virginibus Puerisque and Other Papers*, pp. 63–4.
13. Booth and Mehew, *The Letters of Robert Louis Stevenson 1854–1894*, IV, p. 189; V, p. 85.
14. Ibid., IV, p. 307.
15. R. L. Stevenson, *The Amateur Emigrant*, introd. J. Raban (London: The Hogarth Press, 1984) p. 15. As I explained in Chapter 3, when Stevenson traveled to America in August, 1879, he sailed on the *Devonia*, a ship carrying emigrants from Scotland, Ireland, England, Scandinavia, Germany, and Russia who 'had been unable to prevail against circumstances' at home.

16. Booth and Mehew, *The Letters of Robert Louis Stevenson 1854–1894*, I, p. 330.
17. Ibid., IV, p. 260.
18. Stevenson, *Virginibus Puerisque and Other Papers*, p. 160.
19. Stevenson's experience is the opposite of Mary Barton's in Elizabeth Gaskell's novel discussed in the previous chapter. When Mary Barton travels by train, she senses that she is losing her surroundings and becomes anxious.
20. Booth and Mehew, *The Letters of Robert Louis Stevenson 1854–1894*, II, p. 49.
21. In *The Master of Ballantrae*, the Master returns to his estate twice after being thought dead; the third time, however, he does not survive. In New York the Master arranged with his Indian servant, Secundra, to bury him alive and then when all is well to bring him out of his grave, but the plan does not work. With the assistance of Secundra's frantic attempts to resuscitate his body, the master revives but only briefly. The narrator describes the episode:

> Of the flight of time, I have no idea; it may have been three hours, and it may have been five, that the Indian laboured to reanimate his master's body. One thing only I know, that it was still night, and the moon was not yet set, although it had sunk low, and now barred the plateau with long shadows, when Secundra uttered a small cry of satisfaction; and, leaning swiftly forth, I thought I could myself perceive a change upon the icy countenance of the unburied. The next moment I beheld his eyelids flutter; the next they rose entirely, and the week-old corpse looked me for a moment in the face.

See R. L. Stevenson, *The Master of Ballantrae and Weir of Hermiston*, introd. M. R. Ridley (London: Dent: Everyman's Library, 1976) p. 187.
22. Booth and Mehew, *The Letters of Robert Louis Stevenson 1854–1894*, VII, p. 355.
23. Ibid., VII, p. 93.
24. Ibid., I, p. 333.
25. Stevenson met this white 'assassin' when he was on tour of the Gilbert Islands on board the *Equator*.
26. Booth and Mehew, *The Letters of Robert Louis Stevenson 1854–1894*, VI, pp. 327–8.
27. Ibid., VII, pp. 225, 279.
28. One of these fantasies occurred when Stevenson gleefully represented himself as a 'murderer' and impersonated 'William Figg' (one of the ironic personae Stevenson used in his correspondence with friends) who in 'earlier and more thoughtless years' had 'been unjustly condemned for forgery, arson, stilicide, public buttery, and rape followed by murder in the person of twelve infant and flaxen-headed children of different sexes'. See D. Ferguson and M. Waingrow, eds, *Stevenson's Letters to Charles Baxter* (New Haven: Yale University Press, 1956) p. 113.

29. J. H. Buckley, *William Ernest Henley: A Study in the 'Counter-Decadence' of the 'Nineties* (Princeton: Princeton University Press, 1945) p. 7.
30. Booth and Mehew, *The Letters of Robert Louis Stevenson 1854–1894*, IV, p. 259.
31. Ibid., VII, p. 27.
32. Ibid., VII, p. 287.
33. Ibid., IV, p. 259. He wrote the letter to Cosmo Monkhouse on 16 March 1884. It reads:

> To confess plainly, I had intended to spend my life (or any leisure I might have from Piracy upon the high seas) as the leader of a great horde of irregular cavalry, devastating whole valleys. I can still, looking back, see myself in many favourite attitudes; signalling for a boat from my pirate ship with a pocket-handkerchief, I at the jetty end, and one or two of my bold blades keeping the crowd at bay; or else turning in the saddle to look back at my whole command (some five thousand strong) following me at the hand-gallop up the road out of the burning valley: this last by moonlight.

34. Stevenson, *Kidnapped*, pp. 68, 66.
35. Stevenson was too much a realist and too sensitive to contradiction to overlook the fact that violence is not always so enlivening. He understood that it was possible to suffer the consequences of one's actions, and to be left, isolated and diminished like Mr Hyde and Mr Henry. Mr Henry's wounding of his brother in the duel, for instance, reverses rather than advances his fortunes. One moment of actively facing the enemy throws him back upon himself and entrenches him more deeply within the victim's state of compulsive passivity and guilt.
36. Booth and Mehew, *The Letters of Robert Louis Stevenson 1854–1894*, IV, pp. 189–90.
37. Stevenson, *Virginibus Puerisque and Other Papers*, p. 160.
38. Ibid., p. 160.
39. Stevenson, *Memories and Portraits*, p. 268.
40. R. L. Stevenson, *Dr Jekyll and Mr Hyde* (Toronto: Bantam Books, 1981) p. 97.

6

Rooms Without Mirrors: The Childhood Interiors of Ruskin, Pater, and Stevenson

My body, still too heavy with sleep to move, would endeavour to construe from the pattern of the tiredness the position of its various limbs, in order to deduce therefrom the direction of the wall, the location of the furniture to piece together and give a name to the house in which it lay.

Marcel Proust, *Remembrance of Things Past, I*

For as I look deeper into the mirror, I find myself a more curious person than I had thought.

John Ruskin, *Praeterita*

Among the intimate spaces of childhood are the rooms of home. Not surprisingly, then, those who are nostalgic for their early years often attempt to describe these interiors and repossess them through their words. John Ruskin, Walter Horatio Pater, and Robert Louis Stevenson are among those who, in this manner, have tried to re-enter the rooms of their youth. Their autobiographical writing delineating these spaces are vivid and often beautifully rendered instances of this impulse to write toward home. In their texts they dwell not only upon their idiosyncratic relationship to the interiors of their childhood but also upon how a consciousness of one's physical being defines the sense of one's surroundings. Bodies, not objects, structure the spaces of home.

While composing these descriptions, Ruskin, Pater, and Stevenson transform their texts into mirrors through which they see reflections of what they had once been. They illuminate what, in childhood, they had no need to see. They remind one that occasionally in the act of retrospection, visibility replaces the invisibility of being. To recollect the spaces of childhood is to bring into perception what once had no need to be seen.

THREE MODELS OF INTERIORITY

Years after they had left their childhood behind them, Ruskin, Pater, and Stevenson continued to reflect upon the homes in which they had passed their early lives. In particular they thought about their interiors – the rooms of their childhood. When they described these spaces, they did not simply re-present the contours, features, and things that had composed the drawing rooms of 28 Herne Hill, the interiors of the house in Enfield, or the day nursery and bedrooms of 17 Heriot Row. Instead, when seeking to bring these interiors fully back to life, they considered how they themselves had once occupied the spaces of home – how their physical being had related to the walls and windows of childhood.[1] They let their memories resuscitate the dialogue their bodies had once had with these interiors and recalled how their bodies had given voice to the silences of the enclosing architectural lines. Like the painter who sees through his body, who diminishes the gap between himself and what he perceives, Ruskin, Pater, and Stevenson understood that it is the child's being that shapes and illuminates the interiors of home.[2] Articles don't define interiors; bodies that move and feel their way among these objects do.[3]

Although Ruskin, Pater, and Stevenson are all sensitive to the defining function of the body, each, not surprisingly, experiences the phenomenon in a different way. The result is that their autobiographical texts (Ruskin's *Praeterita*, Pater's 'The Child in the House', and Stevenson's *A Child's Garden of Verses*) offer three distinct models of how the consciousness of one's physical being illuminates the interiors of home. Ruskin's speaks of the invisible body; Pater's of the æsthetic body; and Stevenson's of the ubiquitous body.

John Ruskin

In his uneven, often grumbling yet graceful autobiography, Ruskin describes the houses of his childhood: he writes briefly about the one at Number 54 Hunter Street (London) where he lived until he was four and more extensively about the house at Herne Hill (four miles south of London) where he and his parents remained until 1845. He describes, for instance, the commanding views from their garret windows, the front and back gardens, and the setting of the Herne Hill residence from which he could see the Norwood Hills on one side and the River Thames on the other. His prose has a keen immediacy, as if he had just closed the door behind him or latched the attic window shut. Even after more than four decades of absence, these images remain undimmed. They have not, to borrow Ruskin's metaphor, been swept up into the dustbin of oblivion.[4]

These particular passages, however, are not what give the reader an understanding of Ruskin's experience of the interiors of home, for with their emphasis on prospect they belong more to the public Ruskin, the figure whose carefully selected words guided the British around Venice, directed the readers' eyes to a more truthful view of the Alps, and described the settings of cottages and villas in Europe. What best reveals his experience of interiority are the sections in which he once more steps inside and glimpses the child and his relationship to those surroundings. No longer preoccupied by how light and shadow fall on a cathedral's delicate tracery or concerned about the continuity of a building's structural lines, he dwells, instead, upon a few intimate moments of home – the small temporal and physical spaces he once inhabited. As he had after his travels with his parents in foreign lands, Ruskin in *Praeterita* returns to the recesses of the house, to its 'sacred' niches where during the winter and summer evenings he had listened to his father reading to his mother. He recalls how as a five or six year-old he had passed his days contentedly inside the rooms of Herne Hill tracing the squares and comparing the colors in the carpet or gazing at the patterns in the bed covers, and how in the enclosed garden he had watched the 'ways of plants' and full of 'admiring wonder' pulled the flowers to pieces so that he might stare 'at them, or into them'.[5] He also remembers how he had once stood by the windows and watched a wasp on the window pane, observed a bird in the nearby cherry tree and looked repeatedly at the iron post out of which the water-carts were filled – the mystery of which never wearied his infant eyes.[6]

In all these spaces Ruskin is half prisoner – half free to let his imagination and powers of concentration develop. Like the recess, with its restraining yet supporting table, in which the young Ruskin placed himself and sat night after night in the corner of the drawing room, the interiors of home both confined and liberated him. They set limits to his physical being, yet allowed him to explore his own thoughts. As Sheila Emerson points out, within the 'press and bruise of constraining circumstance', he enjoyed 'the sense of an infinitely inviting prospect and of the incipient power to meet it'.[7]

Protected by the monastic world his parents created, he lived in what he later described as the 'sweet selfishness' of childhood.[8] In *Praeterita* Ruskin rarely speaks of the outside penetrating the carefully guarded interiors of Herne Hill, and never recalls its grazing the skin of his life.[9] There are notices of the occasional visitor (partners in his father's sherry trade)[10] and there are several passages in which he acknowledges (often in an affectionate way) the addition in 1828 of his cousin Mary. (Mary, the daughter of his father's sister, came to live with the Ruskins after the death of her mother.) However, with few exceptions, these figures from elsewhere never permanently touched the inside, never completely upset its protective intimacy, nor properly agitated its 'beloved sameness'. Even though, at first, Mary's entrance into the household disturbed its tranquility, the threat and inconvenience of her presence receded and soon, in Ruskin's mind, his cousin became, as he baldly admits, no more than 'an additional neutral tint'.[11]

In 1845, when the family moved to a grander home on Denmark Hill, the intimate spaces of his childhood retreated. Overwhelmed by the aura of their new dwelling's 'stateliness' and its 'command' over seven acres of 'healthy grounds', the family, in Ruskin's words, was never more 'at home'.[12] As if turning the previous houses inside out, he concentrates, this time, on the dwelling's exterior – the places that open up onto the meadows, the orchards, and the wood-walk with its blossoms. It is here, and not inside, that he finds intimacy and sees his body winding its way contentedly among the trees. Rarely does he move about inside. And when he does, he remains only long enough to direct the reader's attention to what leads back to the outside – to the windows in the breakfast-room, the bedrooms, and the western rooms.

The comfortable recesses and corners of his childhood have disappeared. Ruskin now experiences an 'awkwardness' when he walks around his study.[13] In a sense, the house is not a home but a public monument. (Ruskin appropriately entitles his chapter on this more elegant house, 'The State of Denmark'.) Its rooms pose as public settings in which to display his and his father's collection of paintings (the Turners, the Hunts, the Copley Fieldings). These paintings come too close, perhaps, to being portable commodities

– extensions of his father's mercantile world. They belong to the same kind of stately space as does the large dining room, the scene, as Ruskin explains, of 'our grandest receptions'. What, as a boy, Ruskin had associated with anticipation, argument, excitement, longing, and narrative (he had once eagerly listened to his father tell stories about the subjects of paintings), in this context threatens to become the disembodied subject that speaks to the public rather than to the subjective self and has little to do with the person who inhabits and finds his way around the rooms. They have now more to do with what Ruskin calls the 'industry of middle life'.[14]

In the stately rooms of Denmark Hill, there is less sense of a living being moving about inside. Within the earlier interiors of Herne Hill, however, he had breathed and watched within their moments and corners, yet he had not occupied these spaces with the full visible presence of his body. As if replacing metaphor with synecdoche, Ruskin describes his younger self by focusing exclusively upon his eyes.[15] Paradoxically, then, within the rooms of his childhood, he is almost invisible, for Ruskin desired no vehicle outside of himself to define or reveal himself. As John Dixon Hunt remarks, he required 'little exchange and mutual involvement with others'.[16] To observe was enough. As they were to do in his writings throughout his life, the eyes replace the physical body by standing in for it. The eyes 'rest', 'fall', 'measure', and 'reason'; they are 'careless', though they can be 'guided', 'informed', and 'told'.

As if conscious of this substitution, Ruskin recalls the time he frightened his mother 'out of her wits' by announcing that his eyes were coming 'out of his head'[17] – an almost literal truth, for, in *Praeterita*, he says that it is with a child's eyes that he studies the flowers in his garden, counts the spaces in the carpet, looks deep down into the swift-eddying river, and stares into the holes he liked to dig. His seeing eyes reach out as far as they can, through the window pane, and leave the rest of the body behind, untouched, unobserved, uninterrupted. (Significantly, throughout *Praeterita* Ruskin often speaks of his displeasure at being interrupted – to shed the visible body is a way of ridding oneself of this annoyance and, possibly, of protecting oneself by 'de-eroticizing' the visual order.[18]) And for Ruskin it was the sealed hazel eyes – not the young man's frail, limp body – that signalled the premature death of his friend Henry Dart.[19]

As a boy Ruskin moved through the rooms and interiors of home as inside a frame supporting a glass that hides the body in its dimness while allowing the eyes to peer through its dusk. When he sat observing, his eyes wandered into the patterns of the floors and walls; he traveled within the portchaise and stared out of its panoramic window; setting out on holidays, he took his position on a 'little box' between his mother and father and enjoyed the prospect appearing piece by piece before him.[20] Disappearing into the supporting brackets, his body released his eyes and gave him the freedom to stare, unnoticed, in 'rapturous and riveted' attention.[21] They granted him a protective invisibility that allowed him to observe without being engaged by anything other than himself. He watched without being seen; he existed as a spectator, not as the observed. Later in life he was always to value those moments when he could take note of his surroundings away from people's sight and consciousness. For instance, in his autobiography, he recalls the pleasure he felt as a young man when in 1835 he entered the empty churches in Abbeville and, fancying himself 'a ghost', peeped 'round their pillars, like Rob Roy'; knelt in them; drew in them, and disturbed none.[22] Even later in 1842, alone in Champagnole, Ruskin recalls that his 'entire delight was in observing without' himself being 'noticed'.[23] (He did not always object to people watching him paint if they had their eyes upon his canvas and not on him.) Longing to return to the bodilessness of his childhood, Ruskin says, 'if I could have been invisible, all the better'. Significantly, he admits, 'My times of happiness had always been when *nobody* was thinking of me.'[24] Part of Ruskin's nostalgia for his childhood is to return to its monastic invisibility that allowed him the privacy of his visual ecstacy.

This invisibility is the sweet selfishness of his childhood that he longs to recapture. It was, perhaps, only when his cousin Charles drowned (on 2 January 1834) off the coast of the Isle of Wight that the young Ruskin was forced, for a moment, out of that mode within the boundaries of his own home. In *Praeterita* he recounts the episode. He had been working on a project alone, upstairs, when his Cousin Mary, his mother, and father returned from town. Upon hearing them Ruskin ran eagerly downstairs to tell them about his work. Still revolving in his self-enclosed world, he did not notice their grave expressions. He continued to boast of his accomplishments until Mary captured his attention. Ruskin describes the moment: 'She turned round suddenly, her face all streaming with tears, and caught hold of me, and put her face close to mine, that I might hear the sobbing whisper, "Charles is gone".'[25] Mary recalls Ruskin from his bodilessness by touching him and pressing her tearful face up to his. Through her gesture she performs a metamorphosis and transforms his sensibility. She puts Ruskin, temporarily, back into his body, makes him visible, so that he can participate in an exchange with her and comprehend that Charles' body has been thrown ashore at Cowes; it has not simply vanished into the invisibility of the sea.

In this act Mary also touches him into remembrance, for implicitly she seems, momentarily, to take Ruskin back to the other intimate interiors of his childhood – the household of his Scottish Aunt (Mary's now dead mother) and the more humble home in Croydon belonging to the mother of the drowned Charles. If not in his own home, at least in Perth and Croydon Ruskin was less invisible. Throughout the passages describing his visits to these places, there is a sense of his being connected to others. Often speaking in the plural 'we' and the possessive 'our' he shows himself to be part of the sensual world.[26] His body moves with and is affected by his young companions, especially his cousin Jessie. They grind corn and knead bread together. In addition, his enthusiasm for his Croydon aunt (the one who insisted on buying him the toys his mother, Ruskin claims, later confiscated), whom, in his own words, he 'entirely loved', and his pleasure in remembering the 'happy, happy days at Perth'[27] suggest that in these surroundings there was more of a substance or a fullness to the feeling body than at Herne Hill where he willingly kept it in hiding and lived as the observing eye within his home's protective walls. In either case, though, it is through his attitude towards the interaction between his body and its surroundings that Ruskin expresses his longing for the interiors of childhood.

Walter Horatio Pater

Pater's rendering of his childhood experiences (in the semi-autobiographical portrait 'The Child in the House') is naturally different from Ruskin's. Although Pater's interiors, like Ruskin's, radiate an almost monastic or cell-like aura, they by no means resemble Ruskin's, for the body that inhabits and forms them has a distinctly different affect. It is a sensuous presence. In his rooms the child, Florian, does not have to be touched into recognition, for his sensuous body is alert; he does not require Mary's mediating hands to comprehend fully what is outside of him. And although for Pater the visual experiences are just as essential as they are for Ruskin – for him too the eyes are a determining influence[28] – these visual moments are not detached or bodiless. They emerge from and return to a body through which images move along the nerves, touch the organs, and bring vitality to his being. The child sees feelingly and 'inwardly' ('The Child in the House').[29] In Pater's interiors, therefore, the child's body is just as significant as it is in Ruskin's, but not because of its inquisitive invisibility; it is conspicuous because of its sensuality and its willingness to be affected by what lies outside of it. Here the haptic and the visual conjoin to create an impressionistic body – one that carries on 'the brain-building by which we are, each one of us, what we are'.[30]

When Pater portrays Florian Deleal, the young boy in 'The Child in the House', he dwells upon the boy's willing, though sometimes unconscious, acceptance of the visible, the tangible, and the audible encircling him. Within, the winds from outside the house play on him, and through the open windows the coming and going of travelers, the shadows of evening, the brightness of day, the perfumes from the neighboring garden, and the scent of the lime tree blossoms awaken his senses. The sensitive young boy looks at the fallen acorn and the black crow's feathers that his sister has brought in from 'some distant forest' and discovers intimations of places beyond – these 'treasures' speak the 'rumour of its [the wood's] breezes, with the glossy blackbirds aslant and the branches lifted in them'.[31]

The outside and the inside come together in his body[32] that risks being wounded by the tyranny of the senses and the surrendering of its boundaries – something, of course, the sheltered Ruskin could not expose himself to. From over the high garden wall sentiments of beauty and pain float into his consciousness and penetrate, what Pater calls, the 'actual body':[33] the cry of his aunt on the stair when she announces his father's death strikes and quickens him; the wasp in the basket of yellow crab-apples stings him. (Ruskin, recall, only watched the wasp at his window.) The receptive Florian listens to the voices of people below speaking of the sick woman who 'had seen one of the dead sitting beside her' and then brings the ghostly figure into his own space so that the *revenant* sits 'beside him in the reveries of his broken sleep'.[34] Similarly, he goes outside so that he may bring what is there inside. He passes through the garden gate, fills his arms with red hawthorn blossoms (the scent of which had already reached him), and returns to arrange these brilliant flowers in old blue-china pots along the chimney piece.

Later in two other imaginary and semi-autobiographical portraits, 'Emerald Uthwart' and *Marius the Epicurean*, Pater echoes many of the details describing Florian's experiences within his home. Like Florian these children breathe, feel, touch, move, and see with their bodies. No eye, as in Ruskin's example, leaves the body to reside in the half-concealed recess of a drawing-room. The young and solitary Emerald ('Aldy'), for instance, is also a child who, in the context of his home, responds to the sights and sounds surrounding him – to the 'rippling note of the birds' and to the flowers in the garden that yield a sweetness when the 'loosening wind' unsettles them.[35] When flung open, the windows in the attic where he sleeps admit the scent of the roses and of the faint sea-salt air. Their breath envelops and touches him as he sleeps under 'the fine old blankets'.[36] Similarly, the child Marius in the solitude of his early dwelling (the old country place not far from Rome) feels the wind that blows from the distant harbor, inhales the scent of the new-mown hay that the sea air sweeps into the room, and takes pleasure in the view of the purple heath.

The affect of these children's sensuous bodies is complemented by the interiors of their home. Like Florian who sees and touches what is outside the boundaries of his body, these interiors, as if they were themselves bodies, extend and incorporate what is beyond them – what is outside the windows or the enclosing walls. These interiors do not shut themselves off; they resist exclusiveness. Like a shuttle in a loom, they move continuously inside and out of each other. In Florian's childhood home, for instance, the staircase moves the reader from floor to floor and up to a broad window, out to the swallow's nest that hangs beneath the sill, leads him back down into the house, into the closet, and then back up to the unexplored treasures at the top of the house, and out again on to the open, flat space of a roof that offers a view of the neighboring steeples. Interiors and exteriors mingle. They pass through the intermediary spaces – the windows and gates left ajar – to meet and lie over and press against each other. Outside Florian's bedroom heavy blossoms, pushed by the wind, beat peevishly on the window; the penetrating sun lies warm upon his pillow, and the sounds of voices float into the garden below.

Taking its form from the child's receptive body, these interiors become intricate sequences of superimposed sensations. They replicate or reflect the inextricably woven texture of the child's consciousness and being. As the title suggests, the child is *in* the house.[37] Consequently, just as it would be impossible to render a conventional portrait of Florian, it would be difficult to draw his home. Neither the body of the child nor the structure of the rooms he inhabits is conventionally visible, for each lacks the defining, uninterrupted lines of shape that, for instance, explicate the statuary of the Renaissance. Like a writer's elusive style, that according to Pater's understanding, is transparent and resists an outline, they exist primarily as gatherings of impressions that are continuously overtaking one another. In this manner, the child's body and the rooms of home engage in an exchange – in a sense, each passes into the condition of the other.

When Pater describes this exchange, he is, of course, participating in a familiar metaphor. Throughout his work, Pater often draws upon the recognized comparison between the body, the soul, and the house. As Perry Meisel observes, this metaphor is 'an overarching' one for Pater.[38] Frequently he uses various architectural images or details in order to describe 'the walls' or 'the cells' of personality, to consider 'the chambers' in the 'house of thought', or to refer to the activity of personality building ('The Child in the House').[39] He attaches himself to a tradition that includes the Palladian notion of designing a building in the form of the human body, the sense that in a novel a house and its rooms are, as Samuel Richardson said of his work, virtually interchangeable with the body, and the nineteenth-century psychoanalytic theories that discover, in dreams, affinities between the body's organs and the attributes of a house and its rooms (K. A. Scherner, *Das Leben des Traumes*).

Pater's interest in the metaphor, however, is less indebted to these images than to the writings of those mystics who consider the body to be the raiment of the soul as the house is the raiment to the body. In his description of Cecilia's house in *Marius the Epicurean*, Pater refers to one of these philosophers – probably a fictitious one. Replicating the inextricable bond he had previously portrayed between the soul, the body, and the house in Florian's dwelling, he describes the affinity between Cecilia and her home in these terms:

'The house in which she lives', says that mystical German writer quoted once before, 'is for the orderly soul, which does not live on blindly before her, but is ever, out of her passing experiences, building and adorning the parts of a many-roomed abode for herself, only an expansion of the body; as the body, according to the philosophy of Swedenborg, is but a process, an expansion, of the soul. For such an orderly soul, as life proceeds, all sorts of delicate affinities establish themselves, between herself and the doors and passage-ways, the lights and shadows, of her outward dwelling-place, until she may seem incorporate with it: until at last, in the entire expressiveness of what is outward, there is for her, to speak properly, between outward and inward no longer any distinction at all; and the light which creeps at a particular hour on a particular picture or space upon the wall, the scent of flowers in the air at a particular window, become to her, not so much apprehended objects, as themselves powers of apprehension, and doorways to things beyond'.[40]

In this passage and, especially, in the earlier portrait of Florian, Pater does more than participate in a convention. He also transforms metaphor into action, for in his mind, the person is quite literally the house. The interiors of Florian's childhood do not merely reflect his body; they are actual extensions of it. The two are embedded in each other. Pater's conviction of this phenomenon expresses his desire for a pulsating harmony between matter and form. It brings to life what, within the boundaries of convention, exists only as ideal, abstraction, or possibility.

Robert Louis Stevenson

The rooms of Robert Louis Stevenson's childhood reveal a third possibility. His example suggests yet another way in which the body's affect converses with and gives shape to its surroundings. This time, though, it is neither Ruskin's curious invisibility nor Pater's receptive body that defines or intermingles with the interior; instead, it is the moat of sickness encircling the child's body that structures the spaces of home and creates the sense of the ubiquitous body.

Stevenson, who began writing these poems during a particularly difficult time with his health, returns to these interiors in *A Child's Garden of Verses*. He re-enters the rooms that recall the fevers, the weakness of chest, the coughing, the chills, the severe bronchial infections, the earaches, and, eventually, the hemorrhaging that from the age of two often kept him for long periods in bed. Confined within Howard Place, Inverleith Terrace, and 17 Heriot Row, the young Stevenson periodically missed school and passed his days 'exiled' from the company of other children. Jenni Calder, one of his biographers, offers an example of how these illnesses followed 'one after the other'. She writes:

> In September 1858 [Stevenson would have been about eight], for instance, a long illness began; for five weeks he was unable to sit up in bed. He couldn't sleep and had little appetite. A year later he had chicken pox, and then for most of the following winter and spring, he was ill again. In 1861 he was in bed for six weeks with whooping cough... and so it went on.[41]

Most of all the memory of the feverish nights stayed with him. Stevenson never forgot what he called the 'terrible long nights' through which he lay awake, in his words, 'troubled continuously by a hacking, exhausting cough, and praying for sleep or morning from the bottom of my shaken little body'.[42]

Stevenson's early sickness left its physical memories too. He was, as his friend Sidney Colvin remarked, 'a bag of bones, a very lath for leanness'.[43] Of all the photographs and paintings of Stevenson, none captures his fragility more than John Singer Sargent's 1885 portrait – painted the year *A Child's Garden of Verses* appeared – in which Stevenson's lank and almost transparent body moves through the shadows into darkness. His long thin fingers touch his face and his leg as if having to confirm their actuality. (In moments of cutting, yet playful, bitterness, Stevenson referred to himself as a 'pallid brute'.)

The interiors described in *A Child's Garden of Verses* recall the scenes of his early confinement. The poems take place in the night nursery; they inhabit the land of counterpane; they climb the stairs; they go into the walled garden, and they look through the broad window of 17 Heriot Row. In a sense, each verse is a room shaped by the sick body's desire to escape from itself. The poems and the spaces they describe offer release from the enclosures of the body's frailty. Like the children, in one of the verses, who break through a breach in the wall and go down to the mill ('Keepsake Mill'), or like the river that flows 'out past the mill,/ Away down the valley,/ Away down the hill' ('Where Go the Boats?') – out 'A hundred miles or more' into foreign lands – to Babylon, Malabar, Africa, and Providence ('Pirate Story') – and like the swing that takes the child up high so he can look over the garden wall and 'see so wide' ('The Swing'), these poems reach beyond to places afar; they break through their limits and climb the cherry tree to look abroad ('Foreign Lands').

In these poems, the interiors of home do not isolate the convalescing child. Through his desire to be rid of what threatens to exile him the ailing child shapes the rooms and enclosed gardens so that they carry him to places beyond. As suggested in the previous chapter, the young Stevenson willingly and convincingly substitutes one object for another; he transforms the chair, the stairs, the bedclothes, the windows, and the flickering of the coals' embers into vessels of escape. The bed-room chairs stuffed with pillows become ships; a basket in the sun turns into a pirate's boat; the counterpane assumes its own topography of hills, dales, and plains, and the sheets merge into seas. At night, in his room, the child goes abroad, for his bed is a 'boat' and his room a 'port' ('My Bed is a Boat'). With his nurse's help he launches himself and steers across to unknown, distant places.

No longer need the child be envious of the birds who, once they leave their nest, fly high over his head and look at him below, 'Plodding and walking' ('Nest Eggs'), for within these transformed interiors he too may sail through the skies. In these spaces the stars glistening outside come through the window to shine inside his head ('Escape at Bedtime'). The enveloping and transforming darkness momentarily eradicates the opacity of the enclosing walls and breaks down the barriers between here and there. The half-light of night splinters the boundaries of time so that the rooms of home do not bind the child solely to the feverish now. In them the child may, as in 'Keepsake Mill', anticipate a time when he and his cousins will come back to meet again – he may look forward to remembrance. He may foresee kingdoms where he lives to name rather than to be named, and glance ahead to the time when he has 'grown to man's estate' ('Looking Forward') and guide his own vessel. These interiors, then, not only liberate the sick body from itself but also let it exempt itself from the ailing and extinguishing present. Most of all, though, the desire of the sick child to find release from himself creates situations in which the child identifies with other children and, in that way, becomes part of an ubiquitous body. Within that larger perspective, he can, for a while, forget or lose his fragility and, perhaps more significantly, be less alone, excluded, and strange.

As I have already discussed in the chapter on *A Child's Garden of Verses*, within these rooms is a larger landscape that collapses the distant into the contiguous and, simultaneously, expands the immediate into the distant. The child senses, although he cannot see them, the presence of other children whose activities are similar to his. These children may live away in the far East or in the West beyond the foam of the Atlantic Sea ('The Sun Travels'), and they may eat 'curious' food rather than 'proper meat' ('Foreign Children'); nevertheless, the sick child senses that they share a common physical rhythm: all 'dine at five' ('Foreign Lands'); like him but in an inverted pattern they go to bed, and at dawn they awake and dress ('The Sun Travels'). These parallels in their lives form the larger, more inclusive body so that all children, even when confined and alone, belong to an unseen, unconscious, yet animated inter-textuality of being that is theirs. Just as the sickly young Stevenson once looked out of the nursery window, through the darkness of the night, to see the lit windows where other sick 'little boys' were also waiting for the morning, the child in the verses finds comfort in inclusiveness. He knows there are others ready to receive and understand him so that, for instance, when he launches his boats, he is aware that little children 'A hundred miles or more' away will bring them into shore ('Where Go the Boats?').

Because of this sense of ubiquitousness, the potentially lonely and isolated 'I' of the poems' interiors frequently joins the more inclusive 'We'. In 'A Good Play', 'Pirate Story', 'Farewell to the Farm', 'Marching Song', 'Happy Thought', 'The Sun Travels', 'The Lamplighter', 'My Bed is a Boat', 'Keepsake Mill', and 'Picture-Books in Winter', the child attaches his being to others so that 'we' are afloat, 'we' swing upon the gate, 'we' march, 'we should all be happy as kings', 'we' play round the sunny gardens, 'we' are very lucky, and 'we' see how all things are. Perhaps the most telling example of this modulation is in 'My Bed is a Boat'. In this poem the child begins with the 'I', for he alone embarks on his boat, but in the last stanza he slips, unconsciously and momentarily, into the key of the companionable plural: 'All night across the dark we steer'. What has caused the young boy to move from the singular to the plural is the act of play through which the child transforms himself into something else.[44]

It is, of course, this metamorphosis that empowers the child in *A Child's Garden of Verses*. Like the shadow that follows or jumps ahead of the child, his sick body is almost always a silent, threatening presence among the verses' lines. However, within the context of the poems' transfigured interiors, the child is able to reach beyond himself and connect with others and join the ubiquitous body of childhood. Through play and fantasy, the child alters the rooms of home and releases the suffering 'I' from the fragility of itself and realizes the possibilities of a more encompassing and restorative 'we'. Stevenson's child, in a sense, brings to life one of the most vital experiences of interiority – the understanding that an interior does not exist for its own sake but, instead, for the desire of reaching something or going somewhere.[45]

ROOMS WITHOUT MIRRORS

In all these models of interiority, many of the familiar landmarks of the inside are visible: the windows, the doors, the staircases, and the fireplace. In none, though, is there the usual mirror – an absence that is significant since mirrors and looking glasses were considered an important fixture in the Victorian household. Unlike the genre paintings of nineteenth-century interiors that draw attention to a large framed mirror hanging over a fireplace, to oval mirrors in decorative frames, and to the fashionable convex mirrors displayed in more modest settings, Ruskin's, Pater's, and Stevenson's depictions of their early homes ignore this convention. The mirror's reflecting and revealing eye is notably absent, for the child in their texts does not require its integrating attendance – its way of digesting and making complete the area and contents of a room, its way of bringing interiors and exteriors together. (For example, in Joseph Clarke's *The Labourer's Welcome*, the small mirror hanging among the pictures reflects and frames the image of the returning husband as he walks through the cottage door. In this way the mirror mingles what is out of view – the exterior – with what is directly before the viewer's eyes inside the cottage.) In addition, from their perspective, the child has no need of the mirror's deflecting, interrupting images that comment upon the presence of something other than what is in view. And, most importantly, neither does their child require the mirror suspended above a mantelpiece or the looking glass hung inside its gilded frame to affirm his sense of belonging – to feel his own materiality. The looking-glass world is irrelevant. The child does not need to see its image in the mirror to gain a sense of totality, to understand, rightly or wrongly, a feeling of coherence, and especially to develop a sense of self that distinguishes it from others.

For these reasons the confirming, surveying, and integrating mirror is not a focal point in these autobiographical texts as it is in paintings like August Leopold Egg's *Past and Present, I* (1858), Charles Hunt's *My 'Macbeth'* (1863), or in Frederick Daniel Hardy's *Playing at Doctors* (1863). In these paintings the mirror, placed dead center, reveals how the various subjects relate to their interiors, to the outside, and to each other. The grand mirror in *My 'Macbeth'*, for instance, radiates like a halo around the artist, confirming and enclosing – safeguarding – his success. The small convex mirror in *Playing at Doctors* parallels the family's benevolence and with that the experience of belonging and inclusion. It overlooks the temporary untidiness of the children's play and in doing so emphasizes the unruffled security of home. And, of course, in *Past and Present I*, the mirror simultaneously unfolds the past and the future. Within its opulent frame the glass not only reveals what has been but also shows what is to be. Its reflected images lead to the open door and to emptiness – to a space devoid of objects and the security of home. Caught in adultery, the 'fallen' wife lies prostrate outside the mirror's surveillance – exiled from its field of vision and soon to be ostracized from her husband's society and the household in which the mirror hangs. Significantly, once she is exiled from home, no mirror confirms her space, for in the immediate sequence, *Past and Present II*, the mirror is darkened, and in the last painting of the series, *Past and Present III*, of course, no mirror appears for the wife no longer has a room to be in.

The childhood interiors of Ruskin, Pater, and Stevenson exclude the mirror because it is not needed either to confirm or exile those who inhabit what would have been caught in its field of reflection. The child in these interiors does not make a spectacle of the self – the self is not something to be seen. The disembodied, 'invisible' young Ruskin, for example, is not something to be looked at. On the contrary, as pointed out earlier, he is the one who does the looking. His eye, not the mirror's, is the mediator, the interpreter, the surveyor. Ruskin's child does not engage reflection; instead, with his own eye – the 'true eye' – he looks down into what lies before his field of vision, and absorbs the world through sight. Indeed, he overlooks the reflected image. For instance, when the young Ruskin watches his father shave, he observes his actual father and ignores the image in the shaving mirror that must have been there. He moves his attention, instead, from his father to the watercolor drawing that hangs above the dressing table and waits for his father to tell stories about the picture's subjects. He does not let the mirror trip him. Ruskin describes the moment:

I was particularly fond of watching him shave; and was always allowed to come into his room in the morning (under the one in which I am now writing), to be the motionless witness of that operation. Over his dressing-table hung one of his own water-colour drawings.... It represented Conway Castle, with its Frith, and, in the foreground, a cottage, a fisherman, and a boat at the water's edge.

When my father had finished shaving, he always told me a story about this picture.[46]

The reflected image promises no narrative for the curious child.

In his adolescent poetry and prose of the 1830s, Ruskin did occasionally speak of reflection; however, it is either to disparage the mirror or to engage a form of seeing that the ordinary mirror – the one that hangs in a room – does not permit. For instance, in 1837, when Ruskin was in residence at Christ Church and suffering from Adèle-Clotilde's refusal to return his ardor, he wrote a poem he entitled 'The Mirror'. In the poem Ruskin speaks of the mirror's inability to include her 'loveliness' within its frame. He himself plays no part on its reflecting surface. He stands outside as the spectator–surveyor who passes judgment on the looking glass and finds it guilty of inconstancy, for, unlike him, it has no memory with which to retain the 'living vision' of her beauty.[47] Its reflection is merely transitory. Other poems like 'On Skiddaw and Derwent Water' and a passage from *The Poetry of Architecture* also speak of reflection. In these texts lakes and small bodies of water become looking glasses through which to view the landscape. These are not, as John Dixon Hunt suggests, the Claude glass – the tinted convex mirrors carried by picturesque tourists[48] – for when Ruskin looks into the water's reflection, he does not limit himself to what images the surface reveals, nor does he turn his back (as was the practice of those holding the Claude glass) on what he is staring into. Instead, especially in *The Poetry of Architecture*, he lets the images reflected in the water draw his eye down to what is underneath and fall unfathomably into 'the blue sky'.[49] In a sense, this natural mirror creates an illusion; it draws the eye and, with it, Ruskin's being inside; it does not leave his body standing, separated and gazing. The image is no longer a reflected one. Ruskin quickly bypasses that more superficial state so that his eye may actually enter the landscape and be a part of its immediacy. So intent is Ruskin to rid himself of the idea of mirror, in fact, that in the passage from *The Poetry of Architecture*, he instructs his reader to eradicate the 'edge' of the water – to keep it out of sight. Ruskin does not want to think of the conventional mirror; at this moment he does not want a framed reflection.

Pater's Florian also inhabits a nonreflecting space. He is neither a spectacle to be looked at nor a participant in a world that makes a spectacle of what is in it. He knows images not through their reflection but by the way the visual experiences interpenetrate with his body. The image for Pater's child, therefore, is not so much to be seen as it is to be felt. It does not dwell, exclusively, outside of his body, merely to be observed, for, almost compulsively, the child opens his arms to gather, to hold, and to take in to himself what he sees. Like the young Florian who collects the hawthorne blossoms, the child brings these images close to his body. When he touches their brilliance, he transforms what before was a purely visual moment into a haptic experience, the sensations of which work their way into the nature of his being.

Stevenson's child displays yet another form of the unreflected image. His young boy looks out; others do not look back at him. He is not a spectacle (the lamplighter goes about his task and ignores the child standing at the window). In addition, he is a child who resides somewhere beyond the conventional visual field. In the half-light of his evenings, in the darkness of his nights, and in the metamorphic fantasies of his play, the reflecting images of mirrors are irrelevant. Shadows overwhelm them and so does a circumference of experience and distance too large for the confining, duplicating arena of the looking glass. Even when, in *A Child's Garden of Verses*, the young boy looks down into the 'Looking-Glass River', it is not his disappearing reflection in the darkening water that arrests him. When the ripples disturb the smooth surface and the water turns black, the child does not bemoan the loss of his image; instead, he laments the slipping away of an opportunity to see down into the river's depths and imagine himself there, united with its mysteries. He desires to look through, not into, the looking glass – to engage the less visible. He wants to see and be beyond what is given.

Because of their disregard for the conventionally reflected image, these children do not participate in the mirror's community that necessarily separates the self from itself and imposes a moment of estrangement or divergence – what is commonly called 'otherness'. In Ruskin's, Pater's, and Stevenson's texts, the child communes primarily with himself. Whatever 'otherness' exists, whether in the form of a mirror image or in the form of other people, does not take him away from himself nor cause him to question his identity. On the contrary, the child and his body are connected in various ways to each other and to what surrounds them. Stevenson's child might for a minute feel isolated and want Leerie, the lamplighter, to pause and look at him standing in the window, but, on the whole, he, like Ruskin's and Pater's child, lives in the community of his own mind and inside the frame of his own body. The consequence is that what might, as in a reflected image, be always 'over there' is not; it is also 'here', attached in some way to the child. The young Ruskin, secure and conceited, 'occupies the universe' and knows he is its 'central point'.[50] Only his eyes mediate between the inside and the outside; they are the intermediary organ that binds interiors and exteriors – they contract space. Through their censorship and acuity, they eradicate what otherwise could be disturbing distinctions between the child's sense of himself and his surroundings. Led by his eye and his ear the child easily experiences the intertextuality of the inside and the outside. There is, in Ruskin's experience, a continuous bond between his mind and 'the world that is not himself'.[51]

This same sort of interconnectedness is visible even in some of the most alienating moments of Ruskin's adolescence. When Ruskin was separated from Adèle-Clotilde and was worried about his being 'here' and her being 'there' in a convent school in Chelmsford, he finds comfort by looking at the sky that he knows also stretches over the city where she resides and by reminding himself that, shut up in the school, she is invisible to any one else.[52] In this way his eyes close the distance between what is absent and present; furthermore, they rid his mind of a lurking otherness. He can still include her in his inner space.

Pater's Florian also does not reside within a world irretrievably disrupted by its otherness. Florian does not step back to look at himself, for he is too entwined in the continuous weaving of his own sensations that connect and harmonize with his surroundings. Threads of what lie outside and inside continuously intermingle to bind the self. This continuous overlapping of his bodily sensations with what lies outside of himself smudges experience so that, ultimately, no fissures separate him from what otherwise would be alien; and the boy in Stevenson's verses because he attaches himself to what exists beyond the immediate, succeeds in smearing many of the boundaries that usually separate the 'there' from the 'here', and the introspective from the visual self. The reflexive 'I' is not necessarily a factor in any of these children's early lives.

For these young subjects, then, the looking-glass world seems irrelevant. Contrary to what theorists like Henri Wallon, Jacques Lacan, and Maurice Merleau-Ponty suggest, for these children, the mirror, whether real or metaphoric/symbolic, is not the necessary attendant to their sense of identity and relation.[53] Without becoming unnecessarily involved in the intricacies of these theories, it is sufficient to point out that Ruskin, Pater, and Stevenson are not, for instance, participants in Lacan's mirror phase; their sense of their own unity and of being at one with their surroundings does not depend upon the illusory wholeness that the mirror image initially projects or allows. In addition, they do not require the mirror to experience a discrete separation from others. The looking glass does not catch the young Ruskin, Pater, and Stevenson and cause them to turn round and engage the disturbing world of objectification. Nor does the mirror cause these children to cope with what Merleau-Ponty terms 'the unsuspected isolation' that reveals itself when the child suddenly notices two subjects facing each other in the reflection.[54] For them, consequently, the subsequent work to reclaim a wholeness that the reflected image has divided is irrelevant. Their embeddedness in themselves and their interiors obviates that necessity. In their youth, because they are not spectators of themselves, the mirror is not a factor in their relationship with themselves, their rooms, and with others around them. It is simply not present.

It is only when Ruskin, Pater, and Stevenson have become adults and left behind the rooms of their childhood that the specter of the mirror appears and the discrepancies of experience penetrate. Interiors and exteriors separate, and the body, even though it may share the same memory with its childhood self, requires a mirror image of itself. Now, like Stevenson's Mr Hyde, the individual must consult the mirror to look at himself and see who he is. Ruskin, Pater, and Stevenson must pick up the looking glass of their autobiographical texts in an attempt to re-integrate or reclaim themselves. They must use the mirror as a mediator and a translator. Ruskin, anxious, disoriented by attacks of madness, saddened, partially puzzled by the realization that no one outside of himself either parallels or complements his sensibility, and finding himself to be, in his own words, more 'curious' than he thought, turns to the mirror of his text for affirmation.[55] He leaves the arena of the 'subjective me' and enters the framed, self-conscious space of the 'specular I'. No longer is he the *camera lucida* – the lens or the eye. In *Praeterita* he is now the observed. Looking at the past, he stands outside of himself and the experience of belonging to its rooms. Otherness diffuses what once had been central. Ruskin had, of course, always felt alienated. Jeffrey L. Spear in *Dreams of an English Eden* speaks of him as 'The Outsider' – how Ruskin was always, in one form or an other, out of place. The following passage from *Praeterita* is, therefore, typical:

> I used to fancy that everybody would like clouds and rocks as well as I did, if once told to look at them; whereas, after fifty years of trial, I find that is not so, even in modern days; having long ago known that, in ancient ones, the clouds and mountains which have been life to me, were mere inconvenience and horror to most of mankind.[56]

A similar sense of alienation presses upon Pater. Overwhelmed by feelings of fragmentation, sensitive to the divisiveness emerging from the succession of selves[57] that never seem to catch up to one another, that rarely overlap, but leap ahead, and anxious that the thickening walls of experience are closing in around him – segregating him from the sensual world like Emerald Uthwart imprisoned in his cathedral school – he too turns to the mirror of the autobiographical text to arrest what is fleeting and, perhaps, for a while, to draw closer to what is now an otherness. Pater creates the mirror of his imaginary portraits, the fictions of which acknowledge the distance he desires to overcome and which objectify his sense of having become a spectator of himself.[58] Through the imaginary, semi-autobiographical portrait of Florian, Pater attempts to return, as an adult, to the affirming harmony of childhood. As if anticipating Gaston Bachelard, who, in *The Poetics of Reverie: Childhood, Language, and the Cosmos*, suggests that reverie enables one to re-enter the childhood that has been abducted by the shadows and forgetfulness of experience, Pater, through his dreams, comes through from the back of the looking glass (the opposite of what Alice does[59]), into the rooms of his childhood and turns to look through the mirror of his text at what had been there. Like Leonardo da Vinci in Rome (*The Renaissance*), he brings his former, more cohesive self back to life by surrounding his subject with mirrors (the reflecting, interpenetrating style of 'The Child in the House') that reveal all sides of the young Florian. And through this three-dimensionality, like the sculptors in the School of Giorgione, he sets his subject into 'instantaneous motion'. He discovers, as he explains in his essay on the School, 'some momentary conjunction of mirrors and polished armour and still water, by which all sides of a solid image are exhibited at once'.[60] In a sense, Pater's semi-autobiographical portraits also recall the procession (in *Marius the Epicurean*) in which mirror-bearers, carrying large mirrors of beaten brass and silver, follow the image of the goddess Iris. They hold the mirrors at an angle so that the goddess's image and the faces of the worshippers lined up in the street advance toward one another.[61] Like these ritual mirrors, the text brings Pater closer to his ideal – it lets him approach the icon of his childhood.

Even the adult Stevenson, who endeavored to stay within the sphere of his childhood, must resort to the mirror of his autobiographical text. He must create the looking glass of his poems through which he tries to set his eyes on the child reflected in their frame and replicate what once had been his playful world. Just as one used to hold a mirror under the nostrils of a failing life, Stevenson, like Ruskin and Pater, places his verses under the breath of memory in order to reveal the evaporating moments of the past and make visible to others what is present to none but his own remembrance.

Although these textual mirrors function as sanctuaries from forgetfulness, they are imperfect and inadequate, for just as nostalgia, paradoxically through its experience of longing, distances a person from what he or she desires, the mirror separates the subject from its own reflection. These texts cannot replicate the cohesiveness of childhood. Rather than re-integrate the self, they expose the gaps between what is and what was or between what is and what should be. They surrender to the fact that the child has grown up and gone away.[62] Furthermore, like mirrors, these texts hold their images within a frame that exiles the peripheral or what connects the image to its surroundings. The mirror segregates rather than integrates. In this way, of course, its images contradict the cohesiveness that the one who holds up the mirror desires. Allowing one image at a time, the looking glass fails to admit the blending of the one into the other – the continuous overlapping that is part of the past's becoming.

Given the distinctive constitution of Ruskin's, Pater's, and Stevenson's childhood, however, the principal failing of the text as mirror is that it is compelled to make visible, through language, what had been invisible for them. This is where the poignant discrepancy lies, for, as I have previously suggested, it was the un-self-conscious invisibility of the bodily experience that was distinguishing and that, for them, created the wholeness – the sense of completeness and possibility – that has subsequently split into the fragments and objects of the spectral, adult self. For Ruskin, this invisibility was, of course, the bodilessness that could see; for Pater it was the body that never saw itself but lived in its sensations, and for Stevenson it was the unseen presence of the 'we' – the larger imperceptible body of which he once imagined himself a part. Now all of this invisibility must be eclipsed by the reflected image; it must be objectified through the written word. Ruskin, Pater, and Stevenson have now to look at themselves. Yet, what choice is there, for outside the less public and tangible alternatives of reverie and longing, the textual mirror is the one authoritative space left. Within its boundaries, Ruskin, Pater, and Stevenson attempt to recapture what is lost and bring back from exile the interiors of home – the ultimate authoritative spaces.

Full of longing, Ruskin undertakes his autobiography. As if trying to replicate the moments when, after a long trip abroad, he would first catch sight again of Herne Hill and feel 'the sick thrill of pleasure' run 'through all the brain and heart',[63] sixty-two years later, he re-enters, through his writing, the sacred and comfortable interiors of his early years. To compose much of *Praeterita* he returned physically to the nursery of Herne Hill and wrote its Preface on 10 May 1885, the day that would have been his father's hundredth birthday. Mainly, though, he traveled toward home by rereading himself, by looking again at his past and by going over, sorting, and discarding old journals and letters. As in *Las Meninas* these mirrors restored visibility to that which had been out of view.[64] This reviewing, however, had little to do with the narcissism that a cartoonist in a 18 December 1880 issue of *Punch* found in Ruskin's continual references to himself ('Mr Narcissus Ruskin'). This activity reflected his despair, for the more the darkness of his manic episodes threatened to envelop him, the more he desired the relative peace of reflection and needed to re-enter the interiors of the past. Outside of these mirrors' frames stalked that which threatened to destroy him. The moments that he had hoped to keep invisible – out of sight – might suddenly make themselves visible. Significantly, Ruskin's first attack of madness (in 1878) was marked by terrifying delusions in which 'the Evil One' in the form of a large black cat sprang at him from behind a mirror and 'commanded him to commit some fearful wrong which he was powerless to resist'.[65] At the same time, then, that the retrospective mirror was offering Ruskin a safe itinerary, it

was also taking its revenge for his selectivity and reminding him
that although he might try to evade the painful and disturbing
events of his life, he might still unexpectedly come face to face
with their visibility – outside the mirror's frame.

Throughout his imaginary portraits, Pater, like Marius who leaves
home only to seek to regain it, travels towards its sanctuary. Influ-
enced by what he calls somewhere 'the enchanted distance fallacy',
Pater idealizes home.[66] Home becomes the fixed point of time within
the bewildering flux of the disappearing present. In a sense, home
actualizes the myth of unity that Pater explores in his The Renaissance, for within its rooms the child lives less separated from himself.
He is, perhaps, his own twin, and in being so brings to life the
introductory fable of Amis and Amile – the two friends whose
inward similitude binds them inseparably. Moreover, within these
early interiors, the child personifies the union between matter and
form that Pater searches for in poetry and in painting and which he
finds in music. Like this ideal, the child's constituent elements are
welded together – they are almost indistinguishable. The inward
and the outward require no translation, for the intermingling of the
inside and the outside creates a fabric of boyhood that folds
the various elements together. In this manner the child personifies
the modulated union of landscape and person that Pater finds so
attractive in the Venetian painters and comes close to the condition
of music.[67]

Now, though, about thirty years later, Pater, excluded from the
harmony of childhood, must translate the more idyllic past into
the perpetual flight of the present by tilting the mirror and catching
the reflected image with his words. He has no alternative. And
neither does the exiled Stevenson. Finding himself separated from
what had been an unconscious and integral part of him and experi-
encing the physical/psychical distance between him and home, Stevenson creates small mirrors out of each verse and, for a moment,
presses close to their reflective surfaces. The poems reveal his
longing to be back inside in the child's half-light of play and, once
more, to dwell among its transparent walls. But, because of the
mirror, instead of being the subject, he must now be the one who
perceives. Visibility replaces being; the material, the unconscious.
As the poet he must step outside the child's room and illuminate
what before he had no need to see. The isolation in the poems is,
perhaps, not the child's but that of the solitary figure who was once
a child.

The desire to recover – to resurrect – the child within the rooms of home impels these autobiographical texts. As if soliciting the aid of the Medusa's head uncovered nearby Marius's childhood villa, Ruskin, Pater, and Stevenson attempt to revivify what is lost. Like Asclepias who with two phials of Medusa's blood (drawn from the veins of her left side) raised the dead, they, with their ink, resurrect the past. But Medusa's petrifying gaze cannot destroy them, for the text's deflecting mirror protects them from an unmediated confrontation with their former selves.[68] Perhaps, after all, there was no need in a period before a 'fit of craze' for Ruskin to crush the head of a viper that had just crossed his path and to announce that he had obliterated for himself 'the last lock of Medusa's hair'.[69] Perseus's shining shield had already done the deed.

Paradoxically, then, in the end, the distorting, segregating, alienating mirror image saves Ruskin, Pater, and Stevenson. Like nostalgia itself, this mirror keeps them away from a direct sighting of the past, and, through that act, prevents what lives in their memory from dying. Their autobiographical texts are examples of how longing keeps the past malleable and alive. Their mirrors urge the eye away from the stare of the direct experience that hardens, stultifies, and even destroys its subject (recall the myth of Orpheus). The only way, then, to try and get back into these interiors that had no mirrors is to add one later, walk back with it through the rooms of childhood, and attempt to blend into its reflection.

Notes

1.   Their orientation anticipates those like Maurice Merleau-Ponty who argue that it is not through thought, absented from body, that one knows oneself and one's surroundings, but through one's 'bodily situation' – that one is conscious through the body's position in space. See M. Merleau-Ponty, *The Primacy of Perception*, ed. J. M. Edie (Evanston, Illinois: Northwestern University Press, 1964) p. 5. See also M. Proust, *Remembrance of Things Past*, trans. C.K. Scott Moncrieff and T. Kilmartin, I (London: Penguin Books, 1988) p. 6. Their point of view also looks forward to twentieth-century theorists, like Kent Bloomer, Charles W. Moore, and Robert J. Yudell, who insist that one measures and orders the world out from one's own body, that the body is in constant dialogue with the buildings surrounding it. See, for instance, K.C. Bloomer and C.W. Moore, *Body, Memory, and Architecture* (New Haven: Yale University Press, 1978) p. 57. It is worth noting that Ruskin's, Pater's, and Stevenson's sensitivity to the rela-

tionship of their bodies to their surroundings might in some way echo the emphasis placed upon the child's body in nineteenth-century guides on raising a child. For a discussion of this phenomenon see C. Steedman, *Strange Dislocations: Childhood and the Idea of Human Interiority, 1780–1930* (Cambridge, MA: Harvard University Press, 1995).

2. Maurice Merleau-Ponty writes:

> The painter 'takes his body with him', says Valéry. Indeed we cannot imagine how a *mind* could paint. It is by lending his body to the world that the artist changes the world into paintings. To understand these transubstantiations we must go back to the working, actual body... that body which is an intertwining of vision and movement.

See Merleau-Ponty, *The Primacy of Perception*, p. 162.

3. It is interesting to note that when Ruskin was discussing the art of landscape painting, he suggested that if a place is to be realized, it needs to include the figure that inhabits it. Even if the body is not completely in sight, one needs the sense of it. See E. T. Cook and A. Wedderburn, eds, *The Complete Works of John Ruskin*, V (London: George Allen, 1903) pp. 255–6.

    Ruskin's, Pater's, and Stevenson's depiction of their childhood rooms has little in common with the cupboard doll houses the Dutch once carried with them so that they might open the cupboard's doors to reveal, in miniature, the contents of their home: its wall coverings and furnishings, its paintings, utensils, and china figurines. See W. Rybczynski, *Home: A Short History of an Idea* (New York: Penguin Books, 1987) p. 62.

4. In *Praeterita* Ruskin writes: 'I am content to seep out of the way of what better things I can recollect at this time, into the smallest possible size of dust heap, and wish the Dustman Oblivion good clearance of them.' See J. Ruskin, *Praeterita: The Autobiography of John Ruskin*, introd. K. Clark (Oxford: Oxford University Press, 1989) p. 214.

5. Ruskin, *Praeterita: The Autobiography of John Ruskin*, pp. 12, 50.

6. Ibid., pp. 34, 7.

7. S. Emerson, *Ruskin: The Genius of Invention* (Cambridge: Cambridge University Press, 1993) p. 18.

8. Ruskin, *Praeterita: The Autobiography of John Ruskin*, p. 28.

9. In response to Ruskin's memory of his uneventful, quiet, and protected childhood, Tim Hilton remarks: 'This is nonsense: there was no such society in Herne Hill. The visitors who did come to Herne Hill were numerous, and they were more interesting. John James's diaries show that he entertained practically every night, including Sundays.' See T. Hilton, *John Ruskin: The Early Years. 1819–1859* (New Haven: Yale University Press, 1985) p. 15.

10. In *Praeterita* Ruskin does offer quite lively portraits of his father's business partners. However, these portraits stand outside the boundaries of home. Ruskin does not place them inside his rooms; he places

them, instead, within the context of his father's small counting-house in East London or in the interiors of their own estates. See Ruskin, *Praeterita: The Autobiography of John Ruskin*, pp. 17–24.

11. Ibid., p. 62.
12. Ibid., pp. 287, 347.
13. Part of the 'awkwardness' that Ruskin experienced during this period of his life was because of the tensions between him and his parents. He was, for instance, questioning his mother's evangelical beliefs and rebelling against his father's mercantile world.
14. Ruskin, *Praeterita: The Autobiography of John Ruskin*, p. 348.
15. Many critics have remarked upon the importance that Ruskin attached to the act of seeing. Elizabeth Helsinger has fully explored this theme. Commenting upon *Praeterita*, she remarks that 'Seeing is an end itself in *Praeterita*, needing no goal and no termination. The sensibility revealed through the *Praeterita* descriptions is not changed by what it sees; it *is* what it sees.' See E. Helsinger, *Ruskin and the Art of the Beholder* (Cambridge, MA: Harvard University Press, 1982) p. 40. Another critic, Robert Hewison quotes a revealing passage in which Ruskin makes quite clear the significance he attaches to the act of seeing: 'the greatest thing a human soul ever does in this world is to *see* something, and tell what it *saw* in a plain way. Hundreds of people can talk for one who can think, but thousands can think for one who can see.' See R. Hewison, *John Ruskin: The Argument of the Eye* (Princeton: Princeton University Press, 1975). See also J. D. Rosenberg, *The Darkening Glass: A Portrait of Ruskin's Genius* (New York: Columbia University Press, 1961) pp. 220–1. Many critics, like George L. Hersey, think of Ruskin as an optical thinker – an intense starer at himself and the world. See G. L. Hersey, 'Ruskin as an Optical Thinker', *The Ruskin Polygon: Essays and the Imagination of John Ruskin*, eds J. D. Hunt and F. M. Holland (Manchester: Manchester University Press, 1982) p. 44. It is worth adding that in *Praeterita*, Ruskin speaks of traveling with his family and says: 'We did not travel for adventures, nor for company, but to see with our eyes.' See Ruskin, *Praeterita: The Autobiography of John Ruskin*, p. 107.
16. J. D. Hunt, *The Wider Sea: A Life of John Ruskin* (London: J. M. Dent, 1982) p. 25.
17. Ruskin, *Praeterita: The Autobiography of John Ruskin*, p. 38.
18. It is interesting to note that Martin Jay suggests that one order of seeing took place when people, fearing St. Augustine's condemnation of 'ocular desire', created a 'disincarnated, absolute eye' that is separated from the bodies of the painter and the viewer. See M. Jay, 'Scopic Regimes of Modernity', *Modernity and Identity* (Oxford: Basil Blackwell, 1992) p. 181. I suggest, though, that Ruskin did not intend to de-eroticize the visual order in this manner, for he keenly felt through his eyes.
19. Ruskin, *Praeterita: The Autobiography of John Ruskin*, p. 350. Helsinger suggests that Ruskin could not continue writing *Praeterita* when he could 'no longer return through memory and his own words to recreate sights'. See Helsinger, *Ruskin and the Art of the Beholder*, p.

40. The implication is that, as in the death of Henry Dart, when vision closes so does the vitality and the force of life.

20. Ruskin, *Praeterita: The Autobiography of John Ruskin*, p. 23.
21. Ibid., p. 50.
22. Ibid., p. 146.
23. Ibid., p. 156.
24. Ibid., pp. 155–6.
25. Ibid., pp. 125–6.
26. Notice the use of the first person plural in the following passage from *Praeterita*:

> The dark pools of Tay, which have led me into this boasting, were under the high bank at the head of the North Inch, – the path above them being seldom traversed by us children unless at harvest time, when we used to go gleaning in the fields beyond; Jessie and I afterward grinding our corn in the kitchen pepper-mill, and kneading and toasting for ourselves cakes of pepper bread, of quite unpurchaseable quality.

Ibid., p. 59.
27. Ibid., p. 61.
28. Harold Bloom is one of several critics to remark that Pater 'was kindled by the exaltation of seeing' – that he was the 'prophet of the eye'. See H. Bloom, ed., *Modern Critical Views: Walter Pater* (New York: Chelsea, 1985) p. 5.
29. W. E. Buckler, ed., *Walter Pater: Three Major Texts* (New York: New York University Press, 1986) p. 224.
30. Ibid., p. 225.
31. Ibid., p. 229.
32. In her study of interiors, Philippa Tristram lists examples of the inter-relation between people and houses, specifically the association between the body and the interior. See P. Tristram, *Living Space in Fact and Fiction* (London: Routledge, 1989) pp. 238–9.
33. Buckler, *Walter Pater: Three Major Texts*, p. 232.
34. Ibid., p. 234.
35. Ibid., p. 344.
36. Ibid., p. 345.
37. Among others, F. C. McGrath points out that 'the title itself ('The Child in the House') suggests the fusion or interpenetration of the thinking child with his physical habitat'. See F. C. McGrath, *The Sensible Spirit: Walter Pater and the Modernist Paradigm* (Tampa: University of South Florida Press, 1986) pp. 168–9.
38. P. Meisel, 'The Chemistry of the Crystal', *Modern Critical Views: Walter Pater*, ed. H. Bloom, pp. 123–4.
39. See, for example, W. H. Pater, *The Renaissance*, introd. L. Evans (Chicago: Academy, 1978) p. 235, and W. H. Pater, *Marius the Epicurean: His Sensation and Ideas*, ed. I. Small (Oxford: Oxford University Press, 1986) p. 84.
40. Pater, *Marius the Epicurean: His Sensation and Ideas*, p. 194.

41.   J. Calder, *Robert Stevenson: A Life Study* (New York: Oxford University Press, 1980) p. 42.
42.   See D. Daiches, *Robert Louis Stevenson and his World* (London: Thames and Hudson, 1973) p. 10.
43.   J. Calder, ed., *Robert Louis Stevenson: A Critical Celebration* (Totowa, NJ: Barnes & Noble, 1980) p. 19.
44.   For a discussion of the importance of play for Stevenson, see chapter three and see his essay 'Child's Play' in *Virginibus Puerisque*.
45.   For a discussion of this principle, see M. Tafuri, *The Sphere and the Labyrinth: Avant-Garde and Architecture from Piranesi to the 1970s*, trans. P. d'Acierno and R. Connolly (Cambridge, MA: MIT Press, 1987).
46.   Ruskin, *Praeterita: The Autobiography of John Ruskin*, pp. 28–9.
47.   Cook and Wedderburn, *The Complete Works of John Ruskin*, II, p. 20.
48.   Bloom, *John Ruskin* (New York: Chelsea, 1986) p. 63.
49.   Cook and Wedderburn, *The Complete Works of John Ruskin*, I, p. 90.
50.   Ruskin, *Praeterita: The Autobiography of John Ruskin*, p. 27.
51.   Emerson, *Ruskin: The Genius of Invention*, p. 40.
52.   Ruskin, *Praeterita: The Autobiography of John Ruskin*, p. 213.
53.   See, for instance, 'The Child's Relations with Others' in Merleau-Ponty, *The Primacy of Perception*. See also J. Lacan, *Écrits: A Selection*, trans. A. Sheridan (New York: W. W. Norton, 1977) and H. Wallon, 'La maladresse', *Journal de Psychologie Normal*. XXV (1928). For a discussion of Lacan's sense of the mirror phase, see M. Sarup, *Jacques Lacan* (Toronto: University of Toronto Press, 1992).
54.   Merleau-Ponty, *The Primacy of Perception*, p. 119.
55.   Ruskin, *Praeterita: The Autobiography of John Ruskin*, p. 221. As if thinking of the image of the mirror, John D. Rosenberg writes: 'To use his own phrase, *Praeterita* describes the effect on his own mind of meeting himself, by turning back, face to face.' See Rosenberg, *The Darkening Glass: A Portrait of Ruskin's Genius*, p. 218.
56.   Ruskin, *Praeterita: The Autobiography of John Ruskin*, p. 221.
57.   Gerald Monsman observes that Pater's sense of the perpetual flux creates a 'circle of self' that 'has no definite boundary that endures through time; moment by moment he changes. Identity, temporalized in this fashion, consists in a succession of selves, each of which merely contains a "relic" of the self that preceded it.' See G. Monsman, *Walter Pater's Art of Autobiography* (New Haven: Yale University Press, 1980) p. 19.
58.   Monsman observes:

> Pater's overriding strategy is to reveal himself covertly by deploying through critical or fictionalized critical utterances 'a self not himself'. The reflexive text is thus a mirror in which Pater causes his own image, inscribed within the textual apparatus, to turn back upon the image of his hero and his hero's age – which, then, once again, turns back upon the author's life.

See Monsman, *Walter Pater's Art of Autobiography*, p. 7.

59. It is interesting to note that in 1894 Pater had 'The Child in the House' privately printed so it could be sold at 'a summer fête at which a performance of *Alice in Wonderland* was to be given in the Worcester College gardens'. Ibid., p. 10.
60. Pater, *The Renaissance*, p. 118.
61. Pater, *Marius the Epicurean: His Sensations and Ideas*, p. 61.
62. See Steedman, *Strange Dislocations: Childhood and the Idea of Human Interiority, 1780–1930*, p. 170.
63. Ruskin, *Praeterita: The Autobiography of John Ruskin*, p. 124.
64. See M. Foucault, *The Order of Things: An Archaeology of the Human Sciences* (New York: Vintage Books, 1973) p. 8.
65. See Rosenberg, *The Darkening Glass: A Portrait of Ruskin's Genius*, p. 113.
66. A number of critics speak of Pater's attitude toward the sanctuary of home. See, for instance, I. Fletcher, *Walter Pater* (London: Longman, 1959) p. 6 and Meisel, 'The Chemistry of the Crystal', p. 124.
67. Pater, *The Renaissance*, p. 153.
68. For discussions of Pater's use of Medusa, see Bloom, *Modern Critical Views: Walter Pater*, p. 7. See also Monsman, *Walter Pater's Art of Autobiography*, p. 59. For a full discussion about the figure of Medusa, see T. Siebers, *The Mirror of Medusa* (Berkeley: University of California Press, 1983).
69. Hunt, *The Wider Sea: A Life of John Ruskin*, pp. 397–8.

Part III
The Idea of Recollection

In explaining causes of Nostalgia, the reason to be considered of near and remote sources, I shall enumerate unusual things, according as I conceive the one to flow from and be derived from the other. And indeed I consider the nearest to be the quite continuous vibration of animal spirits through those fibers of the middle brain in which impressed traces of ideas of the Fatherland still cling. Moreover, I believe that these traces are actually impressed more vigorously by frequent contemplations of the Fatherland, and from an image of it, so that the animal spirits follow continuously from thence by the same impulse and thus raise up constantly the conscious mind toward considering the image of the Fatherland.

From Johannes Hofer, *Medical Dissertation on Nostalgia or Homesickness*,
1688

7

R.L. Stevenson and the Idea of Recollection

So shall this book wax like unto a well
Fairy with mirrored flowers about the brim,
Or like some tarn that eager curlews skim,
Glassing the sallow upland or brown fell;
And so as men go down into a dell
(Weary of noon) to find relief and shade,
When on the uneasy sickbed we are laid
We shall go down into thy book, and tell
The leaves, one blank, to build again for us
Old Summer dead and ruined, and the time
Of later autumn with the corn in stook.
So shalt thou stint the meagre winter thus
Of his projected triumph, and the rim
Shall melt before the sunshine in thy book.

R. L. Stevenson, 'Lines to be Sent with the
Present of a Sketch Book'

When writers reach toward events and places from their past, they, of course, inevitably reveal their attachment to recollection. Among those who are more than usually conscious of this indispensable companion is Robert Louis Stevenson who, because of his sensitivity to the subject, frequently punctuated his nostalgic passages with commentaries on the nature of remembrance. His remarks allow one not only to reflect upon the moment of recollection but also to become more aware of its visual elements – to notice the optical metaphors that help structure the experience of it. Stevenson's comments remind one that recollection is not merely a looking back; it is also a commitment to a particular way of seeing. With this principle in mind, it is helpful first to focus upon Stevenson's visual orientation before moving on to discuss his thoughts about the act and the character of recollection.

WITH REVERTED EYES

Throughout his life, Stevenson scanned experience with reverted eyes. His passion for the past captured his attention so that he often stared at the present through the glass of memory. As if still studying the stationer's window where, on Saturday mornings, he and his nurse Cummy attempted to read, through the pictures, the 'forbidden' sequels to the stories in *Cassell's Family Papers*,[1] Stevenson at a later time continued to recapture and, sometimes, extend the 'golden moments' and places of his youth by looking at the remembered images displayed within his mind's eye. These pictures brought him closer to the life he had left behind. They helped him re-embody the absence and break the silence of the glass that stood between him and his earlier years. Consequently, the recalled sight of Miss Broddie, a seamstress who had once come to the Edinburgh house and sewn with Cummy, 'sitting with her leg crossed in a masculine manner; and swinging her foot emphatically' made audible the 'thin perpetual shrill' voice of her gossiping,[2] and, thereby, nearly forty years later (7 December 1893), breathed life into a detail and resuscitated a moment belonging to an earlier time.

Although it recalls only a fragmentary moment in his life, this example of Stevenson's retrieving and concentrating upon an image is significant, for it reflects the importance the visual experience always had for him. In his autobiographical pieces, Stevenson frequently comments upon the fact that as a young boy, he was more than usually attracted to images. He remembers, for instance, that he once coveted the 'gaudily coloured' Indian pictures hanging in his grandfather's study and, as a result, learned to recite a psalm well, hoping that Dr Balfour might reward his efforts with one of them ('The Manse'); and he recalls that during every Sunday of his childhood, he studied 'enchanting prints, full of wood and field and mediaeval landscapes'. These were the prints 'for imagination to go a-travelling in'.[3] Like many young people, he wandered not only into the pictures he looked at but also into those he drew. Drawing absorbed his attention and occasionally served to relieve the distress accompanying his bad health. Consequently, just as recollected images were eventually to protect him from the isolation of exile and were later to ease the discomfort of his chronic illness, his sketching shielded him from the isolation and inactivity that inevitably attended the periods of sickness and recovery that interrupted his childhood.[4] Through these pictures, he turned the 'idle seasons' which 'hung most heavily' upon his youthful head into 'the most pleasant hours'[5] so that when he was with his mother in Torquay for his health (2 April 1865), he was able to reassure his father that, 'I sketch allways [*sic*] when we're out, so there's no danger of my being dull.'[6]

In these early years, though, sketching was more than an antidote for difficulty; it was also a necessary accompaniment to his writing – image was the way to and through the word and it was a significant means of recording a moment gone by. When he was six, for instance, Stevenson composed a *History of Moses* not only by dictating the words to his mother but also by drawing watercolor sketches that brought his narrative to life. And a few years later when he was temporarily away from home, he sent his parents letters to which he added illustrations that were as much a part of his text as the words themselves. For example, from Mentone where he had gone for a cure, he sent his father letters in which he included pen-and-ink sketches of his mother and various guests at their hotel. And at the age of twelve, when he was an unhappy border at Burlington Lodge Academy (at Spring Grove, Isleworth, near London), he appended drawings to his notes home. One is of students (one of whom is homesick) playing a 'Game of Dibbs'[7] and the other is of what seems to be a rugby match or a soccer game (Figures 7 & 8). In the latter picture, the stick figures of the distant boys rushing over the playing fields cluster like miniature letters or hieroglyphs to give voice to the young Stevenson's moment of exclusion.[8]

These images were part of what Stevenson referred to as 'the visionary state' that delineated his childhood.[9] Alone or together with his cousin Robert, he colored pictures, painted, drew, and cut out figures for the pasteboard theaters he purchased at a local stationer's shop. He created narratives and ruled imagined countries that he brought to life by drawing maps and by eagerly dressing up to play his part in these kingdoms' histories. Through these images he realized the invisible, yet compelling, matter of his fantasies. Later in adolescence, Stevenson carried on the spirit of this activity by designing and producing magazines. He created *The Sunbeam Magazine* (1866), 'an illustrated Miscellany of Fact, Fiction, and Fun', for which he not only wrote the serials and articles but also painted lively illustrations. His Cruikshank-Skelt-like watercolor drawings for 'The Banker's Ward' and the sequel drawings he planned for volumes two and three are examples of how eager he was to visualize his characters and situations (Figure 9: *Sudden and*

Awful Catastrophe. Disappearance of Snooks). These brightly rendered
and prominently placed illustrations let Stevenson give voice to the
progress of his story. These images realized what was in his mind's
eye and released the words that followed. They functioned like the
sketches that had given voice to his *History of Moses*, and they served
like the drawings he made in the summer of 1859, when he and his
family took a short trip to Perthshire, that were later to help him
compose an account of his travels to Perth, Dundee, and Crieff
('Travels in Perthshire').

   This attraction to images was not only a part of Stevenson's
impulse to let pictures actualize his words but also an expression
of his desire to exhibit the unseen and to uncover, as he once wrote
to his father, 'something I have not measured, or, having measured,
have not noted, or having noted, cannot find.'[10] As a young man, for
instance, when traveling by steamer with his father to inspect the
lighthouses from Orkney to Shetland or touring alone in the south
of France, Stevenson carried a sketchbook and along with his letters
home sent diagrams and hasty drawings detailing the experiences
that impressed him, that he wanted to know more about, and that
his correspondents could not otherwise see for themselves. His
illustrative diagrams in his 1868 journal letter to his mother, study
and articulate some of the more dramatic moments of the lighthouse
tour and admit his mother into the present of what had passed.
They allowed her to 'feel, as I felt, these little stairs and passages'.[11]
Similarly, while touring in the Cévennes (1878) Stevenson made a
series of pencil drawings of the mountainous country near Monas-
tier in order to reflect upon and more thoroughly attend to his
surroundings.

   In his adult life pictures continued to stimulate Stevenson's imagination and to quicken his correspondence, essays, and stories. His
letters to his wife Fanny and to his friends and acquaintances like
Charles Baxter, Sidney Colvin, and Edmund Gosse often included
drawings and diagrams that brought his correspondents closer to
his mind's eye. The 'visionary state' of his youth also remained. As a
result, he periodically continued to illustrate his own work. When,
for instance, he was filling the empty hours of his convalescence in
Davos (1880), he amused himself by skillfully rendering a series of
humorous woodcuts to accompany his privately printed collection
of little books – his *Moral Emblems* and *The Graver and the Pen or
Scenes from Nature with Appropriate Verses*. Most of all, though,
he continued to engage the cartographic images of his childhood;

consequently, the drawings and the maps that had been an integral part of Stevenson's and his cousin's earlier and multitudinous war games once more came to life when Stevenson and his stepson, Lloyd Osbourne, filled the tables and floors of their various residences in Europe, North America, and Samoa with maps that followed the progress of the Generals, Piffle and Potty, or noted the advance of the enemy on the 10th Scarlet (Figure 10: *Defeat of Napoleon on the afternoon of the 17th*). At other times with the aid of out-spread maps and the pictures in Findlay's *Directories of the World*, Stevenson and Lloyd sailed in their minds to the remotest bays and chartered the exposition of their stories.

It was this kind of activity, of course, that initiated *Treasure Island*. Stevenson's description of his drawing a treasure map on a rainy highland day in 'Miss M'Gregor's cottage' reveals his pleasure in the image and, perhaps more to the point, demonstrates how the map set his words in motion and unveiled the unseen so that the places and characters actually 'peeped out' upon him and let the events of his novel unfold. Stevenson writes about the experience in his essay, 'My First Book':

> On one of these occasions I made the map of an island; it was elaborately and (I thought) beautifully coloured; the shape of it took my fancy beyond expression; it contained harbours that pleased me like sonnets; and with the unconsciousness of the predestined, I ticketed my performance *Treasure Island* ... as I pored, upon my map of *Treasure Island*, the future characters of the book began to appear there visibly among imaginary woods; and their brown faces and bright weapons peeped out upon me from unexpected quarters, as they passed to and fro, fighting and hunting treasure, on these few square inches of a flat projection. The next thing I knew, I had some paper before me and was writing out a list of chapters.[12]

It is interesting to note that this map of *Treasure Island* 'went astray' during the preparation of the book for publication and had, therefore, to be drawn again. For Stevenson this was more than an inconvenience; it was also a disturbing matter, for having to reconstruct the map forced him to reverse his usual process of bringing words into view. The loss made him find images in words rather than the reverse. Stevenson was accustomed, as he explained, to writing up a story 'to the measurements' of his images, but not used to making a visual inventory of his words. He complained that the new map was 'never *Treasure Island* to me'.[13]

In his last years in Samoa when the war games had ceased, Stevenson still turned toward pictures and maps to summon his narratives and inform the course of his writing. In January, 1893 Stevenson wrote to Charles Baxter asking him to go to the family home at 17 Heriot Row to fetch and send him two prints from Rowlandson's *Dr Syntax* and *The Dance of Death*. Stevenson explained, 'I hate to risk losing them, but they would really be of great use to me for a story I have in hand.'[14] Obviously Rowlandson's figures were to let him more precisely see a part of his narrative. And in September when he was about to embark upon his history of Scotland, he wrote again to his friend, this time requesting that he send him various sheets from 'Black's new large map of Scotland'.[15] He also asked him to send a map of the Great North Road so that he might sketch out the characters and the plot for 'A Tragedy of the Great North Road', a novel he never completed. As the examples suggest, images never competed with or subverted Stevenson's texts; instead, they stood behind them, engendering their narratives.

In spite of his sometimes nagging anxiety about 'descriptive writing' and his desire while composing *David Balfour* to destroy 'the optic nerve' and pay more attention to the way people sound or converse – a wish he expressed in an 1893 letter to Henry James – Stevenson was always to be dependent on images and to be continually attentive to the visual elements in his writing. He, consequently, displayed a remarkable sensitivity to color, light, and shade. His consciousness of such nuances created the settings for his words, shaped the descriptive passages in his prose, and caused many of his contemporaries and subsequent admirers to regard Stevenson not necessarily as a writer but as a painter. For these critics he is a skillful illustrator, a 'novelist of place', who is distinguished for his 'topographical imagination', his landscape painting, and his keen eye – John Everett Millais once commented that 'Nobody living' could 'see with such an eye.'[16] So notable is this pictorial aura that for one of his early critics, H. C. Beeching, Stevenson's work emerges as a series of tableau, the more successful of which 'move from picture to picture like a magic lantern'[17] – a remark that parallels the narrator's observation in *Dr Jekyll and Mr Hyde* that 'Mr. Enfield's tale went by before his mind in a scroll of lighted pictures.'[18]

These critics' sensitivity to Stevenson's visual orientation is appropriate because it reflects the idiom Stevenson often selected to characterize himself. Although Stevenson once declared that a 'writer should write, and not illustrate pictures, else its bosh',[19] he did not let this principle interfere with his desire to portray himself as an artist rather than as a novelist or essayist. His correspondence and essays are replete with references to the writer as painter – as watercolorist, sketcher, and portraitist. He speaks of the 'creator's brush', the writer who 'paints thin', and the author who skips 'before his canvas' and occasionally refers to his own writing as a 'picture book'.[20] At other times he refers to himself as 'a literary man' who draws landscapes, a description that complements his tendency to look upon a scene and place it within a frame. His first view of the Isle of Earraid, for instance, remains with him, 'framed in the round bull's-eye of a cabin port',[21] and his sighting of a wooded scene becomes more intense because of 'one small fair-haired child framed in shadow in the foreground'.[22] All becomes picture.

In the context of this 'visionary state' and his own sense of the bond between images and words, it is not surprising that Stevenson showed an interest in the illustrations accompanying his texts. For example, he began, but never completed, an essay on George Roux's illustrations for *Treasure Island*. In his unfinished manuscript Stevenson expresses his admiration for the French artist's 'spirited plates' because they enliven the book's characters and introduce its author to 'his own puppets' and allow him to read his own book.[23] As a consequence of this interest, it was also not unusual for Stevenson to deliver specific instructions to the artist assigned to his work. Even before he had completed *Kidnapped*, he was thinking carefully about its illustrations and sending a letter to the editor of *Young Folks* to say that he would soon send him notes about them.[24] On another occasion (6 January 1888) Stevenson sent a letter to Edward L. Burlingame concerning the illustrations for *The Master of Ballantrae*. His remarks show how meticulously Stevenson thought about the images that informed his words and reveal to what extent he already had pictures in mind when he rendered his characters and settings.

If you think of having the *Master* illustrated, I suggest that Hole [W. B. Hole] would be very well up to the Scottish – which is the larger part. If you have it done here, tell your artist to look at the hall of Craigievar in Billings', *Baronial and Ecclesiastical Antiquities*, and he will get a broad hint for the Hall at Durrisdeer....[25]

Whether or not illustrations accompanied his writing, however, Stevenson wanted to give his audience 'engaging images' to carry with them[26] and wished 'to leave an image for a few years upon men's minds – for fun'.[27] At times so anxious was he for his readers to see the very picture playing within his memory that he turned and requested, as he does in *Kidnapped*, that they consult a particular map: 'the reader would do well to look at a map' to see where the ship lay becalmed to the east of the Isle of Canna.[28]

THE IDEA OF RECOLLECTION

Stevenson created these images, for he hoped that what had once been immediately available to him would come to life again in the imagination of his audience. For Stevenson writing was recollection; it was a way of reclaiming the visionary icons of his past. His poetry and prose evolved from 'the scraps of pictures' ('The Lantern Bearers') that nestled in his memory and crowded his mind's eye; his writing emerged from the recalled pictures he wished to resituate into the present.

Stevenson's desire to recall and revivify images from an earlier time permeated his writing. It led him through the essays that are in *Virginibus Puerisque* and *Memories and Portraits*, shaped his settings, guided the adventures in his novels and short stories, and directed the particulars of his miscellaneous prose and poetry. It is a well-established fact that his *A Child's Garden of Verses* is autobiographical, that many of the scenes in his novels are based upon memories he had of places and events in Scotland, and that the angular posture of many of his characters is indebted to the memory of the figures he cut out for the juvenile dramas he constructed in his youth – as G. K. Chesterton observes, Stevenson, even as an adult, still 'lived inside his toy theatre'.[29]

Recollection, though, was not merely the foundation of his writing; it was also occasionally the subject of it. For instance, 'Ordered South' is an essay that, perhaps, comments as much on the experience of recollection – of being back in a place that has remained in his memory – as it does on the severity of his illness that had sent him once again to the south of France. Stevenson opens the essay by remarking upon how he has kept in mind the view of a valley just before loosing sight of it 'in the disorder of the hills' and goes on to describe how that image during his absence has been with him while he has 'lain awake at night', agreeably tantalizing him with thoughts of corners never turned.[30] In all of his writing Stevenson lingers over these recalled images – the ones that are there before one loses sight of them – and extends their life through his words. As they did in the example of Miss Broddie, these recollections resuscitate the past and let him once more see the world of home and recognize 'the face that was once myself'.[31]

Recollection not only prompted Stevenson's words but also helped shape his sense of the present. As willingly as he recognized the pleasures of the current moment – the times when he experienced Samoa's vividness and benefited from the resilience of Vailima[32] – he often preferred the images of remembrance, particularly those that recalled the clear light of a highland morning and the sight of the gas lamps mapping Edinburgh, the city of his childhood. In a late letter to Will H. Low (15 January 1894), Stevenson admitted that although he appreciated Samoa's beauty and thought of it as a 'spot for a sculptor or painter', he could not help but prefer the 'grey, freezing recollections of Scotland'.[33] As David Daiches remarks, Stevenson lived in Samoa 'under conditions so new and so striking', yet in his mind's eye chose to be surrounded by 'the cold old huddle of grey hills' from which he came.[34]

For Stevenson the present could never be quite as enthralling as the past. It was not, though, without its value, for it served as the occasion for recollection and anticipated remembrance. In the bitter cold spring of 1870 when Stevenson was in Dunoon, he commented, 'If I desire a long life, it is that I may have the longer retrospect. Ninety years of life might be a burthen; but ninety years of recollection must be heaven.'[35] And two years later (5 March [April] 1872) in the midst of a relapse in Scotland, feeling 'uneasy and restless – almost to the extent of pain', he consoled himself by looking forward to recollection. He told Charles Baxter:

but O! how I enjoy it and how I *shall* enjoy it afterwards (please God) if I get years enough allotted to me for the thing to ripen in. When I am a very old and very respectable citizen, with white hair and bland manners and a gold watch and an unquestioned *entrée* to the sacrament, I shall hear these crows cawing in my heart, as I heard them this morning: I vote for old age and eighty years of retrospect.[36]

Stevenson understood that recollection was the compensation for enduring 'hours of wakefulness and pain'.[37] Looking back was the reward for rising from his sickbed and living longer.

THE OPTICAL METAPHORS OF RECOLLECTION

Because of its importance to him, Stevenson thought attentively about the nature of recollection and frequently attempted to understand its idiosyncracies by turning to metaphor and letting its images represent his experience. For instance, when speaking of the act of remembrance, he occasionally chose the familiar metaphor of 'the hour glass of time' that sifts the clutter and chaos of particulars and leaves a few significant pictures for the longing eye to behold. Writing from Dunoon in 1870, Stevenson remarked upon the phenomenon:

> The doings and actions of last year are as uninteresting and vague to me, as the black gulph of the future, the tabula rasa that may never be anything else. I remember a confused botch-patch of unconnected events, a 'chaös without form or void'; but nothing salient or striking rises from the dead level of 'flat, stale and unprofitable' generality. When we are looking at landscape we think ourselves pleased; but it is only... when it comes back upon us by the fire O'nights that we can disentangle the main beam from the thick of particulars. It is just so with what is lately past. It is too much loaded with detail to be distinct, and the canvass of the picture is too large for the eye to encompass. But this is no more the case when our recollections have been strained long enough through the hour glass of time.... All that is worthless has been sieved and sifted out of them.[38]

As the references to a beam of light and a picture's canvas in the passage above suggest, Stevenson was attracted to visual imagery when speaking about recollection. He, therefore, tended to disregard the well-rehearsed reference to the hour glass of time so that he might call upon metaphors that more adequately mirrored his preference and represented his experience. Stevenson, consequently, turned away from this more common image and chose instead various optical metaphors to describe the process of recollection – a choice, of course, that significantly reflects his preoccupation with the visual experience and that appropriately follows his habit of looking back and engaging the image in re-membrance.

The first of these optical metaphors is the magic lantern.[39] In his poems and letters Stevenson sometimes describes recollected images by comparing them to the bright pictures that come out of and return to the darkness in the popular magic-lantern shows. In lines 25–36 'To My Old Familiars', one of his many nostalgic poems displaying the latent romanticism that suffuses his work, Stevenson uses the metaphor:

> Yet when the lamp from my expiring eyes
> Shall dwindle and recede, the voice of love
> Fall insignificant on my closing ears,
> What sound shall come but the old cry of the wind
> In our inclement city? what return
> But the image of the emptiness of youth,
> Filled with the sound of footsteps and that voice
> Of discontent and rapture and despair?
> So, as in darkness, from the magic lamp,
> The momentary pictures gleam and fade
> And perish, and the night resurges – these
> Shall I remember, and then all forget.

The pictures come and slip away as they do in the essays that display a gallery of images and set a series of slides in motion. Each section in 'Some Portraits by Raeburn', 'A Plea for Gas Lamps', and 'Memories of an Islet' resembles an illuminated repre-sentation that elapses into obscurity when Stevenson closes the paragraph and shifts to another image. 'A Plea for Gas Lamps', for instance, opens with a 'slide' of the city, and then moves on from one lighted scene to another – to the city illuminated by oil lights, by gas lamps, and by electricity. Between each illumination lies the inexplicable darkness of time, a space void of image. Similarly, in 'Memories of an Islet', Stevenson moves from one perspective to another. Through his mind's eye he returns to 'the little isle of Earraid' and takes his reader from scene to scene – to the Fiddler's Hole, to the rows of sheds, to the open sea, and to the lighthouse at Dhu-Heartach. Like the changing magic-lantern slides, these views follow without transition. They come as set pieces to behold, to disappear, and be replaced by another.

The second optical figure is the kaleidoscope. Stevenson sometimes thought of recalled images as revolving within his mind's eye
like pieces in a kaleidoscope. He employs the comparison in 'A
Gossip on Romance' when he talks about the 'mind filled with the
busiest, kaleidoscopic dance of images',[40] and uses it again in 'A
Penny Plain and Twopence Coloured' when he tells his readers
that the roll-call of 'stirring names' of the juvenile dramas, such as
The Forest of Bondy, The Wood Daemon, The Old Oak Chest, and *Three-
Fingered Jack*, and the plates of characters, bearded with pistol in
hand, still survive in his imagination.[41] Like 'kaleidoscopes of
changing pictures, echoes of the past', their images revolve with
every turn of remembrance to form altering configurations out of
familiar fragments. This style of recollection is visible in a number of
his essays. In 'An Old Scotch Gardener', 'Walking Tours', and 'Random Memories', images move by association and with a twist of the
author's perspective continuously produce new shapes so that, for
instance, the gardener goes through what might be called a series of
metamorphoses to become his vegetables, his flowers, his bee-hives,
and his 'golden-sayings'. Each 'metamorphosis' is simply a recom-
position of the segments that constitute Robert Young, the Swanston
gardener whom Stevenson admired. In a similar manner images,
moods, activities, and conversations in 'Walking Tours' and 'Random Memories' recompose when Stevenson turns his kaleidoscopic
memory and lets the scraps of remembered pictures and events vary
and fall into place as he moves through his essay.

The third metaphor is that of the mirror. Upon other occasions
Stevenson compared recollection to a looking glass that retains and
reveals the past. When, for instance, he writes about 'Old Lindsay', a
laboratory assistant to Professor Tait, one of his engineering professors at the University of Edinburgh, he speaks of him as being 'a
mirror of things perished'. His presence carries with it reflections of
the past that allow Stevenson to see 'the huge shock of flames of the
May beacon stream to leeward' and to watch his grandfather
(Robert Stevenson) 'driving swiftly in a gig along the seabord road
from Pittenween to Crail'.[42] Lindsay helped Stevenson perceive a
past he, otherwise, would never have seen.

The fourth optical metaphor Stevenson employs is the thaumatrope, a popular nineteenth-century scientific toy illustrating the
persistence of visual impression. The apparatus was composed of a
card with different pictures on opposite sides which when twirled
rapidly, with the aid of strings, combined to form a single image.

Stevenson uses the metaphor in an August 1890 letter to Charles Baxter to explain how images from the past move into the present as a single pattern and leave him with an image, a remembrance, that stands out from all the others – in this case, Baxter's house in Edinburgh.

> There are very few things, my dear Charles, worth mention; on a retrospect of life, the day's flash and colour, one day with another, flames, dazzles and puts to sleep; and when the days are gone, like a fast-flying thaumatrope, they make but a single pattern. Only a few things stand out, and among these, most plainly to me – Rutland Square.[43]

Through the whirling of the card's opposing figures, the motions of retrospect create the single picture that persists and, thereby, eradicates the plethora of competing details that confuse the present and the perception of what is important.

It is this kind of recollection that helps Stevenson cast his essays collected in *Memories and Portraits*. In these pieces, Stevenson often lets contrary or opposing images of his subjects oscillate within his paragraphs until they eventually merge to form a single recollected impression of a person, place, or moment. In the essay 'Pastoral', for instance, the distant swirling rivers, the running streams, the trickling springs of the Hebrides, the Pentland hills, the long-gone drover, the rambling sheep, and the alienating present twirl in Stevenson's memory and in his telling until a solitary, lasting figure emerges to stand forward in recollection. The consequence is that John Todd, the shepherd, with his booming voice and powerful presence dominates both the pastoral landscape and the essay until the final paragraphs when Stevenson relaxes the strings of his thaumatropic memory and once more his past and present separate into differing images. Similarly, in 'Memories of an Islet', Stevenson spins the various remembrances of the little isle of Earraid so that the sound of his 'timorous and hopeful'[44] youthful voice may emerge to still the oscillating fragments of the past and establish a dominating impression. The metaphor also helps structure Stevenson's portraits of individuals from his past, for, in a mode comparable to the essays mentioned above, he pulls the strings of the card with its alternating figures to let the reader see the contrary sides of a personality. For instance, in 'Talk and Talkers' Stevenson describes Purcel and his conversation as being at once 'radiantly civil and rather silent', and speaks in oxymorons of his 'elegant home-liness';[45] and in his portrait of Thomas Stevenson – a 'man of many extremes' – Stevenson exposes the two sides of his father's nature: his 'sternness' and his 'softness', his 'melancholy disposition' and his 'humorous geniality in company', his shrewdness and child-ishness.[46] It is as if Stevenson whirls these alternating traits and features before his readers' eyes and, in this manner, turns his read-ers into spectators who must finally see the lasting single recollected image for themselves. His words revolve so that his audience may see. This is the perspective that Stevenson also tends to use in his novels, for there Stevenson is rarely content to offer a single view of his characters. He keeps them revolving in their dialectical opposi-tions so that qualities like harshness and softness, wildness and gentility, childishness and maturity alternate before the readers' eyes until a solitary synthetic impression comes forth and settles in the mind to create the real 'long- lived' characters such as Long John Silver, Alan Breck, Jim Hawkins, and David Balfour. Like the oppos-ing figures that come together, these individuals 'stamp the story home like an illustration imprinted on the mind's eye forever'.[47] Perhaps one reason that *Dr Jekyll and Mr Hyde* is such a disturbing piece of fiction is that the reader becomes entangled in the revolving figures of Jekyll and Hyde and, in spite of Stevenson's intentions, finds it difficult to catch a glimpse of a unified image and bring the two personalities into the enduring impression of a single body. It is as if the reader is troubled by a slack thaumatrope's refusal to revolve; he or she is caught between absence and presence. When the functioning thaumatrope twirls, it negates such disparity, for it brings both sides – the image that is present and the one that is absent – into view. It does something analogous to metaphor, for through its oscillations it brings what is near together with what is elsewhere and creates a kind of synthesis which otherwise is un-available.

THE CONTRARY STATES OF RECOLLECTION

When Stevenson uses these optical metaphors to speak of recollec-tion, he distinguishes between remembrance issuing from a conscious act of retrospect and that which suddenly appears before the mind's eye. The figures of the kaleidoscope, the mirror, and the thaumatrope seem to belong to a more conscious act of remembrance. One has to twist the images in the kaleidoscope, to choose to look into the mirror, or to pull the toy's strings. The lasting image that emerges is one, therefore, that appears gradually, after preparation. As with the filtering hour glass of time, one has to let the image detach itself from the chaos and arbitrary arrangement of particulars around it.

The figure of the magic-lantern slide, though, suggests a different kind of experience – one in which images from the past unconsciously and suddenly flash brightly into the mind's eye. Stevenson describes this phenomenon in a September 1888 letter to Charles Baxter. He writes that while sailing at sea and preoccupied with navigating a difficult stretch, the image of the Edinburgh Street where his friend lives unexpectedly besieged his mind:

> we were all looking forward to a most deplorable landfall on the morrow, praying God we should fetch a tuft of palms which are to indicate the Dangerous Archipelago; the night was as warm as milk; and all of a sudden, I had a vision of – Drummond Street. It came on me like a flash of lightning; I simply returned thither, and into the past.[48]

This kind of memory comes in an instant, unpremeditated. Like the gas lamps in Edinburgh it flashes into vision the design of the past and like the magic-lantern shows that officers from the English Ship of War put on for the Samoans,[49] its images come without preparation to be viewed in awe and then to perish in the sudden darkness. These are, perhaps, the recollected images that Stevenson attempts to protect from the enveloping darkness by prolonging their brilliance in his narratives.

These contrary states of recollection – the conscious and the unconscious or the gradual and the instantaneous – recall a distinction that Stevenson makes in his youthful prize-winning essay, 'On a New Form of Intermittent Light for Lighthouses'. In this paper that he read before the Royal Scottish Society of Arts in 1871, Stevenson distinguishes between what he refers to as the *flashing* beam of the lighthouse and the *intermittent* one.[50] The flashing light comes gradually into strength and just as gradually fades away. Its recurrent oscillations and revelations move by degrees in and out of view. The intensity of its light warns of its coming and of its going. The intermittent beam, on the other hand, is 'immediate', for, as Stevenson explains, 'a certain duration of darkness is followed at once and without the least gradation by a certain period of light'.[51] One beam comes with preparation; the other, without. In a sense, one is conscious; the other, unconscious. These circling rays of light, perhaps, resemble the beams of recollection that turn in the course of life and shine upon the present, either gradually or suddenly, illuminating what is otherwise invisible. In the context of this possibility, it is interesting to note that in the last year of his life, Stevenson complained to Will H. Low that 'I ought to have been able to build lighthouses and write *David Balfours* too. *Hinc illae lacrymae.*'[52] To some degree Stevenson did what he thought he should have accomplished, for his writing periodically flashes images of the past upon the dark and in this way redeems a former time from the surrounding obscurity of the unseen.

THE BRIGHTEST LIGHTS AND THE DARKEST SHADOWS

When Stevenson writes about his college professors in terms of their 'signalling out of the dark... the images of perished things', when he remembers how the light plays off Professor Philip Kelland's spectacles,[53] and when he composes his nostalgic prose and novels, he does so with the perspective of one who illuminates the darkness and who, like the lighthouse's beam, reveals 'the brightest lights and the darkest shadows'.[54] For Stevenson writing was a casting of the light of recollection. His remembered images are the literary tapers ('Random Memories') that irradiate the subject at hand. He is always the youthful lantern-bearer who carries his bull's-eye at his belt, and who, when he writes, opens his buttoned coat to let the rays of his lamp fall upon the 'black night' ('The Lantern Bearers').[55]

To read Stevenson's work, therefore, is to see spots of light surrounded by shadows. Like the lamp he mentions in an early letter to Frances Sitwell (6 September 1873) that throws light on a beggar's face to reveal its 'ugly reality'[56] or like the gas lamps in Queen's and Frederick Streets that he could see from Heriot Row,[57] his writing sheds circles of light upon certain images and isolates them in their vividness. These bright spheres flash images into vision.[58] They compose the landscape of his narratives so that his characters move from darkness to light through 'a regular pattern of light and shadow'.[59] Like Dr Jekyll and Mr Hyde, they scuttle about the page through streets and pathways of illumination and obscurity. In the darkness they find their way via beams cast by the 'brilliant moon' and the flames flickering in the fireplace. Moreover, like the children in his verses, they sense the disparities between night and day, and distinguish between darkness and brightness. This is the point of view that causes Alfred Noyes to notice how frequently and effectively Stevenson calls upon the 'simple image... of the candle surrounded by shadows'.[60] Noyes, for instance, comments on the use of candle-light in *The Master of Ballantrae* 'where the duel is fought between the two brothers among the frosted trees by the steady light of two candles'. Turning to his readers, he writes:

> You remember what use he makes of those two points of light to enhance the deadly stillness of that scene: how the body of the Master was left lying in their light under the trees; and how, later on, Mr. Mackellar creeps back, guided by their distant brightness, to find one of the candle-sticks overthrown, and that taper quenched; the other burning steadily by itself, making all within its circle of light, by force of contrast with the surrounding blackness, brighter than day; showing the bloodstain in the midst, and the silver pommel of a sword; but of the body not a trace.[61]

Noyes also urges his readers to think of *A Child's Garden of Verses* as 'the poetry of candle-light' and to take a longer look at the candle-lit scenes in *Treasure Island*, particularly the one in which Jim Hawkins and his mother open the treasure chest and using the ring of light from the candle catalogue what they discover there.[62]

In this landscape of contrasts, of light and darkness, recollected images stand forth distinctly. These remembered images are as well-defined as the figures Stevenson cut out with his scissors to create his juvenile dramas and as abrupt and angular as the black and white woodcuts he and his stepson printed in Davos. Like strikingly pictorial incidents in his novels, they are, as Beeching once observed, 'etched in with acid, sharp and unforgettable'.[63] As if removed with a cutlass, they show their edges. Rarely do Stevenson's images belong to or compose an undefined and wavering landscape. Exceptional is the prospect that he describes in *The Silverado Squatters* where the sky has nameless colors and the scene, perhaps because it is actually before him, becomes 'strange, impetuous, silent', and 'shifting'. The familiar landscape changes from moment to moment 'like figures in a dream'.[64] The closer the scene, the more protean it becomes. Removed by time and space, however, recollection stabilizes and names what had once been familiar so that a precise picture of a previous moment stands out like a relief from the unshapely and confusing mass of the past. Like the stranded David Balfour caught on the island in sight of the 'great, ancient church and roofs of people's houses in Iona',[65] Stevenson, though exiled and separated by the tides of time, easily saw the comfortable sights of his homeland, named its places and from a distance watched his friend Charles Baxter moving on the streets of Edinburgh 'by plain daylight'.[66]

RECOLLECTION AND RE-COLLECTION: THE CONDITION OF EMPIRE

Because the recollected image seemed to be focused and available, Stevenson rarely worried lest it might fade into forgetfulness or emerge half-realized out of a past that refused fully to be recognized. On the whole Stevenson trusted memory. Charles Darwin's sensitivity to a vanishing, extinguishing past was not necessarily always Stevenson's. Neither were Wordsworth's tentative 'shadowy recollections' ('Ode: Intimations of Immortality from Recollections of Early Childhood', line 149). Stevenson did not, as did Wordsworth, dwell upon the forgetting and the altering of the past. His recollections are more continuous. He did not think in terms of 'spots of time', of interruption and discontinuity. Instead, he concentrated upon and unselfconsciously believed in the past's durability. Like Hazlitt and Rousseau he trusted that he could gather up the past moments of his being, for they lay protected in the womb of memory.[67] From his perspective 'neither time nor space nor enmity' effaced or weakened memory. Throughout his essays that recall another time Stevenson insists that the past is clear and available. Repeatedly he inserts the word 'still' into his sentences of recollection. He can 'still' see and hear a character in 'Old Mortality',[68] a passage from a book ('A Gossip on Romance' in *Memories and Portraits*), and Magus Muir two hundred years ago ('Random Memories' in *Across the Plains*). The 'sunbright pictures' of an islet stand before him 'still', a childhood game is as vivid to him 'as though it were yesterday',[69] and a remembrance of himself once sitting among his candles in a rose-scented room is as clear as if no time had elapsed between the past and the present.

He never feared that the repeated use of the remembered image would wear out its vividness. Recollections from his childhood endured, for they were unrelenting and inconvertible. In 'Memories of an Islet', Stevenson speaks of their resilience:

> Those who try to be artists use, time after time, the matter of their recollections, setting and resetting little coloured memories of men and scenes, rigging up (it may be) some especial friend in the attire of a buccaneer, and decreeing armies to manoeuvre, or murder to be done, on the playground of their youth. But the memories are a fairy gift which cannot be worn out in using. After a dozen services in various tales, the little sunbright pictures of the past still shine in the mind's eye with not a lineament defaced, not a tint impaired....[70]

In this respect, Stevenson stands apart from many other writers who cling to a past that seems to elude the searching eye or to exist just beyond the vanishing point of recognition. All of Stevenson's memories crowd into a canvas or a perspective that only includes the visible and the 'unfaded visions'.[71] In his rendering of the past there is no sense of a point beyond which it is impossible to see – a place where people, events, sights, and sounds fall into a hole of invisibility and silence, a void in which the viewer knows there is something, yet can neither name nor define it. For Stevenson, the parallel lines of the past and the present never point to the unseen; they are always there, to be counted, constantly beckoning to the viewer who only need shift an eye to follow one or the other's paths. Each is available. Even when Duncan Jopp in *Weir of Hermiston*, on trial for his life, stands 'in a vanishing point',[72] it is an illusion of the moment. This image of the defenseless criminal, for whom Archie, the Judge's son, feels pity and whose trial pits the son against what he perceives to be his father's 'monstrous, relishing gaiety',[73] infects Archie's consciousness and endures throughout his exile in Hermiston. Jopp may hang, but the picture of him lasts; it refuses to slip over the edge of consciousness or sight.

Perhaps it is because Stevenson accepted the reality of the shadow that he sensed the continuous extension or presence of image. He knew too keenly the tenebrous attendant that 'crawls in corners, hiding from the light', and that 'moves with the moving flame' ('Shadow March') and that 'goes in and out' ('My Shadow'), expanding and contracting at will. It is only when one denies the shadow that things go beyond the vanishing point and disappear from view. Without the shadow, there are definitive boundaries;

there are endings. With shadow, there is, instead, an abiding, malleable presence that indefinitely extends the image and stretches the eye.

Because of this orientation, Stevenson's recollected images are not the frail, retreating, slipping, and consumed memories that, for instance, in the next century Michael Ondaatje encounters when in his thirties he returns to Sri Lanka (what was once Ceylon) from Toronto to trace the maze of his parents' and grandparents' lives so he may 'touch them into words'.[74] The 'false maps', the silverfish who eat through the portraits and ingest images of the family, the untitled photographs, the confusion of names in the graveyard, the half-visible records, and the shifting stories of his Aunt's narratives expose many pages of his history but leave a number uncut and unread. Only through his own words, by writing his autobiography, can Ondaatje attempt to repair or replace the damaged, distorted, and elusive images that he has trouble seeing or comprehending.

Neither do Stevenson's precise, clear-cut memories that seem to be easily recoverable belong to Walter Benjamin's sense of his disappearing past – his understanding that what lies behind him or remains with him will be taken away.[75] Stevenson does not have to become the collector that Benjamin was and create 'encyclopedias' out of the world of objects. To see through to the distant past, he does not need a library protected in crates or behind glass bookcases, and he does not have to catalogue his collections as if he were painting a still life of names and bindings out of an uncertain, shifting, and threatening context. In a sense, Stevenson did not have to think, as Benjamin did, of ownership. For him the intimacy of the past was not necessarily threatened; it was somehow available and, therefore, he, unlike Benjamin, was not forced by circumstances outside of his control to link intimacy and legitimacy with ownership. He was not having to watch while others took his cultural possessions away. He was not having to continuously re-collect.

The differences between Ondaatje's and Benjamin's *re-collection* and Stevenson's *recollections* suggest, perhaps, that conditions of empire encourage and permit variations in the nostalgic experience. Like his fellow countrymen, Stevenson was part of a nation that was, of course, expanding, and on the whole impervious to its own fluctuations. The specter of the British Empire's powerful presence surrounded Stevenson wherever he went and legitimized his longing. The land and the people of his nostalgia were, in this context, never far; their availability supported him in his exile. They were not going to move away, and, more to the point, their culture was not, at least during his lifetime, going to disintegrate or be possessed and destroyed by another. Stevenson's nostalgia, therefore, was what Irving Massey calls a 'stable nostalgia'. If he chose, Stevenson could travel home to recover and touch the images of the past. People might die, but the landscape, the history, and the traditions endured. And when there was alteration, the idea of empire remained to reassure individuals that a significant part of their culture would last to challenge the effects of time, change, and distance. It is this sensibility that gave Stevenson the luxury in *The Silverado Squatters* to embrace the illusion that 'There is no foreign land; it is the traveller only that is foreign, and now and again, by a flash of recollection, lights up the contrasts of the earth.'[76] Surrounded by 'so wide an empire' and by an expanding domain, one, in a sense, only momentarily leaves the familiar.

Ondaatje's and Benjamin's circumstances, of course, are quite different from Stevenson's. Theirs is a more fragile world, subject to change and forces that refuse to legitimize home and, instead, impose another order of being or custom. Even though people and objects remain and with them their memories (like Ondaatje's Aunt or Benjamin's children's books), the order and institutions of life around them alter or are compromised; consequently, when the individuals die, the photographs fade, or the pages disintegrate, no larger structure representing that culture which has gone is present to fill in the spaces left by their absence. There is no comprehensive point of reference. Nothing has an easy affinity to anything else or a place to be seen. Those left behind and nostalgic for what has departed, therefore, cannot simply or easily recall images of the past – they cannot dip into a communal pool of alternatives. These individuals must, consequently, launch themselves on a series of acts of recovery. Their nostalgia is not a 'stable' one; instead, it is an isolated, 'personal' one, for it is a solitary rather than a shared act of longing. Like René de Chateaubriand who alone describes the solitary beauty of autumn and who must live separated and disconnected, unsupported by a collapsing and scattered French empire, the individual is left staring at places that can barely give witness to the dead and to their names.[77] The communal memory has been transformed into a self-sufficient, single memory.

Another consequence of the difference between Ondaatje's or Benjamin's circumstances and Stevenson's is that the first two writers tend to circumscribe rather than extend recollection, and, as a result, concentrate on the diminutive and solitary fragments of the past. As if needing to protect what remains, they keep these pieces close to themselves. Ondaatje, for example, closely examines the damaged photographs and faded portions of letters. One feels him enclosing his search for the past within smaller and smaller circles of reference that increasingly exclude what lies outside of them. One senses the diminishing narrative of a former time. Benjamin's example is similar, for he stores his books in crates, holds on to the slight moments of his childhood, and unfolds what he calls the fan of memory to reveal to himself what small remnants of remembrance are hidden within their creases. On the other hand, with the exception of one of his childhood poems, 'My Treasures', a verse that through its list clutches the bits and pieces of childhood (the two nuts, the lead soldiers, a wooden whistle, a stone, and a chisel), Stevenson's writing pushes outward to reach a larger sphere. He links his images to an expanding field of vision. In the other poems in *A Child's Garden of Verses*, for instance, Stevenson attaches the child and his play to a larger domain that reaches outside the garden gate and travels over the seas and beyond.[78] Such, naturally, is the impulse of one connected to the legitimizing community of empire and of one who lives within an augmented frame of reference. Stevenson does not always have, therefore, to keep an accounting of his treasures to protect them from those who threaten to dislocate or destroy them; he can afford to place his recollections in a wider prospect, for he knows they will not be taken away. He can lay things out for others to see and ask his readers, the 'You' in his prose, to partake of his vision. Even though they are his, they also belong to a communal memory.[79]

EXILE AND THE FIGURE IN THE LANDSCAPE

Whether communal or solitary, conscious or unconscious, recollection, of course, serves in some way to bring the places and people of one's past more closely to the present. Recollection, though, however stable it is and however brightly it flashes the past into view, cannot place the nostalgic individual into that setting. The individual will always be just outside the territory of his longing. Stevenson keenly felt the reality of this disparity and painfully understood that one cannot remember experience and be immersed in it at the same time. His nostalgia, consequently, was accompanied by not just a desire to recollect images belonging to a former time or place; it was also coupled with a yearning to see himself among these images and once more find his way among them. His experience is a reminder that nostalgia is a longing not only for the past but also for the self that was once able, unconsciously, to scramble among the hills and walk in the streets with the people one knew and who, in turn, recognized one.

Recollection alone was not enough, for whatever pleasures and accommodations Stevenson's remembrances afforded him, none could completely satisfy him; none adequately recovered the feeling of being a figure within the landscape of home. In 'Memories of an Islet', for instance, he is able to recall 'a little eyot of dense, fresh-water sand', where he had once waded, but he can do no more than merely wish that, perhaps, in time, 'I shall once more be in bed, and see the little sandy isle in Allan Water as it is in nature, and the child (that once was me) wading there in butterburs.'[80] His mind's eye might be capable of seeing the land where he wishes to be, but his feet can never again tread its ground. He cannot resurrect the child. Only the characters in his writing can; they have to suffice as the figures in the landscape. It is, perhaps, this substitution that causes James Wilson to remark on Stevenson's 'intensely visual evocation of' his characters in their surroundings.[81]

Like so many who have been caught between the need to reimmerse themselves in the setting of a distant past – to feel that land once more envelop their bodies – and the reality of that impossibility, Stevenson composed his fiction so that he could vicariously wind his way through the landscape of home. To do this he relied upon the abstracted space of maps. As he had in play, he turned once more toward these images. This time, however, they were not the issue of his imagination; they were the official maps of countries and regions he had known intimately in years gone by. By following their chartered lines, he reached a kind of compromise and re-entered the places of his youth. His impulse bears a similarity to what Benjamin and Ondaatje did later when, for instance, Benjamin sat in a restaurant and drew a map of his past and Ondaatje studied old maps of Ceylon on the walls of a Toronto apartment.

Letters to friends often articulate Stevenson's reliance upon these cartographic images. For example, in one sent from Vailima to William Archer (7 March 1894), Stevenson describes how his writing traces a map. He addresses Archer: 'You must sometimes think it strange – or perhaps it is only I that should so think it – to be following the old round, in the gas lamps and the crowded theatres, when I am away here in a tropical forest and the vast silences!.'[82] In an earlier letter from Samoa to Charles Baxter (27 April 1892), Stevenson is even more explicit about this practice, for he asks Baxter to have a mapmaker 'of some taste in Edinr.' draw one or two maps that would serve as illustrations for *David Balfour*. One would be:

> a map of the environs of Edinburgh *circa* 1750. It must contain Hope Park, Hunter's Bog, Calton Hill, the Molter Hill, Lang Dykes, Nor' Loch, West Kirk, village of Dean, pass down the water to Stockbridge, Silver Mills, the two mill lades there with a wood on the south side of the south one which I saw marked on a plan in the British Museum, Broughton, Picardy, Leith Walk, Leith, Pilrig, Lochend, Figgate Whins.[83]

The particularity of the request reveals that Stevenson already had been traveling in his mind through this map and that in the writing of his novel he had simulated the act of really being there.

Like the glittering hieroglyphs of the gas lamps in the Edinburgh streets, the maps that were spread out before him reattached Stevenson to the surroundings he loved. Their inclusive arena released him from the narrowing funnel of time that pushed life forward and continuously increased the distance between boyhood and adulthood. The encompassing space of these maps spared him from this alienating chronology, for it countered time. As long as a map was in view, Stevenson had the momentary illusion that he could enter and explore Scotland's landscape without having to subject himself to the vicissitudes of each passing moment. Zeus-like[84] the map held time still by exchanging the context of the self from one defined by the ticking of contracting minutes to one devoted to a static perspective that allowed the eye to rove over the fields and streets of childhood.

It was not, however, merely through his own eyes but also through those belonging to the familiar faces of home that Stevenson sought to recover his former self within the hills and streets of Scotland. Like so many who have been separated from their past, he wanted the reassurance that comes from knowing that his old friends, in spite of the distance, could still visualize him – locate him – either by finding him on a map or by imagining his movements through the day. He wanted their 'seeing' eyes to recognize him. When he was living in Samoa, for instance, Stevenson was anxious for his correspondents to consult an atlas and as precisely as possible identify his exact location. In a letter to Sidney Colvin (21 September 1888), he instructed him to 'Get out your big atlas; and imagine a straight line from San Francisco to Anaho, the N.E. corner of Nuka Hiva, one of the Marquesas Islands; imagine three weeks there; imagine a day's sail on August 12 round the Eastern end of the Island to Tai-o-hae.'[85] And in a 19 June 1889 letter to Lady Taylor, he made a similar request: 'Try to have a little more patience with the fugitives [the Stevenson family] and think of us now and again among the Gilberts, where we ought to be about the time when you receive this scrap. They make no great figure on the Atlas, I confess; but you will see the name there, if you look – which I wish you would, and try to conceive us as still extant.'[86]

Stevenson's letters to his cousin Robert also articulate this need, particularly in the last years of his life. Wanting his cousin's legitimizing gaze, he requested, 'I wish you could drop in for a month or a week – or two hours. That is my chief want.... I would sometimes like to have my old *maitre és arts* express an opinion on what I do.'[87] And wanting his cousin, through the mind's eye, to watch him, as he, after being in town, found his way back to Vailima, Stevenson wrote: 'you might see me coming home to the sleeping house – sometimes in a trackless darkness, sometimes with a glorious tropic moon, everything drenched with dew – unsaddling and creeping to bed'.[88] This desire to be seen prompted other letters that contain maps, precise topographical descriptions, and diagrams that made Stevenson more accessible to his friends in Britain. In a number of letters to Sidney Colvin, for example, he drew maps locating himself and his activities in Samoa, charting his course, and diagramming the plan of his home in Samoa. In his own exile Stevenson learned that to be away from home is not only to be absent from it but also to be, himself, so little recollected by those who remain. To be forgotten or overlooked was truly to live in exile.

The eyes of his old acquaintances did more, though, than reassure Stevenson that he was still a figure in the landscape; they also served as looking glasses through which he might view the 'aboriginal' self that linked him to his country's distant past and that resided in the deepest part of his being. Professor Kelland ('Some College Memories'), Dr Balfour ('The Manse'), the old Scottish gardener ('An Old Scotch Gardener'), and his father ('Thomas Stevenson') from *Memories and Portraits* are significant figures, for they carry with them the memory of things perished; they reflect the self that inherits a nation's past. To look at them is to discover what had existed generations before. For this reason Stevenson had an especially strong affection for John Todd ('Pastoral') whose eyes swept over the prospect and history of the surrounding hills and whose alternately rough and gentle presence rooted Stevenson in the past. For Stevenson, then, to recall the image of this shepherd was to recover a place in the land of his forbears and to re-enter a tableau of memory and continuity:

> He it was that made it live for me, as the artist can make all things live. It was through him the simple strategy of massing sheep upon a snowy evening, with its attendant scampering of earnest, shaggy aides-de-camp, was an affair that I never weary of seeing, and that I never weary of recalling to mind: the shadow of the night darkening on the hills, the inscrutable black blots of snow shower moving here and there like night already come, huddles of yellow sheep and dartings of black dogs upon the snow, a bitter air that took you by the throat, unearthly harpings of the wind along the moors; and for the centre piece to all these features and influences, John winding up the brae, keeping his captain's eye upon all sides, and breaking, ever and again, into a spasm of bellowing that seemed to make the evening bleaker. It is thus that I still see him in my mind's eye, perched on a hump of the declivity not far from Halkerside, his staff in airy flourish, his great voice taking hold upon the hills and echoing terror to the lowlands; I, meanwhile, standing somewhat back, until the fit should be over, and, with a pinch of snuff, my friend relapse into his easy even conversation.[89]

THE HALF-LIGHT OF RECOLLECTION

Although Stevenson's recollected images radiate a glimmering clarity, they do not emerge from the brightness of noon. As the references to night and darkness in the lines quoted above suggest, Stevenson was not necessarily attracted to the full light of day to view the distant prospect. He was, instead, drawn towards the evening light when images tend to loose their definition and 'the shadows of night' darken the hills and blear its details, clustering them into 'inscrutable black dots'. This is the time of day for recollection, the interval of half-lit moments when the lamplighter makes his rounds and the exaggerated forms of children dance eerily at nightfall in the marshes in the south of France.[90] Stevenson's was not a clarity that depended upon daylight. Dusk, the time between when he was put to bed and when he fell asleep, appealed to him, for it was the instant when his imagination illuminated the pictures within his mind and like the magic-lantern shows let the images stand out in relief against the encroaching darkness. As Stevenson explains in 'Memoirs of Himself', these were the moments 'when my mind displayed most activity'.[91] It is this experience he hoped his young readers would have when they closed the pages of *Kidnapped*. Stevenson wanted the action and the characters of his book 'to steal some young gentleman's attention from his Ovid, carry him awhile into the Highlands and the last century, and pack him to bed with some engaging images to mingle with his dreams'.[92] When Stevenson searches longingly for the figure in the landscape, it is for this consciousness that stalks between bed and sleep.

Perhaps because Stevenson was sensitive to the half-light of recollection, he was never fully committed to a measured accuracy. In an autobiographical essay, he recalls that as a child he was 'always drawing' but 'from a purely imitative and literary impulse'. He claims that he rarely drew from nature, for he never thought in terms of 'exact forms or plastic beauty' ('Memoirs of Himself').[93] This orientation contributed to his admiration for the Scottish painter, Sam Bough. In an October 1883 letter to his cousin Robert, Stevenson expresses his respect for Bough because he is a painter who disengages himself from the immediate and the measured in order to represent his surroundings more accurately and knowingly. Like the young Stevenson, Bough finds his images in the dusk of daydreams. From Hyères Stevenson wrote:

> Your definition of seeing is quite right. It is the first part of omission to be partly blind. Artistic sight is judicious blindness. Sam Bough must have been a jolly blind old boy. He would turn a corner, look for one half or quarter minute, and then say, 'This'll do, lad.' Down he sat, there and then, with a whole artistic plan, scheme of colour, and the like, and begin by laying a foundation of powerful and seemingly incongruous colour on the block. He

saw, not the scene, but the water colour sketch. Every artist by sixty should so behold nature. Where does he learn that? In the studio, I swear. He goes to nature for facts, relations, values – material; as a man, before writing a historical novel, reads up memoirs. But it is not by reading memoirs, that he has learned the selective criterion. He has learned that in the practice of his art; and he will never learn it well, but when disengaged from the ardent struggle of immediate representation, of realistic and *ex facto* art. He learns it in the crystallisation of day-dreams; in changing not in copying fact; in the pursuit of the ideal, not in the study of nature. These temples of art are, as you say, inaccessible to the realistic climber. It is not by looking at the sea that you get 'The multitudinous seas incarnadine.'[94]

The paradox is that for Stevenson luminosity finally depends upon the mind activated at dusk. The reason that Stevenson's recollections stand so completely before him and his readers is that he removes them from the sunlight and lets them take their shape in the early evening. To be 'partly blind' is to be more vivid. Stevenson understood that if recollection is to bring one any closer to the experience of the past, one must not come too close to it. One needs a judicious distance. To see too fully is to obliterate omission and, thus, to destroy the accuracy of the past and the power of recollection. When Stevenson revisited Rose Manse, a house in Dunoon where as a child he had spent a week, he suffered disappointment, for what he remembered seeing 'as half-way up the slope, seemed to have been left behind like myself', and the places he expected to see were not there. When, for instance, he opened the garden door, he discovered that the slope he had once thought 'huge and perilous' and the pedestals on which he used to walk had shrunk – no longer were they on a level with his eyes. Disillusioned Stevenson complains, 'Aye, the place is no more like what I expected than this bleak April day is like the glorious September in which it is incorporated in my memory.'[95]

As many others have, Stevenson realized that one needs the glass of the shop window – one needs interruption and separation. Through Stevenson's example one comprehends better that although indebted to the images within the mind's eye and although obligated to the optical metaphors that structure its experience, recollection is ultimately and paradoxically dependent upon a darkening canvas and upon a kind of blindness that illuminates the site of longing. Recollection is, finally, only lucid in darkness. The past becomes luminous in the dusk of absence.

Darkness is essential to recollection. In a sense, recollection depends upon the darkroom of the mind to develop the negatives of memory that have been lying dormant, waiting to be realized. In 'The Manse' Stevenson, who was fascinated with photography,[96] refers to the 'aboriginal memory' that remains unrealized 'like undeveloped negatives' in one's inner being.[97] The metaphor suggests that in Stevenson's experience remembrance brings forth the images of the past that have been tarrying, unseen, within one's memory. It is as if the act of recollection exposes the photographic plates that existed before one let words emerge to represent them and allows one to view the pictures taken at an earlier time. It is interesting to note that, half a century later, Stevenson's attraction to the metaphor becomes Benjamin's, for he also speaks of recollection as being an image that comes from the photographic plate of remembrance. In *One-Way Street* Benjamin, who was, of course, sensitive to the frailty of recollection, considers the 'shock' that suddenly isolates a memory from one's deeper self and lets one view the few indelible images that have not been destroyed by habit or by the events that have succeeded it. He describes this sudden moment of recollection in photographic terms:

> It is not, therefore, due to insufficient exposure-time if no image appears on the plate of remembrance. More frequent, perhaps, are the cases when the half-light of habit denies the plate the necessary light for years, until one day from an alien source it flashes as if from burning magnesium powder, and now a snapshot transfixes the room's image on the plate.[98]

Recollection takes both Stevenson and Benjamin, in spite of their differences, into the dark-room of the mind. Perhaps it was Stevenson's sensitivity to this condition of recollection that made him more than usually attentive to the images that surfaced in his dreams and that often gave birth to his fiction. The vividness of *Dr Jekyll and Mr Hyde* emerged from the night. His fiction, as well as his past, came from a recollection that was often born in darkness.[99]

Notes

1.   Stevenson recalls that when the stories from the penny-papers became too much like the forbidden novels, he and his nurse would

> study the windows of the stationer and try to fish out of subsequent woodcuts and their legends the further adventures of our favourites.... Each new Saturday I would go from one news vendor's window to another, till I was master of the weekly gallery and had thoroughly digested 'The Baronet Unasked', 'So and So approaching the Mysterious House', 'The Discovery of the Dead Body in the Blue Marl Pit', 'Dr. Vargas Removing the Senseless Body of Fair Lilias'....

As quoted in I. Bell, *Dreams of Exile. Robert Louis Stevenson: A Biography* (New York: Henry Holt and Company, 1992) p. 26.

2.   B. Booth and E. Mehew, *The Letters of Robert Louis Stevenson 1854–1894*, VIII (New Haven: Yale University Press, 1994, 1995) p. 204.

3.   R.L. Stevenson, *Travels with a Donkey, An Inland Voyage, The Silverado Squatters*, introd. T. Royle (London: J. M. Dent, 1984) p. 136.

4.   In her memoir entitled 'Stevenson's Infancy', Margaret Stevenson, his mother, wrote: 'I had influenza and was confined to bed, so Lou was very much alone and spent most of his time colouring pictures in pictorial papers and with coloured chalks.' See R.L. Stevenson, *The Works of Robert Louis Stevenson*, XXVI (London: William Heinemann, 1923) p. 289.

5.   G.L. Mckay, *A Stevenson Library. Catalogue of a Collection of Writings by and about Robert Louis Stevenson* (New Haven: Yale University Press, 1961) item #6174.

6.   Booth and Mehew, *The Letters of Robert Louis Stevenson 1854–1894*, I, p. 109.

7.   In September or October 1863, Stevenson wrote to his parents:

> My dear Parients [*sic*], I am getting on very well here. You I think asked me what kind of a game dibbs was, there are five stones or bones and you take them in your hand, fling them up and catch as many as you can on the back of your hand, you put all those aside that you have caught eccpept [*sic*] one which you fling up and while it is in the air pick up the others and then catch the flung one. There are other things to be done but all somewhat of the same kind.

Ibid., I, p. 96.

8.   It is interesting to note that throughout his life Stevenson continued to write letters accompanied by stick-hieroglyphic figures. See ibid., III, pp. 301, 146, 348; IV, pp. 3, 7, 9, 42, 101, 133; V, pp. 197, 253, 300; VI, p. 265; VII, p. 418. The style of his childhood remained with him.

9.   Stevenson, *The Works of Robert Louis Stevenson*, XXVI, p. 218.

10. Booth and Mehew, *The Letters of Robert Louis Stevenson 1854–1894*, I, p. 129.

11. Ibid., I, p. 178.

12. R.L. Stevenson, *Treasure Island* (London: William Heinemann, 1924) pp. xxv–xxvi.

13. Ibid., p. xxx.

14. D. Ferguson and M. Waingrow, eds, *Stevenson's Letters to Charles Baxter* (New Haven: Yale University Press, 1956) pp. 320–1.

15. Ibid., p. 341.

16. J. Wilson, 'Landscape with Figures', *Robert Louis Stevenson*, ed., A. Nobel (London: Vision and Barnes & Noble, 1983) p. 73.

17. H.C. Beeching, 'The Works of Robert Louis Stevenson', *Robert Louis Stevenson: His Works and His Personality* (London: Hodder and Stoughton, 1924) p. 108.

18. R.L. Stevenson, *Dr Jekyll and Mr Hyde* (Toronto: Bantam Books, 1981) p. 13.

19. Booth and Mehew, *The Letters of Robert Louis Stevenson 1854–1894*, IV, p. 142.

20. Ibid., VII. p. 232.

21. R.L. Stevenson, *Memories and Portraits* (New York: Charles Scribner's Sons, 1897) p. 123.

22. Booth and Mehew, *The Letters of Robert Louis Stevenson 1854–1894*, I, p. 305.

23. The unpublished manuscript of this essay is in the Beinecke Library, Yale University.

24. R.G. Swearingen, *The Prose Writings of Robert Louis Stevenson: A Guide* (Hampden, CT: Archon Books, 1980) p. 104.

25. Booth and Mehew, *The Letters of Robert Louis Stevenson 1854–1894*, VI, pp. 100–1.

26. See R.L. Stevenson, *Kidnapped* (New York: Bantam Books, 1982) p. xiii.

27. Booth and Mehew, *The Letters of Robert Louis Stevenson 1854–1890*, VIII, p. 92.

28. Stevenson, *Kidnapped*, p. 73.

29. G.K. Chesterton, *Robert Louis Stevenson* (London: Hodder and Stoughton, n.d.) p. 52.

30. R.L. Stevenson, *Virginibus Puerisque and Other Papers* (London: Chatto & Windus, 1905) p. 85.

31. Stevenson, 'Preface', *Memories and Portraits*.

32. Primarily because of his poor health, Stevenson found he could not live in Scotland. As a result, he eventually settled in Samoa where the climate was more comfortable. In 1888 he took his first South Seas voyage, and in December 1889 he bought Vailima, his estate in Upolu, one of the islands of Samoa. With the exception of an occasional trip to Australia and voyages to other Pacific islands, Stevenson remained in Upolu until 3 December 1894, when he died, at the age of forty-four, of a cerebral stroke.

33. Booth and Mehew, *The Letters of Robert Louis Stevenson 1854–1894*, VIII, p. 234.

34. D. Daiches, *Robert Louis Stevenson and His World* (London: Thames and Hudson, 1973) p. 105.

35. Mckay, *A Stevenson Library. Catalogue of a Collection of Writings by and about Robert Louis Stevenson,* item #6174.

36. Booth and Mehew, *The Letters of Robert Louis Stevenson 1854–1894,* I, p. 223.

37. Mckay, *A Stevenson Library. Catalogue of a Collection of Writings by and about Robert Louis Stevenson,* item #6173.

38. Ibid., item #6173.

39. In his article on Stevenson for *The New York Review of Books* (8 June 1995), Richard Holmes remarks that Stevenson had a magic lantern machine 'with which he loved to entertain his visitors as he traveled round the globe'. See R. Holmes, 'On the Enchanted Hill', *The New York Review of Books* (98 June 1995) 14.

40. Stevenson, *Memories and Portraits,* p. 247.

41. Ibid., p. 214.

42. Ibid., p. 29.

43. Booth and Mehew, *The Letters of Robert Louis Stevenson 1854–1894,* VI, p. 399.

44. Stevenson, *Memories and Portraits,* p. 131.

45. Ibid., p. 166–7.

46. Ibid., p. 139.

47. Ibid., p. 256.

48. Booth and Mehew, *The Letters of Robert Louis Stevenson 1854–1894,* VI, p. 207.

49. In a 4 September 1892 letter to Miss Adelaide Boodle's young students, the 'children in the cellar', Stevenson describes how 'There came an English ship of war in the harbour, and the officers very good naturedly gave an entertainment of songs and dances and a magic-lantern' show. He describes the event:

> the great affair was the magic-lantern. The hall was made quite dark, which was very little to Arrick's taste [Arrick was a 'black boy' at Vailima]. He sat there behind the housekeeper, nothing to be seen of him but eyes and teeth, and his heart beating finely in his little scarred breast. And presently there came out on the white sheet that great bright eye of light that I am sure all you children must have often seen [the school was in England]. It was quite new to Arrick, he had no idea what would happen next; and in his fear and excitement, he laid hold with his little slim black fingers like a bird's claws on the neck of the housekeeper in front of him. All through the rest of the show, as one picture followed another on the white sheet, he sat there gasping and clutching at the housekeeper's neck, and goodness knows whether he were more pleased or frightened. Doubtless it was a very fine thing to see all these bright pictures coming out and dying away again one after another; but doubtless it was rather alarming also, for how was it done?

See Booth and Mehew, *The Letters of Robert Louis Stevenson 1854–1894*, VII, p. 372.

50. The distinction that Stevenson makes in this paper is partially based upon the work of his father, Thomas Stevenson, and his grandfather, Robert Stevenson. Both were distinguished engineers and designers of lighthouses.

51. Stevenson, 'On a New Form of Intermittent Light for Lighthouses', *The Works of Robert Louis Stevenson*, XXVI, p. 71.

52. Booth and Mehew, *The Letters of Robert Louis Stevenson 1854–1894*, VIII, p. 235.

53. Stevenson, *Memories and Portraits*, p. 30.

54. McKay, *A Stevenson Library. Catalogue of a Collection of Writings by and about Robert Louis Stevenson*, item #6173.

55. R. L. Stevenson, *Across the Plains with Other Memories and Essays* (London: Chatto & Windus, 1892) pp. 215–16.

56. Booth and Mehew, *The Letters of Robert Louis Stevenson 1854–1894*, I, p. 289.

57. 17 Heriot Row was Stevenson's Edinburgh childhood home.

58. Stevenson, *Memories and Portraits*, p. 191.

59. Stevenson, *Dr Jekyll and Mr Hyde*, p. 15.

60. A. Noyes, 'Stevenson', *Robert Louis Stevenson: His Work and Personality*, p. 217.

61. Ibid., p. 218.

62. Ibid., p. 219.

63. Beeching, *Robert Louis Stevenson: His Works and His Personality*, p. 95.

64. Stevenson, *Travels with a Donkey, An Inland Voyage, The Silverado Squatters*, pp. 250–1.

65. Stevenson, *Kidnapped*, p. 91.

66. Ibid., xiv.

67. McKay, *A Stevenson Library. Catalogue of a Collection of Writings by and about Robert Louis Stevenson*, item #6173.

68. Stevenson, *Memories and Portraits*, p. 43.

69. Stevenson, *Virginibus Puerisque and Other Papers*, p. 161.

70. Stevenson, *Memories and Portraits*, p. 120.

71. Stevenson, *Virginibus Puerisque and Other Papers*, p. 96.

72. Stevenson, *The Master of Ballantrae and Weir of Hermiston*, p. 209.

73. Ibid., p. 211.

74. M. Ondaatje, *Running in the Family* (New York: W. W. Norton, 1982) p. 22.

75. For a sense of this need to become a collector because of a disappearing past see W. Benjamin, *One-Way Street and Other Writings*, trans. E. Jephcott and K. Shorter (London: NLB, 1979) and 'Unpacking My Library: A Talk about Book Collecting', *Illuminations*, ed., H. Arendt, trans., H. Zohn (New York: Schocken, 1969) pp. 59–67. See also Susan Buck-Morss, *The Dialectics of Seeing: Walter Benjamin and the Arcades Project* (Cambridge, MA: The MIT Press, 1989).

76. Stevenson, *Travels with a Donkey, An Inland Voyage, The Silverado Squatters*, p. 231.

77. For a discussion of René de Chateaubriand see Irving Massey, *The Uncreating Word: Romanticism and the Object* (Bloomington: Indiana University Press, 1970).

78. For examples see: 'Pirate Story', 'The Land of Counterpane', 'Where Go the Boats?', 'Foreign Lands', 'The Sun Travels', 'Singing', 'Travel', 'My Bed is a Boat', 'The Swing', and 'The Little Land'.

79. Stevenson's trust in a communal memory is, of course, also very different from Elizabeth Gaskell's sense that the experience of the communal memory has been compromised and that, consequently, people must deal with its remnants rather than with its reassuring presence. See Chapter 4.

80. Stevenson, *Memories and Portrait*, pp. 121–2.

81. Wilson, 'Landscape with Figures', p. 88.

82. Booth and Mehew, *The Letters of Robert Louis Stevenson 1854–1894*, VIII, p. 261.

83. Booth and Mehew, *The Letters of Robert Louis Stevenson 1854–1894*, VII, p. 273.

84. When Zeus made love to Alcmene, he prolonged his pleasure by extending one night to the length of one week.

85. Booth and Mehew, *The Letters of Robert Louis Stevenson 1854–1894*, VI, p. 209.

86. Ibid., p. 322.

87. Ibid., VIII, p. 306.

88. Ibid., VIII, p. 305.

89. Stevenson, *Memories and Portraits*, pp. 104–5.

90. In *Travels with a Donkey in the Cévennes*, Stevenson describes seeing 'black figures, which I conjectured to be children, although the mist had almost unrecognisably exaggerated their forms. These were all silently following each other round and round in a circle, now taking hands, now breaking up with chains and reverences. A dance of children appeals to very innocent and lively thoughts; but, at nightfall on the marshes, the thing was eerie and fantastic to behold.'
See Stevenson, *Travels with a Donkey, An Inland Voyage, The Silverado Squatters*, p. 122.

91. Stevenson, *The Works of Robert Louis Stevenson*, XXVI, p. 214.

92. Stevenson, *Kidnapped*, p. xiii.

93. Stevenson, *The Works of Robert Louis Stevenson*, XXVI, p. 219.

94. Booth and Mehew, *The Letters of Robert Louis Stevenson 1854–1894*, IV, pp. 169–70.

95. McKay, *A Stevenson Library. Catalogue of a Collection of Writings by and About Robert Louis Stevenson*, item #6174.

96. Alanna Knight talks about Stevenson's interest in photography. On his sailing trips in the South Seas, he brought camera equipment with him and took hundreds of photographs, some of which were destroyed in a fire. In her diary, his mother, Margaret Stevenson, who accompanied Stevenson on board the *Casco*, refers to the field camera, the plate film, and the heavy equipment and tripods that were necessary for taking photographs. See A. Knight, *R.L.S. in the South Seas: An Intimate Photographic Record* (Edinburgh: Mainstream

Publishing, 1986). J.R. Hammond also remarks upon Stevenson's interest in photography and 'his gift for describing scenes and locations with photographic distinctness'. He notes that when Stevenson wrote to Sidney Colvin on 25 April 1893 concerning illustrations for one of his books, he specified: 'Atwater's settlement is to be entirely overshadowed everywhere by tall palms; see photograph of Fakarava; the verandahs of the house are 12 ft. wide.' See J.R. Hammond, *A Robert Louis Stevenson Companion* (London: Macmillan, 1984) p. 180.

97. Stevenson, *Memories and Portraits*, p. 119.
98. Benjamin, *One-Way Street and Other Writings*, pp. 342–3.
99. See Stevenson, 'A Chapter on Dreams', *Across the Plains with Other Memories and Essays*.

8

From the Vignette to the Rectangular: Bergson, Turner, and Remembrance

As I have suggested, those who long for another time tend to write toward home. Charles Darwin, in his homesick letters from the *H.M.S. Beagle*; Robert Louis Stevenson, in his essays and poems; John Ruskin, in his autobiography; and Walter Horatio Pater, in his portrayal of the child, turn away from the immediate moment and set out to reach the dwellings and the landscape of their youth. Their words swivel the arrow of attention so it no longer revolves in the present or tentatively ventures into the future, but, instead, points earnestly backwards. Like signs indicating a one-way street, their texts seem to concentrate on a single journey from the present to the past and shift the gaze so it continuously looks back to keep in view the faces, names, and places of a former time.

The implications of this retrospective focus are that remembrance depends upon a directed movement from the present and that the past has to be reached from a place that lies a significant distance from it. Although there is, of course, truth in this – *Praeterita*, for instance, opens with the image of Ruskin sitting in his childhood home and working his way, some sixty-two years later, back into his boyhood – one has to acknowledge that memory has really more avenues into consciousness than those that lead the attention from the now into an incontiguous then. One theory of memory, in particular, challenges this notion of a one-way street by essentially inverting the process described above. In his exploration of memory and recollection (*Matière et Mémoire*), Henri Bergson insists that the arrow of attention points in quite the opposite direction – that 'memory does not consist in a regression from the present to the past, but, on the contrary, in a progress from the past to the present'.[1] Thus, rather than simply waiting passively to be retrieved by a searching or longing eye, memory also moves forward to meet and intersect with a present that either rejects, acknowledges, or uses it.

Significantly, for Bergson this crossing of time is not the occasional, remarkable event it is, say for Stevenson who on board a yacht in the South Seas suddenly finds himself enveloped by a remembrance of Scotland, but is ongoing. There is, as Bergson suggests, a 'continuous thread of memory'[2] that is forever moving into and through the present. From his perspective memory is always searching for its analogue in the now and is, therefore, constantly 'inserting'[3] itself into the experience of it. Conscious pictorial recollection, it seems, emerges from these points of intersection.

In order to explore this alternative paradigm and consider how it comments upon the act of writing toward home, it is useful, perhaps surprisingly, to call to mind a small selection from the numerous etching-engravings and mezzotints of J. M. W. Turner.[4] In their own interesting way, these prints mirror aspects of Bergson's understanding of the relationship between the past and the present, and serve as visual parallels to the process of recollection. In a sense they extend Bergson's own metaphoric context, for they articulate his tendency to think in pictorial terms and to represent memory as an artist's 'sketch' – one 'into which we put the right details and the right colouring'.[5] More significantly, though, Turner's engravings are appropriate analogues because their long series of intermediate proofs (printed before the plate's publication) allow one to see the 'successive degrees' by which, according to Bergson's theory, the 'virtual state' of memory grows into the 'actual perception' of recollection.[6]

Perhaps more than most artists Turner was unusually attentive to the development of his prints and, consequently, closely watched the work of his engravers who often suffered under his demanding eye.[7] He insisted upon their sending him each proof so that he could 'touch' each one by writing directive comments in the margins, marking the impressions with graphite or chalk, and scratching out areas he felt needed to be lightened or better delineated. Because of his vigilance, many of the proofs carry with them a history of an engraving's progress and a narrative of Turner's relationship to it. There is a consistency of voice that one does not usually find in the production of prints; there is a record of the memory as it is brought into picture.

If one considers Turner's prepared copper plates with their thin layer of 'ground' (the protective coat spread over the plate's surface), imagines the tools (the etching needles) scratching out the defining lines of the places Turner wants to bring into sight, and notices how these lines come into being after the plates are dipped in acid, then one draws closer to seeing how the past (the landscapes Turner had once seen) 'gnaws', as Bergson would say,[8] itself into the present and the future (the copper plate that receives or 'adopts'[9] the lines) and begins to develop into recollection. Once these lines are etched into and meet the present, then what had been the non-image of what Bergson calls 'pure memory'[10] gradually starts to materialize or slip into perception so that what had been virtual translates into the actual. The subsequent series of prepared proofs decelerate and isolate what happens when memory not only inter-acts with the present but also emerges, step by step, into sight.

When Turner's engravings go through this process, they particip-ate in what Bergson calls 'rebuilding the object'.[11] They begin with an outline, a hasty memory, of the scene that before had barely existed as image (Turner was in the habit of hurriedly sketching the places he was later to engrave) and, through expanding circles of reference and reflection they slowly come into being. As the proofs emerge, what Bergson calls the afterimages and 'intellectual' additions overlap and comment in 'ever widening systems' upon the object, the memory.[12] Eventually, what had been nebulous, indistinct, and distant becomes clearer, closer, and more ample. Out-lines of images become prominent as if the condensing cloud of non-image were evaporating.[13] They develop into the fuller sight.

Consider, for instance, the sequences in the production of *Long-Ships Lighthouse, Land's End* from Turner's *Picturesque Views in Eng-land and Wales*. The first step after the dominant lines were etched into the copper plate was to make an impression of them. This subsequent 'open etching' is disturbing to look at, for its blocked-out white spaces and flat tones create an almost unrecognizable image in which distance, depth, and movement are scarcely visible. Once the engraving had begun, though, and the burnishing tools had rubbed out and emphasized selected lines, the plate's images became more distinct. Defining forms arose where there had only been nicks in the plate, and, like Bergson's after-images of memory, recollecting shadows emerged and deepened the perspective. If one compares the 'open etching' of this print to the engraver's proof (a) (Figures 11, 12), one notices how the *chiaroscuro* in the second plate replaces the confusing flatness of the first impression and, in addi-tion, orients the remembered image so that the viewer now begins to witness the wildness of the sea and clouds and to realize that the white dots on the right-hand side of the open etching are torches carried by figures who are rushing, in the night, over the cliffs, to examine the wrecked ship. What had been invisible is working its way materially into the present.

In most of the prints, as the engraver's proofs progress, the circles of reference proliferate. Like one who is rebuilding a memory of the past until it 'grafts'[14] itself upon the present, Turner revises, refines, reworks, improvises upon, expands, sorts, sifts, amplifies, and adorns each proof and brings the image closer and closer to the observing eye – until, as Maurice Davies points out in his study of Turner's perspective, the artist presses the spectator's nose against the glass of the picture's frame.[15] Consequently there are, for example, differences between the engraver's proof (a) and the first published state of *Lyme Regis* from Turner's *Picturesque Views of the Southern Coast of England*. In the former the depth of shadow is not as dominant, for the sky lacks the lines, the darkness, and the light that later with the addition of the soaring sea-gull in the upper left hand corner beckon the winds sweeping menacingly across the completed image. In the latter, after Turner has marked and adjusted the previous plates, the picture has grown more distinctive, not only because of the 'touches' to the sky but also because of his reworking of the foreground that now with its enlarged and heavier streaks of darkness draws the observer right up to it. Hardly a frame or a margin comes between the individual/viewer and the memory of the picture it encloses. Perception and recollection have interpenetrated so that what was unseen comes into the sighting of the present – the harbor at Lyme Regis.

Of all the engravings, perhaps, none offers a more comprehensive sense of Turner's participating in Bergson's overlapping circles of remembrance than *Modern Italy* (1842).[16] Throughout the evolution of this engraving, Turner, keeping his object in mind (his memory of the scene), moves his critical and amending eye around each plate so he may instruct his engraver (in this case, William Miller), for example, to lower the 'White Clouds', to darken 'the left-hand upper corner', to transform the foliage in the bottom left-hand margin, to blend the 'Horizon', to attend to 'the Spray from the waterfall below the bridge and small church and wall', to get a better definition in the foreground, to close the lines of the water in the front, to make the broken 'sliver'd' bough more convincing, to lighten the tone of the campagna, to attend to the child in the left foreground, to keep the 'silvery softness' of the water, to give more vigor to the shrine, and to make the trees on the front right 'quieter'.[17] While bringing his memory into image, Turner rotates his attention, in and out of these interlocking circles, and in his rounds returns repeatedly to the sky, the water, the structures, and the various figures that people the landscape.

In the course of these movements, Turner expands his perception of the scene and, in such a way, continues to 'rebuild', as Bergson would say, his object. For instance, the earliest impressions of *Modern Italy* do not include a bird's nest in the left foreground nor do they display sheets of what seems to be swaddling cloth draped over the walls. As the proofs evolve, however, Turner directs his engraver to work in these details. What had only been partially suggested in the lower left-hand corner in the etching/engraving becomes something definite and nameable in the early engraver's proof – the circular forms among the foliage turn into the bird's nest with eggs, and what had been paths of light in the earlier impression metamorphose into cloth.

Tracking the development from non-image to image in these prints, one, of course, cannot help but consider the 'crucial defining element'[18] of Turner's preoccupation with light and the nuances of reflection and how this too offers the viewer examples of Bergson's understanding that during the experience of recollection the 'pure memory' passes from invisibility into the luminosity of sight. Turner's mezzotints offer particularly explicit and dramatic instances of this journey from darkness to light. For example, consider *Shield's Lighthouse* from the so-called *Sequels to the Liber Studiorum*, which Turner himself executed – this time Turner used a steel rather than a copper plate. Recalling his broadly sketched preparatory watercolor (such as the one in the Clore Gallery at the Tate), Turner began to translate the darkness of his memory of the scene into areas of light by burnishing and scraping the roughened plate covered with black ink. In an early trial proof, the rubbed out spaces create a moon whose halo and rays reflect throughout and begin to define the sky and the sea. Crude outlines of boats and the lighthouse start to show through the darkness. Later, as the memory interacts more deeply with the present, the plate (engraver's proof (b)) lightens throughout and what had been roughly recollected softens into recognition (Figure 13). In addition, as had happened before, through the 'progress of his attention' (Bergson), Turner expands and modifies his object. With a dry point he adds the buoy on the right; in addition, he defines more details on the horizon, fills in a space on the extreme right margin, and eventually, in the completed version, alters the diameter of the moon by reducing it $\frac{5}{16}$ inches.

These comparisons between the Bergsonian theories of memory and the evolution of Turner's prints would not have necessarily been alienating to Turner's champion, John Ruskin, for, significantly, whenever Ruskin studied the engravings, he found memory and recollection at work – he saw, what he termed, 'an arrangement of remembrances'.[19] Ruskin believed that Turner, 'assuredly' more than most artists, consciously and unconsciously beckoned remembrance to initiate, develop, and modify his pictures' images. Turner *recollected* rather than *imagined* his compositions. His prints, therefore, do not replicate a factual accuracy; they portray, instead, the impressions of memory.[20] For Ruskin this indebtedness to memory – this 'grasp of memory' – was 'the root' of Turner's 'greatness'.[21]

To illustrate this principle of Turnerian topography, Ruskin, in Volume IV of *Modern Painters*, selects and examines two stages of an engraving depicting a view of Nottingham: *Turner's Earliest 'Nottingham'* and *Turner's Latest 'Nottingham'* (Figures 14, 15). He points out that Turner did not like to loose or disturb 'the impression made upon him by any scene – even in his earliest youth',[22] so in reworking this picture, Turner chose to stay within the boundaries of his memory. Rather than returning to review the town and castle of Nottingham, places he had seen and sketched as a boy, he embraced his memory of them and refashioned the past by 'associating with it certain new thoughts or new knowledge'.[23] The result is that through this 'amplification and adornment'[24] of the earliest etching, the latest comes into being and, in its own way, reflects the Bergsonian progress of recollection. As if following the movements of the interlocking circles Bergson describes when he monitors the growth of a non-image into perception, Ruskin notices how the images draw into themselves complementary recollections – how pieces from the past emerge to compose a picture that is a compilation of memory, recollection, and association. Moreover, Ruskin draws attention to the fact that during this activity Turner never loses sight of what Bergson is later to call the 'object'; he never shakes 'the central pillar of the old image'[25] – there is what Bergson calls a 'solidarity'[26] between the additions or adjustments and the central thought or memory which they complement. Ruskin emphasizes this point in his description of the changes visible in the second engraving (see Figure 15):

Every incident is preserved; even the men employed about the log of wood are there, only now removed far away (beyond the lock on the right, between it and the town), and so lost in mist that, though made out by colour in the drawing [Turner originally sketched the scene thirty-five years earlier], they cannot be made clear in the outline etching. The canal bridge and even the stiff mast are both retained; only another boat is added, and the sail dropped upon the higher mast is hoisted on the lower one; and the castle, to get rid of its formality, is moved a little to the left, so as to hide one side. But, evidently, no new sketch has been made. The painter has returned affectionately to his boyish impression, and worked it out with his manly power.[27]

While considering these alterations to the Nottingham print, Ruskin reminds his readers that Turner, in his other studies as well, summoned images from the past, especially as they were needed to fill out his picture. Therefore, just as Bergson was later to assert that the past comes into the present as the past is useful to it, Ruskin insists that remembrance places itself into Turner's compositions as it is 'wanted', as it is useful and 'harmonious'[28] to the desires of the emerging present. When Turner, for instance, was working on an etching of the Alps (*The Pass of Faido, St Gothard*), he altered a detail so as to make 'the bank on the right...more solid and rocky' – the present signalled a need for 'a firmer resistance to the stream' running through it.[29] Turner, consequently, transformed the bank into 'a kind of rock buttress to the wall', an image that Ruskin notices is not imagined but is 'a facsimile of one which he had drawn on that very St. Gothard road, far above, at the Devil's Bridge, at least thirty years before, and which he had himself etched and engraved for *Liber Studiorum*, although the plate was never published'.[30] Significantly, Ruskin does not consider this recollection from another time to be a mistake or a 'chance coincidence'; on the contrary, he suggests that it is in keeping with Turner's use of memory and his practice of 'after a lapse of years' recalling 'something which, however, apparently small or unimportant, had struck him in earlier studies'.[31] As Bergson observed, the past not only works itself into the present as needed but also acquires 'sufficient vigour and life to abide with it in space'.[32]

It is interesting to note that when Ruskin and Bergson reflect upon these various compilations and conjunctions of memory and recollection, they are both sensitive to their analogous relationship to the dream vision in which remembrances of 'things which we have seen so long ago'[33] associate in new and unexpected ways. An image and its associations move into the present in the same way pictures emerge from the darkness of sleep into the light of dream – 'darkened images come forward into the full light'.[34] For both Ruskin and Bergson there is a sense that, as in a dream vision, when the past comes forward to mingle with other fragments of a former time, the individual who dreams or reconstitutes the past does not always do it wilfully, that he exhibits, as Ruskin says, a kind of 'passive obedience', a spontaneous, unconscious remembering that is distinct from a deliberate rebuilding of the past, step by step – what Bergson refers to as the habitual memory. Images from this spontaneous memory 'flash out',[35] a phrase Stevenson also used, at intervals and disappear independently of the will. When it appears, it cuts across the sequential progress of the voluntary memory as the latter changes from the virtual to the actual.

Ruskin is keenly aware of how these two forms of memory interpenetrate in Turner's work. He is especially sensitive to Turner's willingness to let the 'involuntary remembrances' modify the more consciously recalled and reworked images. (Ruskin, in fact, revered Turner for his 'submissiveness' to his unconscious memories.[36]) His commentary on the engravings, in particular, alerts one to this coupling of the habitual and the spontaneous in the composing of the prints. After reading Ruskin one more clearly senses that both forms of memory are active in Turner's prints and come together to 'lend to each other a mutual support'.[37] One becomes aware not only of the sequential, wilful reworking of the past as Turner moves from proof to proof, rehearsing and altering his images, but also of those recalled moments that, independent of this repetitive, ongoing, and conscious activity, spontaneously cut through its path to structure the composition – as the rock buttress had unconsciously found its way into *The Pass of Faido*. Ruskin's commentary and Bergson's analysis of memory remind one that recollection is replete with these crossings of the voluntary and the involuntary. It is a composite of various planes of remembrance. Like the examples from Turner's prints, remembrance contracts into itself the habitual and the spontaneous, the past and the present.

One aspect of memory that Ruskin and Bergson seem only to touch upon is the role of the peripheral in the experience of recollection. Both refer to the power of the dominant image in memory to expose or bring forth what at first seems extraneous to it – to illuminate and give life to what is marginal. And both speak of how this faculty enriches or enhances perception. Neither of these observations, though, adequately offers a commentary on Turner's attention to the peripheral in his pictures of remembrance, nor, in turn, sufficiently represents the potency of the marginal in recollection.

If one looks closely at some of the marked proofs of his engravings, one notices that Turner, although he always meticulously attended to the entire area of a particular proof, often stressed the details closest to the prints' margins, especially those surrounding or just inside his wide foregrounds. Ruskin seems to have considered this practice a particularly Turnerian one, for he periodically remarked on the 'accumulated débris' littering the margins[38] – that Turner's pictures have a 'cluster or two of greengrocery at the corners. Enchanted oranges gleam in Convent Garden of the Hesperides; and great ships go to pieces in order to scatter chests of them on the waves'.[39] It is certainly true that in a number of prints, Turner did fill in his foreground with the remains of a wrecked ship. For instance, when he was reworking *Long-Ships Lighthouse, Land's End*, he was constantly fussing with the width of the floating mast, and up to the end altering other parts of the wreckage. Similarly, in *Modern Italy*, he devoted more than considerable attention to the lower left foliage, to the crumbling wall in the left foreground, to the water in the bottom margin, to the sliver'd off bough and the front trees. A brief glance at the finished print easily reveals Ruskin's 'greengrocery at the corners' – so much so that one's eye has to make a conscious movement from these well-articulated edges into the center and into the depth and distance of the larger image. It was also not unusual for Turner to add peripheral elements toward the conclusion of a print's evolution. Therefore, in *Shield's Lighthouse* he adds a later, seemingly trivial, detail – the buoy in the right foreground (its wake points toward the right margin) that ends up being, oddly enough, the darkest and, therefore, most prominent and clearly defined detail in the print (see Figure 13).[40] This kind of overarching addition is, of course, not unusual for Turner. Among some of the better known examples of this practice is his *Colchester, Essex*, 1827 (engraved by Robert Wallis), in which a dog chasing a hare headed for the bottom left-hand margin – a destination that, perhaps, comments on their origin and their peripheral nature – pushes the supposed dominant image (the town of Colchester) even further to the right, out of view. Their motion not only initially overpowers the spectator's eye but also thrusts it away from the town. Another example is the mezzotint *Gloucester Cathedral*, 1820–25, to which with white chalk Turner appended a hare. Because of its position in the foreground, this marginal addition looms larger than the named image, the cathedral tower in the left distance.

Critics, of course, have often commented upon this practice. Ronald Paulson, for instance, has suggested that some of these peripheral details 'are meant to draw our attention to an "aspect" of the work of art'.[41] These additions, like the hares and the hounds, are not necessarily an 'integral part of the composition'[42] but a kind of hieroglyph, a linguistic *remarque* that sits on top of the image, deflating it, diverging from it, punning or expanding upon it. A number of commentators also speak of how these marginal elements enhance the composition. Eric M. Lee, for instance, not only recognizes that these marginal details affect 'the meaning of an image' but also believes that occasionally they 'enliven the visual interest' of the print.[43]

More, though, seems to be at work. If indeed Turner was creating pictures that are to be seen, as Ruskin said, as arrangements of remembrance, then what do these striking peripheral images contribute to one's understanding of the relationship between what is marginal and what is dominant in recollection?

To begin with, they support Ruskin's and Bergson's sense that dominant images bring forward items that exist on its periphery – the landscape surrounding the cathedral allots a generous space to the peripheral hare, and the scope of *Modern Italy*, with its layering of the present upon the past, allows the contemporary family to cluster among the vividness of the living foliage. The resilience of the marginal pieces reminds one that a remembrance of something often elevates or emphasizes what had in the initial experience seemed less important. (Recall, for instance, Darwin's astonishment when after his voyage ended, he found himself thinking about places he had thought insignificant or undistinguished.) These moments can unseat the dominant image. Thus, as critics like Paulson point out, one discovers that a number of Turner's paintings tend to place what is named (what is identified in the title) in a shadow of light or away from the center and closer to the margins.[44] In a painting such as *Parting of Hero and Leander*, the two named figures cower like diminutive ghosts surrounded by a bold, lively, moving periphery; in *Michael's Mount, Cornwall*, the titled mount fades with pale yellows, hazy greens, and shades of white into the distance – the dark, well-defined foregrounded figures working on the beach challenge its centrality; in *Ulysses Deriding Polyphemus*, Polyphemus arises, barely visible on the left side, and Ulysses poses as a small red clad figure; and in *The Evening Star*, the rocks, the boats, the man, the fishing gear, and dog on the beach detract from the reflection of the identified center.

The engravings also participate in this displacement. For instance, the lighthouse named in Figure 13 (*Shield's Lighthouse*) is replaced, as I have already mentioned, by Turner's attention to the buoy. And in Figures 11 and 12 (*The Long-Ships Lighthouse, Land's End*), the lighthouse, the print's subject, is pushed into a receding and diminishing distance by the tempestuous waves, the fragments of the wrecked ship, and the scattering gulls. It is interesting to note that when Turner made an engraving (*Bell Rock Lighthouse*) for Robert Stevenson's book on the building of that structure (*An Account of the Bell Rock Lighthouse* 1824), his image of it remained as dominant as its title suggests it should have been (Figure 16). Standing secure in its centrality, the powerfully delineated lighthouse reflects, perhaps, the fact that, in this case, Turner was not working from memory (he never visited the site but relied, instead, on a drawing supplied by the engineer Robert Stevenson).[45] Imitation rather than recollection was structuring his composition; therefore, the peripheral ceased to be a vital, independent factor. It merely served its conventional role to support and complement the dominant image. Thus, the later addition of the lightning streak in the left margin of the first published print (see Figure 16) exists purely to enhance the idea of a well-wrought structure that survives and resists a tempestuous sea. No peripheral elements enter to usurp what is named.

In suggestive ways the vitality of the periphery in these selections from Turner's work resembles Turner's practice of notetaking. In his study of Turnerian perspective, Davies describes the manner in which Turner prepared a series of lectures he delivered at the Royal Academy during his tenure as Professor of Perspective (Turner held the post from 1807 until 1837). According to Davies, when Turner was assembling materials, he apparently tended to ignore the main body of his text; Davies notes that the artist preferred 'to copy a wide range of sources', and easily 'became sidetracked and scribbled down much material relatively marginal to his core subjects'.[46] Moreover, when Turner skimmed through his own text, he altered and deleted 'things as they caught his eye, and liberally' appended extra sheets. The result is that in some cases, the original text can hardly 'be distinguished from later additions, enabling it to be studied separately. In others, it is impossible to reconstruct the contents of a manuscript at a specific stage of its development. Occasionally it cannot even be ascertained where different versions of lectures were intended to begin or to end.'[47]

Although this practice seems haphazard – apparently Turner's lectures were difficult to follow – it is not as fumbling or as pointless as it may at first appear. Turner's fascination with what is peripheral to the text of his lectures is very much in keeping with his willingness in his prints and paintings to acknowledge what moves around and in and out of his central theme or idea. It belongs to his wider practice or habit of surfacing, recording, and visualizing the act of revision in remembrance. It is yet another version of his tendency to honor these marginal matters by allowing them to seep into a more central position in the canvas of the recollecting mind. In various striking examples, the presence of this forthright and expansive peripheral suggests that it is not always the dominant image or object of memory that beckons the marginal into its visibility; instead, it is sometimes the reverse, for there are occasions in recollection when what is on the periphery ushers in the main text – just as the plethora of marginal notes and supplementary materials were supposed to summon the text of Turner's lectures on linear perspective. With this reversal in mind, one more readily attends to the fact that what surrounds the recalled object in, for example, *Long-Ships Lighthouse, Lands End* and *Shields Lighthouse*, is more forceful and active than what is named. The surrounding details in these compositions, not the lighthouses themselves, are what allow the spectator to focus upon the identified image. The marginalia lead the eye to the titled structure. This movement from the outside to the inside resembles Turner's sensitivity to the light that shines from beyond the framed picture and breaks through its border from many directions. From these peripheral positions, this light, of course, brings to life the dominant images that can only exist as the surface of their bodies reflects this exterior, yet forceful and life-giving, element. The margin evokes the center.

Davies's commentary on Turnerian perspective allows one to touch upon yet another aspect of recollection. With their multiple vistas that allow the eye 'to move gently'[48] in directions other than that established by a fixed perspective center, Turner's work makes one more sensitive to the phenomenon that in remembrance the focus of the mind's eye shifts and does not simply settle upon a single point. During these moments of recollection, there is not always a central dominant image or space that pulls what surrounds it into itself; there also can be various and optional points, of equal weight, from which to view the scene. For instance in *Long-Ships Lighthouse, Lands End*, in lieu of a central perspective, the eye's attention slides from place to place: to the lighthouse in the rear, to the darkening sky, to the cliff with figures carrying burning torches, to the disturbed gulls, to the rock with its white- breaking spray, and to the wrecked ship and the turbulent waves. This altering focus glides to the rhythm of the pieces of the past working their way into the composition of remembrance. The print, though, does not suffer from these alterations. Mirroring the elasticity of memory, it holds together, undisturbed. In spite of the multiple vistas, no alarming discontinuities dislocate the object or the spectator. Although the attention shifts, the scene is subjectively always whole.

CONCLUSION

In conclusion, if one moves from these parallels between Turner's work and the act of remembrance and returns to the autobiographical writings of Darwin, Stevenson, Gaskell, Ruskin, and Pater, one can no longer think of their texts as one-way streets, leading the reader and author from the present to the past. Darwin does not simply look back towards home; Stevenson does not merely cast his longing glances behind him – Stevenson, of course, is caught in the duality of the crossing trains, traveling in opposite directions; Gaskell does not smooth out the irregularities of memory; Ruskin does not just work his way backwards via his retrospective vision; and Pater does not retrace the fantasy of his childhood only through a narrative that travels from adulthood to childhood. As the above discussion suggests, texts like *The Voyage of the Beagle*, *A Child's Garden of Verses*, *Cranford*, *Praeterita*, and 'The Child in the House' emerge from a plethora of directions, sources, and shifting images that intersect and revolve in overlapping circles to form a complicated network of roads. Lines leading from the past meet and blend into avenues of memory pushing forward from the opposite direction. Intersecting vertical moments flash spontaneous images and interrupt the exchange. Circles of association and afterimages move around the object of remembrance and expand or alter its presence. From all sides tangential paths cut into the center and dislodge it;

simultaneously, the center ushers in what is beyond it and what completes it. Moreover, as the pure memory grows into the delineated image, and recollection and writing mingle, the center of attention alters so that what at first emerged from nothing (from the non-image of pure memory) and metaphorically took the shape of one of Turner's vignettes – an isolated, concentrated oval image with a single focus that floats unattached to border or margin[49] – becomes, through these intricacies, transformed into the rectangular page on which the words stand attached, framed, and organized in the full view of the present. Like the rectangular prints of Turner, the printed page emerges from the habitual and the spontaneous forms of memory and from the longing backward eye; it simultaneously displays a kind of unity that almost belies the complexity of the various vistas and directions that developed its content. In its multiplicity, Darwin's, Stevenson's, Gaskell's, Ruskin's, and Pater's completed pages give the illusion of singleness. Like the published prints, they contract into themselves the successive proofs and directions of memory. Like nostalgia, recollection revolves the eye in many directions at once – it is not a simple way of seeing and reconstructing the past.

Notes

1. H. Bergson, *Matter and Memory*, trans. N.M. Paul and W.S. Palmer (London: George Allen & Unwin, 1962) p. 319.

2. Ibid., p. 75.

3. Ibid., p. 320.

4. In his Foreword to the catalogue for the exhibit *Translations: Turner and Printmaking* at the Yale Center for British Art, Patrick Noon, Curator of Prints, Drawings, and Rare Books, informs the viewer that the Center houses over 3000 engravings. 'This group, one of the most comprehensive outside Great Britain, comprises two major collections that were assembled independently at the beginning of this century and acquired by Paul Mellon in the 1970s. The richer of the two is nearly 2000 prints amassed by Sir Stephen Courtauld, among which are several hundred proof impressions touched or annotated by Turner.' See E.M. Lee, *Translations: Turner and Printmaking* (New Haven: Yale Center for British Art, 1993) p. 5.

5. Bergson, *Matter and Memory*, pp. 103, 123, 130.

6. Ibid., p. 319.

7. For a discussion of Turner's relationship with his engravers see C.F. Bell, 'Turner and his Engravers', *The Genius of Turner*, ed., C. Holmes (London, 1903); L. Hermann, *Turner Prints: The Engraved Works of*

J.M.W. Turner (Oxford: Phaidon Press Limited, 1990); A. Lyles and D. Perkins, *Colour into Line: Turner and the Art of Engraving* (London: Tate Gallery, 1989). It is also helpful to look at W. G. Rawlinson's description of Turner's engravings in his two volume work: *The Engraved Work of J. M. W. Turner, R.A.* (London: Macmillan, 1908–13). In *Translations: Turner and Printmaking*, Lee summarizes the nature of this relationship:

> Generally, Turner's engravers began working for the artist when they were impressionably young, which enabled Turner to shape their abilities according to his needs. This also assured Turner more direct and sustained interaction with his engravers. Engraving after Turner involved long sequences of intermediate proofs before the plate's publication. First, Turner would produce a watercolor to serve as the model for the engraving. The engraver would then transfer the design to the plate and produce the initial etched outline and afterwards the engraving, whether in line or mezzotint. An impression from the plate at this stage would then be sent to Turner, who would write and draw, directly on this proof, detailed instructions to the engraver on how to improve the print. After reworking the plate, the engraver would then furnish another proof on which Turner would provide further instructions. This process of revision and refinement would continue until the print fully satisfied Turner. Only then would it be issued to the public with its title and identifying inscriptions.

See Lee, *Translations: Turner and Printmaking*, p. 7.
8. Bergson, *Matter and Memory*, p. 194.
9. Ibid., p. 114.
10. In Chapter 3 of *Matter and Memory,* Bergson writes: 'from the moment that it [the past] becomes image, the past leaves the state of pure memory and coincides with a certain part of my present. Memory actualized in an image differs, then, profoundly from pure memory.' Ibid., p. 181.
11. Ibid., p. 128.
12. In Chapter 2 of *Matter and Memory,* Bergson explains:

> It is the whole of memory, as we shall see, that passes over into each of these circuits, since memory is always present; but that memory, capable, by reason of its elasticity, of expanding more and more, reflects upon the object a growing number of suggested images, – sometimes the details of the object itself, sometimes concomitant details which may throw light upon it. Thus, after having rebuilt the object perceived, as an independent whole, we reassemble, together with it, the more and more distant conditions with which it forms one system. If we call B', C', D', these causes of growing depth, situated behind the object, and virtually given with the object itself, it will be seen that the progress of attention results in creating anew not only the object perceived, but also the ever

widening systems with which it may be bound up; so that in the measure in which the circles, B, C, D represent a higher expansion of memory, their reflexion attains in B', C', D' deeper strata of reality.

Ibid., p. 128.

13. In Chapter 3 of *Matter and Memory*, Bergson writes: 'But our recollection still remains virtual; we simply prepare ourselves to receive it by adopting the appropriate attitude. Little by little it comes into view like a condensing cloud; from the virtual state it passes into the actual; and as its outlines become more distinct and its surface takes on colour, it tends to imitate perception.' Ibid., p. 171.
14. Ibid., p. 120.
15. M. Davies, *Turner as Professor: The Artist and Linear Perspective* (London: Tate Gallery, 1992) p. 80.
16. For a full reprinting of Turner's commentary on *Modern Italy*, see J. Gage, *Color in Turner: Poetry and Truth* (New York: Praeger, [1969]), pp. 44–7.
17. Ibid., pp. 44–5.
18. Lee, *Translations: Turner and Printmaking*, p. 7.
19. E. T. Cook and A. Wedderburn, eds, *The Complete Works of John Ruskin*, VI (London: George Allen, 1903) p. 41.
20. Ibid., p. 40.
21. Ibid., p. 44.
22. Ibid., p. 42.
23. Ibid., p. 42.
24. Ibid., p. 44.
25. Ibid., p. 42.
26. Bergson, *Matter and Memory*, p. 127.
27. Cook and Wedderburn, *The Complete Works of John Ruskin*, VI, p. 44.
28. Ibid., p. 41.
29. Ibid., p. 40.
30. Ibid., p. 40.
31. Ibid., p. 41.
32. Bergson, *Matter and Memory*, p. 125.
33. Cook and Wedderburn, *The Complete Works of John Ruskin*, VI, p. 41.
34. Bergson, *Matter and Memory*, p. 97.
35. Ibid., p. 101.
36. Cook and Wedderburn, *The Complete Works of John Ruskin*, VI, p. 44.
37. Bergson, *Matter and Memory*, p. 98.
38. As quoted in D. Birch, *Ruskin on Turner* (London: Cassell, 1990) p. 105.
39. As quoted in J. Lindsay, *Turner: The Man and his Art* (New York: Franklin Watts, 1985) p. 2.
40. For a history of these changes, see Rawlinson, *The Engraved Work of J. M. W. Turner, R.A.*, p. 386.
41. R. Paulson, *Literary Landscape: Turner and Constable* (New Haven: Yale University Press, 1982) p. 64.
42. Ibid., p. 66.
43. Lee, *Translations: Turner and Printmaking*, p. 8.

44.   Ronald Paulson remarks that in this respect,

some of Turner's details are likely to recall Brueghel's *Fall of Icarus*, which is *about* the Flemish peasant ploughing the field, but allows a sidelong glimpse of the tiny figure of Icarus plunging unnoticed into the sea. The detail dissociates or makes peripheral the mythical from the routine of everyday life. We might see Turner's detail of the ploughman and the rabbit (and the boating party far below the train), or of the boys sailing a boat, as reminders of the persistence of natural and human cycles in the presence of a sublime landscape.

Paulson, *Literary Landscapes: Turner and Constable*, p. 65.

45.   The Bell Rock Lighthouse was the great undertaking of Robert Stevenson's engineering career. (Robert Stevenson was the grandfather of Robert Louis Stevenson.) It stands twelve miles off the Firth of Tay (Scotland). His design was the forerunner of all subsequent stone lighthouses. The methods used to construct the tower on a partially submerged reef were revolutionary.
According to Mungo Campbell, in 1816

a Scottish drawing-master, Andrew Masson, spent six and a half weeks on the rock recording the seas and their moods and effects. In 1819 James Skene, who had himself drawn the Light, approached Sir Walter Scott on Stevenson's behalf for an introduction to Turner to produce a watercolour which could be engraved as a frontispiece for the *Account*. Scott (himself a Commissioner of the Northern Lighthouses, with whom Stevenson had visited the rock in 1814) replied that although 'a sketch of the Bell Rock from so masterly a pencil would be indeed a treasure', the artist would 'do nothing without cash and anything for it'.

See M. Campbell, *A Complete Catalogue of Works by Turner in the National Gallery of Scotland* (Edinburgh: National Galleries of Scotland, 1993) pp. 91–2.

46.   Davies, *Turner as Professor: The Artist and Linear Perspective*, p. 19.
47.   Ibid., p. 22.
48.   Ibid., p. 65.
49.   Jan Piggott writes about Turner's vignettes: 'Between 1830 and 1839 one hundred and fifty vignettes from design were engraved on steel and published in books; under commission from publishers he made sketches and finished watercolours in the vignette form for the illustration or, in the idiom of the day, the "embellishment" of editions of his contemporaries – Samuel Rodgers, Walter Scott, Lord Byron, Thomas Campbell, and Bunyan.' See J. Piggot, *Turner's Vignettes* (London: Tate Gallery, 1993) p. 13.

Afterthoughts: Nostalgia and Recollection

Several concepts and definitions of nostalgia and recollection have emerged in the course of this book. They are catalogued here in the order in which they appear. Such a listing may offer the reader an opportunity to reflect more generally upon the experience of nostalgia. If one detaches these thoughts from their specific surroundings, what seems applicable to a particular instance – to events in the lives of Gaskell's protagonists or to moments in the lives of Darwin, Pater, Ruskin, and Stevenson – can reverberate in the experience of others.

1. Nostalgia's memory both resists and requires the obliteration of the past.
2. Nostalgia's desire exempts home from mutability's authority.
3. Nostalgia depends upon forgetfulness as well as remembrance. It is as if nostalgia roams between the tenor of death and the vehicle of life. Like Orpheus, nostalgia attempts to recover what darkness imprisons so that it might lead what is lost back toward the light of the living present. Nostalgia charms death with its bitter-sweet melodies. But, as Orpheus learns, nostalgia can never completely resurrect what it releases. The past can never join the present. It must always remain several paces behind and eventually travel once more through the river of forgetfulness. When nostalgia turns to claim what it has raised, recognition fades. Briefly, the released image inhabits consciousness; soon, though, the vividness weakens, and even though one might reach out like Orpheus, to hold it, the image turns to retread its path to the underworld of the unconscious. Nostalgia, therefore, continually repeats Orpheus's journey and, thus, knows a double death.
4. Nostalgia does not always rid memory of the dangerous or the violent. It does not, as some would claim, consistently reject the negative or cast the unwanted into oblivion. On the contrary, nostalgia occasionally clears away the quieter, edenic moments and surfaces the excitements associated with the more difficult, fearful, and threatening episodes – those that place the individual on the edge of disaster.

5. Nostalgia's memory not only resurrects the dangerous; it also brings what had been peripheral into the center. The things to which the individual had once paid no attention become important and what seemed significant disappears.

6. Like metaphor that recognizes what is present and what is absent from the eye, and thereby, discovers some spontaneous continuity between the two elements, the experience of nostalgia can occasionally bring the conflicting present and past together. It does not always have to trap consciousness between two conflicting points of reference, for just as the so-called 'vehicle' in metaphor refers to what lies outside the boundaries of the described and points away from the named ('the tenor') yet functions to create a single, echoing-reverberating meaning, so too can the distracting present in the nostalgic moment help to secure a single text – one that grows out of the opposition between what was and is. In this context, nostalgia emerges as a figure that can simultaneously acknowledge and dismiss difference or otherness.

7. Nostalgia mourns the loss of a collective memory that glosses over change and differences in time by repeatedly moving the past into the seamless present, and offers, through a shared set of rituals, the illusion of belonging to a communal identity where remembrance occurs among people, not within the solitary individual's mind.

8. There are two kinds of nostalgia: the first creates sites of memory that freeze and attempt to conserve or frame a detached moment; the second evokes places of memory and attaches one's yearning to a wider orbit and multiple dimensions that continually qualify the experience of longing.

9. Because it gathers bits and pieces from the past and assembles fragments arising from the involuntary memory, nostalgia merely offers vanishing glimpses of what was. This incompleteness denies the possibility of substitution by inscribing the sense of loss or absence and, thereby, awakens a longing for the fuller, more lasting picture. With the exception of its abstracting powers, nostalgia usually confirms the presence of a divided self. In a sense, it signifies the ultimate duality.

10. Paradoxically, nostalgia is prevented from ever properly resurrecting the past because it relies on a memory that depends upon comparison and a sense of otherness. It cannot fully recover what lies there, for like the adult who attempts to play,

it cannot adequately move the limbs and quicken the voices of the absent as a child can. Nostalgia, it seems, is always attended by a reference to an 'other' that censors by qualifying the player's gestures and discourages by accepting no substitutes.

11. Nostalgia defeats itself except when it goes around itself to the text and keeps the writer and the reader, for the moment, revolving in a time and a space that is always fully available and needs no otherness, not even a third-person narrator, to explicate or qualify it.

12. Nostalgia keeps one away from a direct sighting of the past, and, through that act, prevents what lives in the memory from dying.

13. Those left behind and nostalgic for what has departed cannot simply or easily recall images of the past – they cannot dip into a communal pool of alternatives. These individuals must, consequently, launch themselves on a series of acts of recovery. Their nostalgia is not a stable one; instead, it is an isolated, personal one, for it is a solitary rather than a shared act of longing.

14. Nostalgia is a longing not only for the past but also for the self that was once able, unconsciously, to scramble among the hills and walk in the streets with the people one knew and who, in turn, recognized one.

15. Sometimes during the act of retrospection, visibility replaces the invisibility of being. Therefore, to recollect the spaces of childhood is to bring into perception what once had no need to be seen.

16. There are contrary states of recollection: the conscious and the unconscious or the gradual and the instantaneous.

17. Removed by time and space, recollection stabilizes and names what had once been familiar so that a picture of a previous moment stands out like a relief from the unshapely and confusing mass of the past.

18. Conditions of empire encourage and permit variations in the nostalgic experience.

19. Recollection, however stable it is and however brightly it flashes the past into view, cannot place nostalgic individuals into that setting. They will always be just outside the territory of their longing.

20. If recollection is to bring one closer to the experience of the past, one must not come too close to it. One needs a judicious distance. To see too fully is to obliterate omission and to destroy the power of recollection.

21. Darkness is essential to recollection. In a sense, recollection depends upon the darkroom of the mind to develop the negatives of memory that have been lying dormant, waiting to be realized.

Index